To Neal

Kurt A. Shallada

Kurt's Journey

Kurt L. Wallach

Kurtell Publishing

Book design and production: Tabby House
Jacket design: Carol Tornatore

ISBN: 978-0-615-20704-9

Library of Congress Control Number: 2008905852

Kurtell Publishing
1717 20th Street, #105
Vero Beach, FL 32960

Dedication

This book is dedicated to all the good people who suffered the ravages and horrors of Mother Nature through the three catastrophic hurricanes, which began early in the century. It is also dedicated to the thousands who died in the attacks on the twin towers in New York, the Pentagon in Washington and those who died in the plane crash in which the passengers fought the terrorists in the skies over Pennsylvania.

Further, I dedicate this book to my dear wife Marilyn, my children and my grandchildren in hopes that as it outlives me, it will remind them from whence the spawning came and my love for them.

Contents

List of Illustrations

Preface

The life of Kurt Wallach has been unique. It differed dramatically from most. It was not mundane but earthly. It reflected mostly different from ordinary and was rarely uninteresting, as the boy escaped the Nazi gangsters in the 1930s from Germany, to almost four years in Holland and then to this strange land in North America. As a man, the military began the real period of maturation along with the years of marital instability, business success, business failure and again success.

My feelings for the Holocaust, its horrors and my desire to educate followed through teaching, countless lectures, lecture series and involvement with the Holocaust Museum. The years rolled on as event after event and milestone after milestone saw tranquility turn to turbulence and back to tranquility. Rarely in the life of Kurt Wallach was there stability that lasted for too many years.

Interesting is the study of varying activities,

similar and dissimilar in nature, that had any longevity. It was the dissimilarity of conditions in life that made this life so divergent and multifarious.

1

The Beginnings

The author, Kurt Wallach, was born in the city of Magdeburg in the province of Saxony Anhalt, a city in central Germany located on the Elbe River, just west-southwest of Berlin. It was chartered in the thirteenth century and was a model for hundreds of medieval towns created in Germany, Austria, Bohemia, and Poland. It had its own court system, elected council, and was exempt from all duties except for the payment of rent to the prince of the land. In 1524, Magdeburg accepted the reformation away from Catholicism, continuing resistance to Emperor Charles V until his fall to Maurice of Saxony, at which time the archbishops were converted to Protestantism.

The family members of the house of Brandenburg ruled the archbishops. *The 'Magdeburger' Centuries,* the first comprehensive detail of protestant history, was edited there in the sixteenth century. In 1631, imperial troops under Hanz Pappenheim stormed the city. Fires broke out in various quarters and soon the entire city had burned down.

Roughly 25,000 people, eighty-five percent of the city's population, perished. The sack of Magdeburg created an immense impression throughout Europe and was responsible for close alliances among princes of the region. The city was rebuilt and its trade revived. From the late seventeenth century Magdeburg was an important Prussian fortress.

Magdeburg was severely damaged during World War II, when its population stood at 350,000. In 1994, population numbers showed 270,564 residents. The city is a large inland port, industrial center, and railroad junction. Manufactured there are metal products, textiles, and chemicals. It is also known as a food-processing center.

Martin Luther spent much time in Saxony. It was his teachings that caused Magdeburg's defection from Catholicism. In years to come, the city gained a reputation as a stronghold of Protestantism, and became the first city to publish the writings of Martin Luther. The emperor quickly outlawed the unruly town.

During World War II, Magdeburg suffered near total destruction from allied fire bombings.

The very impressive Gruderzeit suburb north of the city called the "Nordfront" was totally destroyed. It was the second most devastated city in Germany. Only Dresden suffered more. American and Soviet troops occupied the city in 1945, however, American forces left after a short time, leaving the city under Soviet stewardship.

From 1945 to the end of the century, Magdeburg remained the capital of Saxony-Anhalt in the reunified Germany. Most of the city is now rebuilt exclusively in modern style, rejecting its millennias of spanning history.

It was in this ancient city that the headlines screamed on August 26, 1926, that Rudolph Valentino died. Thousands of women were sobbing next to their radios that day, overcome by the news of Valentino's death. The actor having thrilled them for five years previous with films like *Blood and Sand*, *The Young Raga*, *Cobra*, and many others, was only thirty-one years old. The bursting of a gastric ulcer sent him to a hospital, where he spoke his final words, a sad delirious babble of French and Italian. Paula Negri, the great actress, had ordered four thousand roses for his bier. One fan even chose to shoot herself. It was a sad day worldwide. Two weeks prior to this, Gertrude Ederly became the first woman to swim the English Channel. She accomplished this feat in less time than any of the men who had done it over the previous fifty-one years. The gritty New Yorker crossed the channel in fourteen hours and thirty-one minutes. The best previous time was sixteen hours and twenty-one minutes by an Italian swimmer. Ms. Ederly walked instead of diving into the surf at seven o'clock in the morning and arrived at Cape Gries-Nez, France, at 9:31 at night acknowledging the cheers of a few spectators. She was slowed somewhat, after five hours in the water when the winds increased. However, her biggest delay was recorded at the finish. There, the nineteen-year-old swimmer was held up again, when customs officials insisted on interrogating her before permitting her on the shore. It was these headlines and stories that made August 26, 1926, a day for news in the Magdeburg newspapers.

Not mentioned on that fateful day, was the fact that Mark and Lena Wallach, entrepreneurial Magdeburgers, announced the birth of their third child, who would be named Kurt. Surely, this news was small in comparison to the many other interesting stories in the paper that day. However, in my life, it was the commencement and the genesis. If it were not for the happening on that fateful day of August 26, 1926, this book would not have been written, and you would be doing something else rather than reading it at this time.

Growing up in Magdeburg was not difficult for the youngster Kurt. Mark, his loving father, was a successful businessman, having purchased apartment building after apartment building, all successes, which made the family extremely comfortable financially. Aside from the real estate empire he was building, Mark, the father, owned the city's only leather goods store, which was located on the "Breite-Weg," translated, "Broadway." The leather goods store had had a good run since the horrible inflation days of 1924, and both my parents devoted ample time to that endeavor. Since automobiles were not the mode of transportation in Magdeburg in 1926, Dad had to travel to the various apartment complexes by streetcar. He was not a good loner, and was much happier when accompanied by a companion. As a youngster, even as young as two and three years of age, I was fortunate to have him take me with him as we visited the various complexes, speaking to tenants, nosing around, and just being together. I think he enjoyed these little trips with me, and paid more attention to my antics than he did to the happenings at the buildings.

It was generally a very good afternoon when he said to me, "Come on, Kurtl," his nickname for me, "let's go to the buildings." On occasion, my sister Renée, who was two years older than I, came along. Rarely did he take all three of the children, which would have included my older brother Benno, who was a year older than Renée. In any event, the sojourns to the buildings are still very much remembered by me, as pleasant times that we spent together.

Since the leather goods store was a busy and active operation, my mother, Lena, spent many hours there along with my father. Her presence at the store, I believe, was much needed, and this left us missing her to a great degree.

While Mother and Dad tended the store, they had hired a governess for the three children. The governess was a very lovely lady by the name of Hilda. At this writing, I do not remember her last name, if, in fact, I ever knew it.

Benno and Renée, being older than I, went to school every morning at about eight or eight-thirty, leaving Hilda and me at home. Hilda and I had a marvelous relationship. She loved me

*Kurt in Magdeburg with his Easter basket,
1931.*

like a son, and I have only the most pleasant memories of her. In fact, it was like a love affair between her and me, as we spent the hours together until Mother or Dad or my sister and brother finally came home later in the afternoons. We had lunch, we played games, we went for walks, and generally enjoyed each other to the utmost, almost as boyfriend and girlfriend, although I was still under the age of six.

Between 1926 to 1933, our relationship continued as I've described it. Sometime in 1932, late in the year, after I had turned six, it was decided that I was to start school. This, of course, was very much *not* to my liking. By going to school, I would be missing Hilda. Our walks, our games, our lunches, our fun together, would, for the most part, be over, for when I was to come home from school, Mother, Dad, my sister, and brother would likely also be coming home, and it was no longer a twosome, which I so much enjoyed. School was extremely difficult for me. Previously, Hilda and I just played in the "rote zimmer" at our home, but now, I would have to spend my days in a classroom with thirty-five other children my age. The teacher, a mean middle-aged man, was extremely cruel to me.

We must remember it was the days of the

Renée, Lena, Kurt, and Benno.

SS, SA, and the Hitler movement in Germany. Anti-Semitism was very much alive, which was taught so severely and completely on the radio, in the newspapers, on the streets, and most of all, in the schools. One could not mistake it, nor could one miss it. Life was not easy if you were Jewish.

While attending class in the first grade, my teacher singled me out, obviously as a Jew, the only Jewish boy in the class who was to get *special* attention. And special attention I got, usually by being whacked across my knuckles with a birch stick. I doubt that a day went by that I was not abused by this Nazi fiend. Although only six years of age, I was his victim and his private Jew to molest and violate.

It is almost with tears in my eyes that I remember one day he demanded that I draw a potbelly stove. At age six, this was a difficult task, particularly in view of the fact that his demands were such that my painting was to be an exact duplicate of the potbelly stove in the classroom. I was unable to do it. As I tried and failed, the birch switch found its way onto my back, the back of my head, on my arms, and on my knuckles, until soon, my artwork was wet with tears. Although my recollection of this is

Benno, Lena, Kurt on lap, Mark, and Renée.

ever so vivid, it was only one of so many abuses I suffered by this hoodlum Nazi, who had no other way of showing his hatred than to beat a six-year-old kid. Then I'd go home to Hilda and mother, who were usually at home by the time I arrived. I gave them a detailed description of my beatings. Hilda, I found, was more sympathetic and at one time, I recall her crying with me over the abuse that I had to take. Looking forward to going to school in the morning after breakfast was almost like living a daily nightmare—until I finally came up with a solution to the problem.

It came to my mind that I should throw-up my breakfast on the way to school, by heaving it all over my clothing. Surely Hilda would not be able to take me to the classroom in my soiled condition. The day after my plan, I made up my mind that this would be a permanent solution to the problem. I became quite expert at puking and in no more than three to four minutes out of the house, I saw to it that the big breakfast that I had eaten was to wind up on my small shirt and short pants. The ploy worked. The first day that I was able to pull this off, Hilda took me back home and attempted to change my dirty clothes. I fidgeted and protested to a point where probably forty-five minutes or more went by and she finally said to me, "Kurt, I'm afraid it's too late. You've missed school. I cannot take you now." There was not a day from the beginning of this neat trick that I did not repeat it, and there was not a day she was able to get me to go back to the classroom. Finally, after about three weeks or more, I was victorious in my battle and I was taken out of school, not to return. I had won.

While this was my young life at age six, the propaganda for the presidential election between Adolph Hitler, the representative of the National Socialist German Worker's Party, the "Nazionale Deutche Arbeiters Partei," and the president of Germany, Paul Von Hindenberg, was raging. As Hilda and I passed the days, we saw trucks filled with Nazi hoodlums riding up and down our street with horns blaring, dispensing Nazism and anti-Semitism. There were daily motorcycle brigades with sidecars on each motorcycle decorated with swastikas, as well as trucks carrying armed men, shouting Nazi slogans and singing "Die Fahne Hoch" ("The Flag up High"). Also, they played the German National Anthem, "Deutchland, Deutchland, Uber Alles."

Nationalism was on the front page of every

newspaper in Germany. In the runoff election for the presidency of Germany, the uncommon Paul Von Hindenberg was beating Hitler by several million votes. Hindenberg had improved upon his showing in the primary election, but Hitler had an even better beginning and an additional two million votes more than in the primaries. When the final count was in, Hindenberg had received fifty-three percent of the vote and Hitler had received nearly thirty-seven percent. The traditionalists in Germany hoped the result would be a catalyst for liberal forces, but Hitler called it a race to victory for National Socialism.

He had stated, "Victory obliges me to thank all who work to create the basis of this victory, but it carries a heavy obligation. National Socialists know not what loss is, and must not rest until the goal of German liberation has been reached."

These times in Germany were not good as far as the Wallach family was concerned. Hitler's National Socialists had doubled their strength in the legislative elections and became the biggest party in the Reichstag. The Nazis increased their seats from 107 two years previously, to 229 representatives.

The German legislature was now badly divided. The election ended as it began, with fierce battles in the streets. At Altona, Hamburg's seaside port, "Bloody Sunday" erupted as the Communists attacked the Nazis with guns. It did not take long for the Social Democrats to join in and turn the battle into a blood basin.

Talks between the German government and Adolph Hitler, who had received thirteen and a half million votes, had broken off with Chancellor Von Papen's refusal to give the Nazi leader a cabinet seat. Earlier, President Hindenberg had denied Hitler's demand that he be made dictator. Addressing the 230 Nazi Reichstag members, by far the strongest block, Hitler said he could no longer tolerate the present government and that the Nazi party's total victory was only a matter of time. It was with this background of political news that my father, Mark, began to panic.

My sister, Renée, and brother, Benno, suffered in school as I had, although very likely not so severely. But life was made miserable for them also. Father's apartments were being filled with Nazis and recruiting in his buildings became almost a nightly affair. The Social Democrats at one time had outlawed Nazi recruiting and during those times, my father, along with some friends and the police, would actually raid apartment by apartment where recruiting parties were held. The following day evictions were served. My father had become a marked man. He and my mother, and most likely my brother Benno and Renée, recognized this more than I did. I had not yet turned seven years of age. It was near the end of January in 1933. After a month of secret negotiations, Nazi leader Adolph Hitler became chancellor of Germany. The flamboyant powerhungry Hitler had taken over the job at a very volatile moment in the German history. The country seemed poised on the brink of civil war. Almost daily, bloody street battles erupted between Hitler's National Socialist followers and their hated adversaries, the Communists. Hitler was feared by most of his opponents, but many hoped he would be less dangerous if he were in office than in the streets commanding his storm troopers. It was believed Hitler's thirst for power would be checked by the coalition cabinet that was largely assembled by the deft political skills of the former Chancellor Franz Von Papen. Hitler showed little restraint in his first proclamation. "The National Socialist Party knows that the new government is no National Socialist government," the chancellor declared in a proclamation, "but it is conscious that it bears the name of its leader, Adolph Hitler." He placed himself at the head of the government to lead the German people.

Communist agitators started milling in the streets of Berlin as soon as the news of Hitler's title was no longer a secret. They plastered walls with handbills calling for a nationwide general strike. Violence erupted one day as one hundred Nazis were walking home after a pro-Hitler demonstration.

A police officer accompanying them was shot to death. One of the Nazis was also killed. Hitler would surely not forget the incident. He had made the elimination of the Communists one of his key goals. The new government press chief, Walter Funk, had already made an oblique attack on the Communists, stating the cabinet would not tolerate any experiments of a financial or economic nature.

Scenes of Nazi jubilation in Berlin greatly outnumbered the Communist demonstrations. Large crowds greeted columns of Hitler's storm troopers as they marched in torchlight parades through the Brandenburg Gate. The crowds raised their hands in salute to President

Hindenburg, who stood in one lighted window of the chancellery. In another, stood Adolph Hitler, next to his new aviation minister, Hermann Goering.

Hitler, Hermann Goering, and Dr. Wilhelm Frick were the only Nazis in the cabinet for some time. It was put together by former Chancellor von Papen, after President Hindenburg gave Hitler and national party leader, Alfred Hugenberg an ultimatum and ordered the two adversaries to form a coalition. At that moment, von Papen acted quickly and drew up the cabinet with Hitler as chancellor, himself as vice chancellor, and Hugenberg as minister of the economy and food. Two Hitler allies played key roles in the month-long secret meetings that brought the Nazi leader to power. They were Cologne banker, Kurt von Schroeder, who had been impressed by Hitler's anticommunist rhetoric, and Nazi bureaucrat Joachim von Ribbentrop.

With this political background, going to the store daily was a frightful thing for my father. He never knew who would come in to attack or possibly even murder him.

Renée and Benno, my sister and brother, were now taken out of school for they too were in danger. Times were difficult indeed. Both my parents spent much more time at home than at any time previously. Even there, I am not sure that they, or the children, were safe. We were a family of five living in fear.

On February 28, 1933, smoke was first noticed by a police officer on patrol in the Reichstag at nine o'clock in the evening. Before sending an alarm, the officer fired several shots at men seen running from the scene. The officer said he seized one of them. The young suspect was said to be a Communist who was identified as Marinus van der Lubbe.

By the time the firefighters arrived, the blaze had spread in many directions. Whoever started the fire apparently had set a match to furniture piled on rugs. The wood paneling, chairs, and desks in the Reichstag's chamber were all very dry and burned easily. The flames crawled to the very top of the elegant Italian Renaissance chamber and caused the ornate glass ceiling to crash to the floor. Ten thousand Berliners heard the fire alarm and rushed to police barricades around the burning Reichstag. In the crowd were Hitler, Goering, and Vice Chancellor Franz von Papen. The brave firefighters stopped the fire before it burned through the coppola on the top.

They also saved the library and reading room, where countless priceless documents were stored.

Chancellor Hitler placed Goering in charge of the investigation into the fire. Before dawn, police were rounding up Communists and locking them up until the investigation had been completed. President von Hindenburg signed an emergency decree, which suspended constitutional guarantees of individual freedom, freedom of the press, private property, and the secrecy of postal communications. The Communist newspapers were shut down until the election and suspected Communist meeting places were closed. Parts of Berlin had begun to look more and more like a police state. The regular police backed up by Nazi auxiliaries armed with rifles patrolled many neighborhoods in armored cars.

Hitler's opponents questioned his accusation that Communists were responsible for the Reichstag fire. They wondered what the Communists could have hoped to gain. They also asked why a twenty-four-year-old Dutchman accused of the arson would have allowed himself to be captured with all his identification and his Communist Party card. The new crackdown on Communism was an outgrowth of the government's repression, which had been on the rise since Hitler became chancellor a month earlier.

Three days after he took power, he ordered the homes of the Communists searched without warrants. All their meetings had been either banned or strictly controlled. After the fire, scores of Communists disappeared underground because of increasing harassment and fear. Communists were not the only targets. Catholics had also been attacked by Nazis. Two dozen provincial governors and police chiefs were dismissed by Goering and replaced by National Socialists.

Much of the German population was in a state of panic as the elections approached. Hitler apparently hoped that they would turn to his Nazi party and the program of National Socialism as their only possible hope for salvation.

With this being the political scene, news had leaked to my father that he might be assassinated that day. This came from a loyal employee, and my father believed what was told to him. Within two hours, he had seen to it that my mother packed up our belongings and the five of us (not counting Hilda) marched ourselves off to the railroad station where we caught a train taking us to Cologne. Cologne was quite a distance. It is near the border of Holland and became our refuge for twenty-four hours. A bit of sightseeing was done in Cologne, where we viewed the famous dome and its interesting surrounding areas. That evening we were on the train again and headed west into Holland. I still do not know how it was possible for my dad to make arrangements for us to go across the border. This was usually a very complex thing to do requiring various papers to be signed and permission given. However, we did cross the border and within twelve hours we were in the town of Scheveningen, a suburb of Hague. It was March 1933.

Money was of great importance and although my father was an extremely wealthy man by most standards in Magdeburg, I am almost sure that he did not have any more money than he had in his pockets and a bit at home, which he took with him when we left Magdeburg. We were in a precarious predicament being in a strange country, with no one speaking our language, and funds at an absolute minimum.

We found an apartment and dad arranged for the five of us to move in. I believe he had saved our lives at this juncture as the Nazis shortly thereafter ran rampant in Magdeburg and destroyed many Jewish businesses, burned synagogues, beat Jews, and killed many of them as a prelude to what was to come. The Wallach family was now safely ensconced in Scheveningen.

2

Our Life in Holland

The clouds hung low and the rain came down in torrents on the first day of March 1933, which found me in this very strange environment in Scheveningen. The unknown surroundings made me homesick. Everything was so different here. No one could understand me, speaking only in the German language. Conversely, I could not understand the jabbering in guttural tones of these Dutch people who appeared so different to me. I missed my Hilda, who was no longer with me. I have always thought of her as my first and greatest love. Here I was in these far away surroundings without her. Would I ever be able to communicate with the children in school? I often wondered what things would be like when I was enrolled in first grade at the elementary school about three blocks from our apartment. My first day was very difficult, with the language barrier, of course, being the biggest problem. The jabbering kids looked at me curiously without any understanding as I just stared at them when they spoke to me. I hadn't an inkling about what they were saying. When I tried to respond, the words came out in German. Of course they looked at me in surprise. My teacher in school was a very large woman by the name of Frau Deroes. *Deroes* in Dutch means "giant," and surely she was well named. I looked up to her as one would look to the top of a tree. Although awesome, she was sweet and I liked her very much at first blush. I felt that the feelings were mutual as she escorted me into the classroom amongst the children and introduced me as the new little boy from Germany. Frau Deroes taught in Dutch, of course.

The children were very curious about me. They appeared to be kind and surely not like the Jew-hating children in Magdeburg. It would not be necessary for me to regurgitate every morning on the way to school. It wasn't long before I actually looked forward to coming to school, since I felt a kindness from most of the children, who appeared not to have a mean bone in their bodies. Frau Deroes also made me feel very much at home as she paid a little extra attention to me on a daily basis and took great interest in my ability to pick up a Dutch word here or there. After a couple of weeks, I was actually uttering a sentence or two in this strange language. At such an early age, the language barrier was not as great as it would be were I much older.

I actually picked up the language rather quickly, and after a couple of months, was able to communicate with the children, who appeared to understand and had no qualms at all about being my friends. How different this was from school in Magdeburg, how different the attitude of my teacher, and how enjoyable were the kind and understanding people I found in this new school.

One day after a couple of months, I met a boy whose name was Harry Spitz, who had a friend by the name of Kurt Berman. Kurt was a chubby rascal, whereas Harry was a skinny blond boy who, like Kurt, had also escaped the Nazis and came to Scheveningen. I was able to speak to him freely in German, and we became a threesome with so much in common. To the best of my knowledge at that time, there were no Jewish kids in the entire school except the three of us who had, by now, formed a bond. School was fun, but it was just a little bit of the overall enjoyment that I found in Scheveningen.

Our apartment was approximately a half-a-

Kurt on Dad's lap, Holland, 1934.

mile from the Strand, which was a beach on the North Sea. When the weather was good, the three of us would romp in the sand and play football (soccer, as we call it in America). Many times, some of the other kids from the school would join us and there were as many as eight or nine of us rolling in the sand, which made for happy days. Up until this time, I had never been on a beach and living within half a mile of one and being able to play there was a joyful experience.

The beach was due west of our house. About the same distance to the east was the city of The Hague itself. When the summer came, the beach was our second home as we swam in the North Sea on an almost daily basis if possible, at least three or four times a week. My mother and dad, along with sister, Renée, and brother, Benno, all partook of this wonderful venue.

Scheveningen was a summertime resort. People from all over Europe came to spend countless hours daily basking in the sun and in the sand. The surf was high, since the North Sea is one of the most vibrant bodies of water in the world. Oh, how we enjoyed it. When not there, we spent our time at the Bosches, a forestlike park east of Scheveningen, where we had an equal amount of fun in a different way.

Going up a walkway on a little hill in the Bosches, one wound up at what appeared to be the top of the world, where a structure was built called the *paraplu*. This was a plateau, possibly 150 feet in diameter, with a wooden umbrella in the middle and benches underneath. The paraplu was the highest spot in Greater Hague and one could see forever.

Looking south, we saw the outline of the town of Katwyk in the distance. Katwyk was a little obscure fishing village eight to ten miles south of the Bosches to which somehow nobody had ever been. It was not until many years later on a trip back to the old homeland that I found out that the reason none of us, nor anyone that we knew, had ever been to Katwyk was because there was no road from Scheveningen, or, for that matter, from The Hague, going to this little fishing village. We made many jokes of it and vowed that one day, we would, indeed, visit Katwyk. Actually, this did not happen until almost forty years later when my wife and I took a trip back to Holland from the United States and made an effort to get to this little place to which I had never been.

Generally speaking, my life at Scheveningen

was wonderful. I found a popularity that I had now known before. I found friendships that I had never experienced, and life was a joy. Frau Deroes was my teacher in school all the way up to the fourth grade. She was always extremely kind to me. Apparently, she had taken a liking to me and enjoyed the developments of a strange German kid who was turning into a regular little Dutch guy that everybody loved. With her as my friend, all the kids around to play with, and to be in this school, life could not have been much sweeter.

Although life was good for me and for my brother and sister, my father and mother had a more difficult time. When the five of us came from Germany, Dad had almost no money except what he had in his pockets. The escape from Nazi Germany had been quick and without hesitation. He had absolutely no time to gather worldly goods or take care of finances, which would be needed. As a seven-year-old, I could not give an analysis of my father's plight of not having a job, or a business, or for that matter, income of any kind. For some time it was actually much more difficult for him and my mother than I could comprehend. The store and the apartments in Magdeburg were gone. There was no cash flow from there. The apartment buildings that they had owned, although fully occupied, brought no rent since we were not there. My father was not there to collect, and the collector of rents was no longer in his employ.

One day my dad announced that he had been able to communicate with his major manager, a gentleman by the name of Fritz Bromann. Fritz Bromann was Dad's righthand man in Magdeburg. In his apartment business, Bromann was in total charge of the operations. The stroke of luck of being able to communicate with Bromann was likely a turning point in my family's life. Until now there were no funds for us to live on. Dad wasn't working and there was no business to bring monies needed to exist.

Mr. Bromann was not only an excellent employee, but now also a friend who was sympathetic to my father's plight. Surely he was not one of the Nazis who would hate us, but appreciated our family for what we were. It was his intent to help us in any way that he might be able. A constant stream of correspondence ensued and Bromann promised that monies from the buildings would somehow be funneled to us in Scheveningen, although this was very much against the law. It is my belief the Bromann was

Kurt, at left, with his mother, grandfather, brother, and sister.

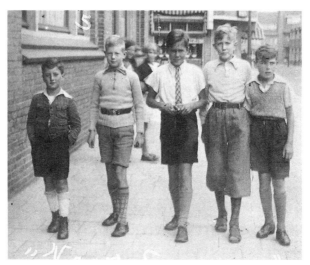

Scheveningen (Holland), 1933, on the way to school.

actually taking his life in his hands by this action. It was not too long after the initial contact and ample correspondence that some funds came to the family from Magdeburg. Paying the rent, putting food on the table, and all the general expenses soon did not present a burden any longer. Our financial well-being was assured by this German gentleman, whom I thought in later years actually saved us from destruction in Scheveningen. He had known of my father's financial plight. The eventual funding of monies from the apartment buildings through Fritz Bromann had opened my eyes to the realities of the day.

The funding came on a regular basis, along with news of what was going on in Magdeburg. The news was always highly distressing as he told of what was happening to our Jewish friends. I recall vividly hearing of so-and-so, a friend of my mother and father, having been incarcerated. My mother and dad would have arguments, sometimes heated, as Dad would say he was put in jail because he was a Jew.

Mother, on the other hand, was a little bit more naïve and argued vehemently that, " . . . they don't throw people in jail because of their religion." In the news from Bromann, it seemed that hardly a letter arrived without information about a friend who was jailed or beaten by the Nazis. World news became a highlight of almost everyday, as family, even I at the age of nine, sought information about political happenings not only in Germany, but throughout the whole world.

About a year and a half after our settling in Scheveningen, the Nazis declared the Nuremberg Laws in 1935, which took almost all freedom from the Jews. They could not work for the government, they could not have domestic help, they could not intermarry, they could not teach in public schools, the children were not allowed in school as students, etc. Though much of this had been going on prior to the Nuremberg laws, actually being introduced by government, it was now Nazi law and no longer practiced in a willy-nilly fashion. The forbidden was illegal and punishable by incarceration. Thousand of Jews throughout Germany who had violated the laws were incarcerated and severely punished. That news became a big thing in my life. The news had spread to Holland also of the horrible economic conditions in the United States, among them the dust bowls in the Midwest. The economic conditions in America were such that people were homeless and living on the streets with no food to eat. News of the day came that the United States agents had killed Dillinger, the infamous outlaw, as he left a theater in Indiana.

The Italian government had declared war on Ethiopia. A war of major consequence was being fought in that country. Cities were being bombed by Italian airplanes, and countless thousands were killed as Emperor Haile Selassie opened the prisons to increase his army. Italy's motorized legions advanced on the North and Eastern Front with mechanical precision, rolling back crumbling Ethiopian outposts. Planes were overhead, shelling military and civilians alike in great numbers. Emperor Haile Selassie had complained to the League of Nations that the Red Cross hospital had been bombed and women and children, helpless noncombatants, perished in the raids by Italian aircraft. It appeared Mussolini was trying to regain the old Roman Empire.

In 1934, Marinus Van Der Lubbe, the young Dutch man convicted of arson and the German Reichstag's fire a couple of years ago, was executed in Leipzig. Anywhere else in Nazi Germany, his head would have been lopped off with an axe, but Leipzig is in Saxony, and the Saxons used only the guillotine. His execution was unannounced, unlike publicity surrounding the arrest of the young communist. Dutch authorities had pleaded with Germans to spare Van Lubbe's life, but it was to no avail.

The revolt by Social Democrats in Austria had collapsed, and the government declared a state of emergency there. In Vienna, fighting was particularly violent as the army attacked workers with machine guns and howitzers. Hundreds were killed or wounded. The Socialist mayor of Vienna, Carl Zeiss, and many other party leaders were put under arrest. Foreign newspapers were confiscated. The government's handling of the crisis had reminded observers of Nazi Germany. Many Jews had already left Austria, possibly some had come to our new hometown of Scheveningen.

In 1935, early on in the Nazi regime, there were reports that Hitler might move to annex Austria. This news shocked Europe to a point where Britain, France, and Italy issued joint statements calling for an independent Austria.

In America, a new star came onto the scene. His name was Clark Gable. He took Hollywood by storm. Also in the news, it was reported that fighting occurred in New York City as Nazis rallied, shouting, "Heil Hitler," and Nazi sympathizers clashed with opponents during and after a New York City rally held by supporters of Germany's Adolph Hitler. The Pro-Nazi rally in Queen's stadium attracted a crowd of over 9,000 persons, most of who were there to protest the United States' boycott of German goods. Police estimated that there were eighteen clashes in and around the stadium between the Nazis and those who opposed the German regime, including several hundred Communists. Many were arrested, and a resolution was passed asking President Roosevelt to end the boycott of German goods.

The United States was much in the news in Scheveningen as word came of the killing of Bonnie and Clyde in a police ambush in Shreveport, Louisiana. They were speeding at eighty-five miles an hour in an automobile when officers opened fire from the roadside. Clyde Barrow and Bonnie Parker were found crumpled up, their guns clutched in their lifeless hands. Bonnie and Clyde had menaced the Southwest for four years, holding up banks, gas stations, and luncheonettes. It ended an era of heinous crime. A year earlier, Bromann reported that the

SS in Germany had murdered the leadership of the SA storm troopers in a bloody purge. Adolph Hitler had moved quickly and mercilessly to stamp out what he called a revolt ready to happen by the leadership of the storm troopers. Hitler himself flew from his home in Munich early in the morning to deal with Captain Ernst Roehm, chief of staff of the storm troopers. Roehm, who was reportedly caught in a compromising position with a top aid in the bedroom of his country house, was given a chance to commit suicide. When he refused, he was executed in a Munich prison. Karl Ernst, the leader of the Berlin storm troopers, was found in a house near Bremen. He was shot trying to escape from Berlin.

The Gestapo under the command of Prussian Premier Hermann Goering said they tried to arrest former Chancellor Kurt von Schleicher at his home near Potsdam. Police said both he and his wife were killed when they tried to resist.

World news was a big thing in the Wallach household by mid 1935 as always. Most of the family members, including myself, had learned to read the Dutch newspaper. One day we read that the Chinese government, in Nanking, had acquiesced to Japanese demands that it remove one of the armies from northern China. Japan, which had laid down an ultimatum to the Nanking government, also had demanded the right to approve all Chinese administrators.

The Japanese moves were similar to those in Manchuria earlier before the establishment of the Japanese-sponsored empire of Manchukuo. In complying with the Japanese demands, the Nationalist government of Chiang Kai-shek lost all political and military influence in northern China.

We were to learn in the newspaper one day that Rudyard Kipling, son of Great Britain's foremost authors, had died at the age of seventy in a Middlesex Hospital in London. Perhaps best known for his masterpieces about India, Kipling wrote volumes of prose and poetry. He was denied the poet laureate award for his negative references to Queen Victoria. Kipling was the first Englishman to win the Nobel Prize for Literature in 1907. His work was voluminous.

The English language is left with scores of Kipling's phrases, like "The White Man's Burden" to "East is East and West is West and never the twain shall meet," etc. We also read in the paper one day that Chancellor Adolph Hitler had declared open the Winter Olympics in Garmisch-Partenkirchen. Sonja Henie of Norway had won the figure skating title for the third straight Olympics and helped to attract many of the half million spectators who attended.

The program was expanded to include Alpine events with women competing for the first time, as well as in the crosscountry relay races. Norwegians swept all of the major titles.

The newspaper had become a big item in my life. The whole family was now reading Dutch without problems, and speaking the language at home at all times. It was not quite a year and a half after our arrival in our now beloved Scheveningen that my sister, brother, and I had totally given up German. We refused to speak it and conversed only in Dutch. Mother and Dad were a little bit perplexed by this, but it was not too long thereafter that they, too, communicated with each other primarily in Dutch. Holland was, in every way, "HOME." As 1936 rolled around, war in Spain was winding down with the country still talking about the heroes of the German rebel soldiers. Insurgents had seized control of the palace fortress. Hundreds of cadets and officers, together with hundreds of women and children, had been holding out there.

In America, the right-wing priest Father Coughlin was rebuked by Rome. The political activities of Charles E. Coughlin, a radio priest from Detroit, had been severely criticized by *L'Osservatore Romano,* which usually reflected the opinion of the Vatican. The newspaper said that Father Coughlin had violated proprieties in his harsh attacks on President Roosevelt's effort to aid the poor and bring America out of the Depression. Father Coughlin was a self-styled champion of the poor and had been an ardent Roosevelt supporter in 1932. Later, the Catholic priest's sermon broadcast from the Shrine of Little Flower was highly critical of the president, saying that his programs have done far too little for the poor. He was an anti-Semite who would remind us very much of the German Nazis whom we had fled from just two years earlier.

One day as I was moseying around our apartment, I noticed that my dad was in the kitchen with some ice cream being mixed together with such things as cherries and then bananas and strawberries. Some nuts occasionally were put into these mixtures with which dad was playing. Occasionally he would have berries squeezed into pulp and would mix them with his ice cream. In fact, there was hardly a fruit known to me that dad wasn't putting together with virgin ice cream to create a newfangled idea that he had, that this could become a great dessert, and could be commercially used and become popular, possibly creating a business for him. He had played with all these various fruits mixed with virgin ice cream to a point where he had literally perfected fruit ice creams. Shortly after all his experiments, dad had gone to Amsterdam where, unbeknownst to us, he had rented a store downtown. For the next few weeks, he remodeled it completely to become an ice cream parlor. There were approximately twenty tables with possibly seventy or eighty chairs. It had a bar and cash register that reminded us of the old-time kitchens in the castles.

Although we lived in Scheveningen outside of The Hague, and Amsterdam was twenty-five miles away, we heard daily of dad's new business that he had created, selling fruit ice cream to the public for the first time ever. Up until this time one could purchase any kind of ice creams that was wanted, so long as it was chocolate or vanilla. No such thing as fruit ice creams existed. My father decided that the newfangled desserts that he had created in our kitchen could be sold and indeed, they would be sold by the thousands in the months to come. He opened the Ice Cream Palace of Holland in downtown Amsterdam. It was not too long before lines formed outside the new business.

Hundreds tried to get in to taste these delicious desserts, which became the hit of Amsterdam. There was not a newspaper in town that was not talking about the new desserts that were being served by one Mark Wallach, a refugee from Nazi Germany.

Dad occasionally came home on weekends, and at times he would bring pictures back of crowds in front of the ice cream parlor wanting to get in to taste his creations.

The fruit ice cream business became an instant success as people came from all around the town to taste this new delicacy. I don't know what the cost of purchasing a cup of this ice cream would be, but no doubt it was not a cheap delicacy. It was not too long before Dad was slowly but surely becoming a successful businessman. We were happy as pigs in the mud as we lived in our beautiful little town of Scheveningen. A certain amount of wealth had come to the family, allowing us all types of luxuries we had not had recently. It was all good, and we lived at the top.

The distance from Scheveningen to Amsterdam about twenty-five miles, seemed no less a distance than possibly from Miami to Chicago in the United States. Transportation, as we know it today, was not to be had. In order to properly operate this wonderful new business Mark had created, it was mandated that he would get there on Sunday traveling via bus and working until Friday night, at which time he would pack up and come back to Scheveningen to be with the family for the weekend. He was a very hardworking, industrious individual who had always and once again made success his way of life, giving his family the financial comforts that anyone would wish to acquire.

On a winter day, when the ice cream parlor was not filled with customers seeking the fancy dessert, a middle-aged couple came into the establishment and sat down at a corner table. Normally, the average customer might consume one, possibly two dishes and then leave, or just take the dish with them. Rarely did a customer stay for more than ten or fifteen minutes at most. This day, however, it was a little bit different. This couple had ordered one dish after another for two hours. It is my belief that there were about twenty dishes of different flavors including nuts, etc., being served. They had sampled almost all of them since sitting down a couple of hours earlier. After this length of time, my father came over to their table and introduced himself as the owner and asked if he might join them. The task of the introduction was quite difficult since the gentleman and his wife did not speak Dutch, nor could they speak German.

Neither of them could communicate with my father, who, in turn, was unable to understand their language, which apparently was English. Somehow, however, they could communicate a little and Mark sat down at their table. They told him that they had come to Holland from a far-off country called "Pennsylvania," somewhere in the western hemisphere. My father, of course, had no idea where this country of Pennsylvania was, but knew it had to be somewhere in America. Obviously, they communicated rather poorly, but somehow got their thoughts across to each other. One was that this gentleman was going to build ice cream stores on highways in the United States. The government had allowed him to put one ice cream store every twenty-five to fifty miles on a new highway being built. It was his idea to come to Amsterdam to see what this ice cream my father was making was all about, and it was therefore that he was in the ice cream parlor to taste it. Apparently, he and his wife had enjoyed eating almost every flavor when my dad, despite the poor communication, took him in the back and showed him how he was making it. Dad was sharing his recipe.

The gentleman and his wife stayed almost three hours, at the end of which he shook hands with my father and wished him good luck. His name was Howard. Dad had introduced himself as Mark. Howard and Mark had become friends. Howard decided to come back the next day, prior to boarding a ship back to America. My father looked for him, but he never came back. It was the last that he was to see of him in Amsterdam.

It is interesting to note that many years later, after we had immigrated to the United States, we heard this chap, Howard, had indeed opened a number of ice cream parlors on what was to be the Pennsylvania Turnpike running from Philadelphia, westwards through Ohio. The restaurants all had an orange roof and were named after him. His last name was Johnson. It was thus that the Howard Johnson Ice Cream Parlors and later, hotels, came into being—from Mark Wallach's initial discovery of fruit ice creams. At the time of this occurrence, none of us, including my dad, had any inkling of the fame which was to come to Mark Wallach's fruit ice cream in America. Dad was enjoying his huge business, which had now grown to where there were great number of employees and hundreds of customers on a daily basis. We, in Scheveningen, were enjoying the Bosches daily, living the good life. What could be better?

3

An Ordeal

It was late in 1935 that my dad became almost paranoid over what was happening in Germany as news came from Fritz Bromann and others about the harassment and torturing of Jewish friends in Magdeburg. The Nazi movement, which had spread so quickly, had made its way into our home in Scheveningen. There were daily discussions on what was to come with this maniac at the head of the government in Germany. Although nobody would pay much attention, my dad would say that this crazy man would one day declare war and conquer all of Europe and that the madman would round up all the Jews in all the countries in Europe and have them killed. When my father would utter these wild tales, my mother just shrunk and couldn't bear seeing the faces of people hearing this "idiot" telling such crazy stories. It was as if in today's world, President Bush would say, we are going to kill every Baptist in America. When my father would say Hitler would kill every Jew in

Germany, there was little difference between these two statements. He would come off as crazy, and my mother was ashamed to be with him when he would tell of his crazy ideas of what he thought the fuhrer of the German people would do. It was just too wild a story, and it met with disgust from my mother. Likely, rightly so.

One day in late 1935, my dad had tried to convince his wife that he should go to America because this is where he wanted to take the family. My mother thought of this as a big sham. There was no way that she would ever agree to her family leaving their wonderful nest in Scheveningen to go to that heathen country across the ocean where people were starving in a horrible depression. Nevertheless, she gave in eventually and did not voice great objections to my father traveling alone to America to visit his brother Joe in Detroit and his other brother Adolph in Cleveland, Ohio, America. Dad's thoughts were quite different. For him, this trip was an exploration for possible future settlement. For my mother, this trip was a nonsense. She felt that, after all, he had not seen his brothers for thirty years, and was entitled to be with them and visit them before too much more time elapsed. Dad came to America and spent two weeks with Joe, his brother from Detroit, and A. T. as he was called, his older brother who lived in Cleveland, where he stayed. Joe Wallach came over with his family frequently.

There was a wonderful reunion that lasted a couple of weeks while dad was there. During the visit, much was discussed about the possible emigration from Holland to America and how Mark might be able to learn to speak the English language and make a living in this country. It was at this time that the depression of the mid 1930s was at its height. The unemployment rate in the United States had become astronomical. Nearly a million persons had been made homeless, and thousands killed by one of the worst floods in the history of the Ohio and Mississippi rivers. Louisville, Cincinnati, and other cities, were under water and the army engineers had drawn up plans to evacuate as many as three-quarters of the million people living across Mississippi from Cairo, Illinois, to the Gulf of Mexico.

Property damage was estimated in the hundreds of millions in what was called the greatest emergency of the nation. Beside this huge tragedy, unemployment reached unthinkable heights as men roamed the streets hungry. Soup kitchens were set up throughout the country to feed the starving. It was to this country that my father was introduced when he visited with Joe and A. T. After a couple of weeks in America, Dad made his way back to Scheveningen to his wife and children to report that he had just come from the land of "milk and honey." He described that there was money in the streets and it was the most wonderful place in the world to be as everyone was well off, happy, and cheerful. It was the biggest lie of the year as he told my mother that this land of plenty could be their home for the years to come. My mother was totally, utterly, and completely opposed to any crazy notion of leaving the cozy life that we had in Scheveningen and going to this God-forsaken country in America. We had it all. The children were happy, my father's business was thriving, and we led the good life. Surely no better life could be had than what we were living in Scheveningen. My father found it difficult to disagree with her assessment. On the other hand, he was almost paranoid about the daily news that we were getting from Germany as to the state of the anti-Semitism that was sweeping that country. The government made laws which, when violated, would cause violators to

Mark, seated second from left, coming to the United States, 1935.

go to work camps and prisons and often to their death. The agony suffered by Jews was such that it became almost impossible for them to remain where they were. They could not work; they had no jobs and no way of leading normal lives, nor could they, by any stretch of the imagination, support themselves.

The Jews suffered so terribly with anti-Semitism, that life could not be lived. My father saw this as a disease which would spread not only throughout Germany, but in the not too distant future, would find its way into Holland and the rest of Europe.

As I had written previously, he was almost paranoid with the thought of Nazism spreading over Europe and the German armies conquering the neighboring countries. With his intention to get out while there was time, where could be better than the United States of America, where he had family? This message was to be hammered into my mother's brain for weeks to come. She did not take kindly to it, and the arguments which became a daily happening between my mother and father were so vociferous and heated that I do not believe I shall ever forget them. My father insisted that for the sake of the family, for the sake of our livelihood, and for the sake of our lives, we would have to leave Holland and be gone from the Nazi monster, which he felt was going to take over Europe soon. My mother, on the other hand, was of an entirely different mind, as she saw nothing my father saw. She could not imagine Hitler conquering Europe by any means. She could not imagine the violent anti-Semitism existing in Germany spreading across the boarders into Holland, and refused to even hear of any crazy thoughts of leaving Europe for America.

My mother had three sisters in Vienna with husbands and children. Her father was also in Vienna, and it must have been in the front of her mind that should she ever acquiesce to my father's wishes and come to America, then she would never see her family again. This thought was a driving force with her, I am sure. Why would anyone leave the comforts that we had, she thought, and go into unchartered waters to once again experience what we had four year earlier before coming to Holland without the knowledge of language, without money, without knowing the customs, etcetera? No, no, no way would she consider it, and the battles continued.

One day after a rather heavy lunch, my father had a terrible stomachache. It was so bad that mother insisted that he should see a doctor. He was at the doctor's office being examined when the doctor decided that there had to be a major problem in his abdomen and that exploratory surgery was called for. My mother agreed to this. Dad entered the hospital in late 1935. The surgery was performed, I believe, by an unskilled surgeon who opened a wound from bellybutton to the groin. The surgery was extremely severe. Dad stayed in the hospital for weeks recovering from the trauma the surgeon had inflicted. They found nothing and luckily, he survived the ordeal, although there was much suffering. His life was very much in question at the time.

After two months, Dad was back to the ice cream parlor in Amsterdam. Things were never the same. The serene togetherness of mother and father had somehow disappeared since the daily battle waged as to the family remaining in Holland or moving on to the United States of America to an unknown life, had taken a toll.

It was at this time that the Olympics were held in Berlin, Germany. They ended with record crowds, record receipts, and record performances, a smashing success for the German

organizers and the fifty-three competing nations.

Five thousand athletes competed. Sixteen
records were set and one equaled in the twenty-
three events on the track and field program. The
United States took twelve first places, more than
any other nation. However, the Olympic quest
for peace and harmony among nations was once
again strained, this time by Chancellor Adolph
Hitler. Jews not only contributed to the United
States Olympic coffers, they were also among
the visiting American athletes, much to the dismay of Hitler and his anti-Jewish National Socialist Regime. In addition, ten blacks showed
up on the talent-laden American team. Hitler
had called Negroes an inferior race. But they
more than just showed up. They made shambles
of the sprints and hurdles and dominated the
field events as well.

The undisputed star of the show was a mod-
est black athlete from Ohio State University,
Jesse Owens. He won the 100- and 200-meter
dashes, the running broad jump, and was on the
winning 400-meter relay team. He also was in
a drama with Hitler. When Hans Woelike won
the shot put on opening day, Hitler had the first
German champion of any Olympics paraded

before him. But when Owens and his "black auxiliaries," as Hitler called them, exploded on the scene, it was a far different matter. Owens ran the 100 meters in a record 10.2 seconds. Other blacks also dominated their events. This put the fuhrer on the spot. Hitler, who had congratulated other Olympic visitors publicly, was faced with a dilemma to recognize the blacks or flout world opinion by ignoring them. His solution was to leave the stadium hastily, ostensibly because of threatening rain and lateness of the hour. Hitler congratulated other Olympic champions publicly. When the Germans finished one and two in the hammer throw, he received them under the stands. Even when Lutz Long finished second in the broad jump, Hitler congratulated him privately and ignored Owens completely. When Owens completed his triumphant performance at the Olympics by winning the 200-meter race in a record 20.7 seconds, spectators rose as one to pay tribute to the American athlete from Ohio State. The applause was thunderous, but by that time, Hitler had again left the stadium.

Americans Archie Williams and John Woodruff won the 400- and 800-meter races respectively. Another American, Glenn Morris, won the decathlon. Clouds of doom floated over Europe in the eyes of my father. As days went by, he was more determined by the hour that he would take his family out of Europe and bring his children to America. He had previously conquered his financial problems in Holland and felt that when taking his family to the United States, he would not have a problem in doing so there as well. My mother disagreed totally, saying that she could not speak the language there, that the country was in a very bad state of affairs, which was true, and that we would suffer greatly if we came to America.

The battle was ongoing for months, and there was no peace in the Wallach household. The children suffered from the goings-on between Mother and Father, which went on day and night with no end in sight.

My father had a very strong personality, as did my mother. In the end, however, he prevailed. To come to America was his goal to save his family. The idea of coming here, penniless, of course, was not one that he relished and somehow he felt there had to be a solution to the problem of not being able to take any money out of Holland and to bring it to the United States. His solution was found and he began to exercise it.

Instead of going to Amsterdam on Sunday nights as he usually did, he would leave Scheveningen and our home. For the next five days, he traveled Holland, not going to the Ice Palace in Amsterdam at all. What he was doing was buying all the herring and all the cheese that he was able to purchase. He bought the herring and cheese by barrels wherever he could and sometime completed the week having purchased fifty to sixty barrels of cheese and possibly the same number of barrels of herring. He piled these up in huge inventories and saw to it that these barrels of herring and cheese were to be shipped to South Hampton, England, where the world's largest ship was under construction and was scheduled to sail to America.

He had made arrangements with the Cunard White Star Line to purchase five cross-Atlantic tickets for his wife and three children and rent part of one of the lower decks to transport his herring and his cheese to the United States. Most of this plan was unknown to my mother. It is my belief as I look back that he had her totally convinced that he was in the ice cream parlor doing business every day of the week that he was gone. He had not gone there week after week and had instead purchased the herring and cheese. When the fateful day came, Mark took his three children and his wife to a small ship in Rotterdam.

We traveled to London, a one-day trip. It is not necessary to describe in detail the trials of the journey, which saw almost every member on the passenger list dirtying the decks with previously swallowed food, and seeing passengers hanging over the sides of the ship, feeding the fish from their stomachs. The ride on this small ship from Rotterdam to London had to be one of the roughest rides anyone had ever taken. There was not a soul aboard the ship, with the exception of me, Kurt, who was not totally seasick.

My mother, father, sister, and brother—and everybody else—were throwing up or were yellow in the face like the color of a banana. Thank goodness the trip ended and we arrived in London. It was October 26, 1936.

The following day was my sister's birthday. Renée had now turned twelve and was enjoying the sights of London. The family toured London, Southampton, and the surroundings for approximately three days enjoying the sightseeing of our life. It was very educational, although nobody spoke the language of these funny Englishmen who resided there. After the third day, we headed for South Hampton, where the *Queen Mary* was docked, and the family boarded. What an experience this was for a kid who was not quite eleven years of age—to be standing up high on the deck looking down over South Hampton from the *Queen Mary's* highest point! The thrill of that trip, the first in my young life, is hard to describe. It was the thrill of a lifetime. My dad had bought good tickets and after a few hours aboard, the ship was guided out by a pilot tug.

We were at sea for the major voyage across the ocean.

4

Cleveland, America

The *Queen Mary* was just great. Not only were the luxurious lines on this magnificent vessel eye-catching, but the interiors were out of this world. There were three classes for passengers with the highest priced being first class having superior service, the finest meals and the very best the Cunard-White Star Line was able to offer. Second class was good in every respect and as a matter of fact, so was the third class. Dad chose to go second class for the five of us and we did enjoy luxuries sometimes not available on land. The experience of seeing nothing but water in every direction day after day was exciting. The seas were rough at times but surely nothing like crossing the North Sea, which made everybody so sick. This was a joyride in comparison. The luxury, comradery and a general happy atmosphere aboard made the trip a marvelous one. Renée and I chased each other around from port to starboard and from stern to bow almost every day. We were most likely little pests as we scampered around.

As was a part of most cruises, the food was more than excellent. We were served some things I had never eaten before, i.e., shrimp, lobster, etc. What a joyride this was. At the end of the fifth day we pulled into New York harbor and saw the Statue of Liberty, a sight about which we had heard much, but could not imagine seeing in person. Again, the ship picked up a pilot tug and it was guided slowly in. It took a little while to get the ship moored. As we stood on the top deck we looked down and saw hundreds of people, obviously Americans, waving their arms, screaming, yelling and generally making merry. We stayed there, not ready to get off, as my father was not in a hurry. Looking down from the top deck I saw them taking out what appeared to be hundreds of barrels from a lower deck. My father came by and said, "Look, that's ours, all of it," herring and cheese.

It was the cargo that my dad had put on the ship to bring to America to try to sell and have some liquid cash available for our sustenance after our arrival. There was a delay of about two to three hours that we children did not mind at all. At the end of that time, we got off and were met by my father's cousin, Anchel, who had come to greet us. The reunion and the joy between them were wonderful to behold.

Anchel and his wife lived in New York City. It was they who would be our hosts for the first few days in America. After all the routine discharging from the ship was complete and all our luggage, I believe eighteen pieces, was gathered together we got into an automobile to take us to Anchel's apartment which was in midtown Manhattan. The ride was quite an experience for us kids since we could not even imagine these highrise buildings that we passed. As we looked up we could see thirty, forty, fifty even seventy stories high buildings that were totally strange to us.

We had heard of skyscrapers in America but found our first view of them to be beyond words. We pulled into Anchel's apartment in about an hour and finally settled in with them. The communication was not too difficult for my father as Anchel spoke a very broken German. He was able to understand nearly everything that was said to him. His replies were slightly lost but both mother and father picked up almost everything. As evening came the kids were put to bed ending what was the journey of a lifetime for all of us. What an experience!

The following morning we woke up and looked around in an entirely new environment, one that we had never experienced. It was like being on another planet with all the buildings, the high rises, the traffic, all of which was strange to us, since obviously we had none of this in Scheveningen.

I went with Anchel and my dad to the pier where arrangements were made for shipping of the barrels of herring and cheese to various places in New York City from where they would be sold. Currently Anchel had made connections with food brokers here and within three days of being in the herring and cheese business my father had sold the entire product that he had purchased in Holland. We were ready to leave the big city for Cleveland, Ohio where his brother and family awaited us. After the third day at Anchel's home we boarded a train and again experienced a whole new life of seeing what was in the big cities in America. Smokestacks, high-rises, and the elevateds in the hubbub of the metropolis were obviously strange to us all. Not a moment of the past eight days was lost as we kids traveled, enjoying one new experience after another. The train ride from New York across Pennsylvania to Cleveland was another highlight of the odyssey which we were experiencing and were so very much relishing. Benno and I did not get along on this trip, either on the ship, at Anchel's house or at home, but then again that was not an unusual happenstance as he and I had never been comfortable with each other, nor enjoyed each other, though we were brothers only three years apart. Renée and I on the other hand were like two peas in a pod as we had always been. We enjoyed what was to be seen as a pair, not so much individually. The arrival in Cleveland that day was another fantastic event which is to be remembered as my uncle, A. T. Wallach, my father's brother, and his wife Florence, met us at the train station.

They picked the five of us up and took us out to their lovely home in Shaker Heights, which once again became an experience, since we had not lived, nor had any family members lived, in so sumptuous and luxurious surroundings as A. T. and Florence had. Their home was large on a huge corner lot with landscaping that was beautiful. We looked around and again marveled at the new experience that we were having. We were shown to our rooms. My brother and I shared one, my sister had another, mother and

Mark, A. T. and Joe in Cleveland, Ohio, 1937.

dad had theirs and Adolph and Florence had theirs. They took their three-year-old, my cousin Claire, in with them. It was a full house. We were tired, worn out, and had a great night's sleep.

The following morning again had us all excited as we walked up and down the streets viewing the beautiful homes in the neighborhood, sights to which we had not been accustomed. The neighborhood we traveled that day as we walked around in the town of Shaker Heights was dotted with magnificent homes, the types that none of us children had ever imagined. Although it was cold and snowy we insisted on continuing with our walks going up one street and down another viewing new neighborhoods.

We passed the elementary school and wondered what it would be like if we were to attend. Of all the experiences in Holland and Germany during my younger years, I had never before been made aware of what life could be like here, and what appeared to be living in the lap of luxury.

Cold as we were, our walk must have lasted five hours before we returned to A. T. and Florence's home where two worried parents and my aunt and uncle sat wondering what had happened to the kids.

Much thought was given by me to the prospect of once again being in a school with many children, and being looked upon as some strange bird who could neither understand the language nor speak it. How would my teacher react to a new student who understood nothing? How would it be for me to progress and learn when in fact I could not understand anything? These thoughts ran though my head that evening as I crawled into my cozy bed, tired out almost totally from what was probably a six- or seven-mile walk around the heart of Shaker Heights.

Living with my uncle A. T. and Aunt Florence was a fine experience, although I realized that there must have been many times that I got on my aunt Florence's nerves. After all, a ten-year-old does not take to discipline as one would like him to. The time at my uncle Adolph and Florence's home was actually quite short since we stayed only a period of three weeks, when one morning my dad announced that we had found a place of our own to rent and that we would shortly be moving to a three bed room second floor apartment, actually quite spacious, on East 147th street. This move took place some time in early December or late November 1936.

All the boxes and all of the belongings which

had been stored after we came off the *Queen Mary,* were now being delivered to 147th Street. It took the family less than a week to settle into our new surroundings. Were they as sumptuous and luxurious as my uncle Adolph's house in Shaker Heights? No, they were not. However, they were nevertheless at least as comfortable and spacious as where we lived in Holland. Everyone seemed quite satisfied. Our landlord, Mr. Kirnig, lived downstairs in this duplex. We had the upstairs including a porch, which was probably about forty feet long and fifteen feet in depth. My brother and I shared a room, my sister Renée had her room and mother and dad had theirs.

There were two bathrooms and no one suffered in the least. The difficulty lie ahead of course, in our being enrolled in a new school. This school was called Andrew Jackson Rickoff. It was at the end of our street, probably about a half a mile to the north. Being enrolled in "Rickoff," as it was known, once again created trauma. The neighborhood in which we lived was middle class and the children were not of the kindest nature as they related to this new kid who couldn't speak the language. I couldn't communicate at all and had no idea what was going on in the classroom. Keeping in mind that we were still in the height of an economic depression, it can be noted that the lives of the children in the fourth grade were not as pleasant as they might be in different economic times from those in which we lived.

Many of the parents suffered badly due to lack of money, as jobs were very scarce. Parents who were well employed earned less than what would have been acceptable in different times. All felt the stress of a lack of money very severely. This came right down to the children who were denied what children of today's parents would consider to be easily obtained and routinely purchased as compared to similar items being considered luxury by the children of 1936.

The weather in Cleveland was a little bit harsh for me because Scheveningen did not have nearly the severe cold, sleet and wind of Cleveland, Ohio. We found it extremely difficult to get used to the cold, although with the strength of youth, this ten year old sometimes more than slightly enjoyed the frigidity. I felt it quite interesting to be able to comb my hair wet in the morning, very wet, and then march off to school which was about a ten to fifteen minute walk. By the time I got to school my hair was frozen

Back row: Benno, Lena, Mark, Margaret. Front row: Kurt, Renée, Claire, Carolyn, Cleveland, Ohio 1936.

solid as I sat in class. Many times I took the little pieces of ice I was able to pick up off my head and used them to throw across the room. This bad habit soon gave me a bad reputation with the teacher who didn't necessarily agree with my antics. Since she was a bit frustrated at not being able to reach me verbally, and since I understood nothing, the situation at times was quite difficult. My indulging in this practice gave me a thrill and her a headache.

It was not too long after coming to Rickoff that I slowly but steadily started to pick up words and sentences in this new language, and after several months was able to communicate.

Due to the fact that I had changed languages once before, from German to Dutch, there was very little accent that could be detected. Within the year, I believe it would have been difficult for anyone to know that I was not born in this country, as I spoke the language just as fluently as all the other children. School had become a routine, although I was a bit angry over the fact that they put me back one year since I was initially unable to speak English. It was felt I was not fit to be in the fifth grade where I really belonged, instead, the fourth grade was where I landed.

The year lost stayed with me all the way through high school. At all times I was a year older than my classmates and this disturbed me to no end. In learning the English language I reveled in the daily newspaper the *Cleveland Plain Dealer,* which I read with uncommon interest for a kid of my age. I believe, in looking back today, that my reading so vociferously daily helped me a great deal to learn English. There was so much news of interest. Once I started reading all the things that were happening in this country, I became quite educated, likely more so out of the newspaper than out of the classroom.

The news of the day in 1936 and 1937 were quite ample and interesting as I read about the abdication of King Edward of England, who had broadcast his farewell to throngs unwilling to believe that their ruler was retiring. The king was marrying a commoner as thousands swarmed around the car of the next monarch, the Duke of York, returning from dinner with Edward. A future course was in doubt, as we heard reports that he would take a castle in Denmark. Many other reports, mostly unfounded and untrue, were to be found in the pages of the *Plain Dealer.* The king was about to marry Ms. Wallace Simpson, a commoner.

Interesting also was the crash of the *Hindenburg* over in Lakehurst, New Jersey, which killed thirty-three people leaving sixty-four alive after static electricity from the engines, ignited hydrogen gas. The captain, one Ernst Lehmann and the commander, were critically hurt, as were many of the sixty-four survivors, most of whom leaped out of the *Hindenburg* after the explosion. The *Hindenburg* had her silvery bulk shattered by a terrific explosion. The German dirigible plunged down in flames at the United States Naval Air Station. Explosions continued to tear her twisted aluminum skeleton apart and rip into her fabric for hours afterwards.

Harry Bruno, the press relations counsel for the Zeppelin Company, which operated the luxurious modern dirigible, said that sixty-four of the persons aboard her maiden voyage in 1937 had in fact been reported safe. The Navy Department of Washington said it had heard that at least forty-eight persons were killed. Oil-fed flames horribly burned many of the dead. Hospitals for miles around were crowded with the injured.

It appeared that a spark had ignited the engine of the *Hindenburg*. Captain Ernst Lehmann had his Last Rites administered by a Roman Catholic Priest. Lehmann, the skipper of the ship's 1936 flights made the ill-fated flight as an observer. Captain Max Pruss, the commander, was listed as an injured survivor who eventually lived to tell the tale. This was one of the interesting stories of the time. As I recall it was only one of many.

Another interesting remembrance was the saga of the power of Joseph Stalin in the Soviet Union. Stalin had at this time executed sixteen of his political opponents, all of whom were said to be Trotskyites. All of them were former Stalin allies, but that seemed to make no difference. The defendants were tried for high treason. They were not allowed defense attorneys, but 200 spectators including foreign diplomats were permitted to watch the proceedings.

Sergey Zinoviev and Stanislav Kamenev had already been in custody for assassinating Sergey Kirov, the Leningrad boss and Stalin confidante. During the trial, both confessed to plotting with the exiled Leon Trotsky who had attempted to overthrow Stalin's government.

In Spain there were no trials and all jails were emptied. Rebel troops in the civil war did not bother to take prisoners when they stormed into towns bordering Portugal. They lined loyalist up against the wall and fired. The streets were running with blood. There was no mercy in the civil war, which raged there. Portuguese journalists reported that every street was barricaded and each was heaped with corpses. Women were searching amongst the dead for their husbands. Moroccan troops under the command of Colonel Yague backed up the Legionnaires and the Fascist militia when they were surrounded. Rebels opened fire with artillery and fired for the final assault. All were then murdered. Most of these young men did not plead for mercy.

Many did ask for a priest. Spain was soon to be divided in half. Franco's troops held the south, west and the north of the country. They were trying to open up a line to connect the divided forces. The government was in control of Madrid, the northeast part of the northwest and both sides were trying to expand their control by appealing to civilians for support. The battle in Spain was murderous, ambitious and almost beyond description at times. The fascist rebels were backed by Adolph Hitler, the German dictator.

As we settled into our new country, President Roosevelt was elected by a landslide, defeating

Alfred Landon in the greatest outpouring of votes in the nation's history. Returns had shown that the President had 523 electoral votes, while his Republican opponent had just eight. The election proved to be an overwhelming endorsement of the new deal featuring the president's innovative program that sought to bring the nation out of the depression. Vast numbers of workers as well as the unemployed went to the polls, many of them for the first time. Governor Landon, from Kansas, had stepped up his attacks on Roosevelt and accused the president of trying to be a dictator. All his efforts failed as the country elected the incumbent president. Those were only some of the many stories of my early arrival in Cleveland. I took to all of them with great enthusiasm.

I played with the kids at school, but it was not nearly as much fun as playing football (what we call soccer) in Scheveningen with my buddies. Here in this strange country I found even stranger an oblong object that the kids threw to each other, which they called a football. How could they be so ignorant as to call this thing "a football"?

Everyone knew that a football is round and made of patches. Yet these kids didn't know anything about what a real football looked like. It took me quite some time to understand this funny game that they played where we tagged each other when we ran with this thing. What I heard being played in high schools was that instead of being tagged by the opposition player, they were to be knocked to the ground before play would stop. Instead of continuity in the "real game of football," these kids in America stopped every time they did what they called a "play." What a funny game it was! However, it was not too long before I decided that I would also play this strange sport, and it was soon after that I was enjoying it to no end. Running with this oblong object and knocking other players down was indeed a fun game. Surely I could not connect it to what I had all my life known as "football." It seemed that as the winter waned that year, they stopped playing this game altogether. I had a difficult time in figuring out why since everybody seemed to be having so much fun doing it. I then found that instead of "football" they were now playing a game where there were nine people standing out on a field. One of them had a ball in his hand that he threw at a player representing the other side. That player who was the opposition, stood there all by himself with one of the opponents behind him as this fellow in the middle threw a ball at him. It was his job apparently to hit this ball with a round stick that he had in his hands. If he was successful in hitting the ball he than an down the sideline to what they called a base. Strange?

Yes, it was a strange game that I found extremely difficult to understand. Why would they do this? How much fun could you have with a round stick in your hand trying to hit a ball that some fellow on the other side throws at you? But then again I did not fully understand these odd American kids anyway. I did not partake of this strange game that they called baseball for quite some time. However, I did view it many times in all of its stupidity. Throw a ball at somebody, hit it with a round stick and then run for your life toward a destination so many feet on the side of the playing field. Peculiar! Odd for sure.

Being an athlete all my life, I found it difficult to just stand by and watch this silly goings-on. I decided one day as long as they are doing it, I will do it too and I got into the game. I think they put me way out in what they called the right field. I was given a glove with which I was to catch this baseball in case the fellow with the stick would hit the ball in my direction. I was told if I got the ball before it hit the ground I was really doing the right thing for our side and would be hurting the other team. However, if I did not catch the ball and it hit the ground I was likely to be blamed, nevertheless I had to pick it up and throw it to one of the other guys on my team.

Playing in this right field, I learned before too long was almost a punishment since rarely did the guy with the round stick hit the ball out there. So I had very little to do playing on this side rather than taking my turn with the stick to swing at the ball. Of course this took place also and the first few times that I did all the kids yelled at me because I was not able to use this stick right, apparently since I did not hit the ball at all, but swung at it and the chap standing behind the plate said I was "out." I don't know what exactly that meant, but I suppose it meant that I wasn't allowed to swing at the ball any more and I was told to sit down on the side until everybody else was also called out and then I had to run back out to right field where I was never, or rarely ever, to see the ball come in my direction. Well, it was not really too long before I got used to this art form of sports.

Surely they never did anything as silly as this back home in Scheveningen. If they did, they would have laughed them out of town. I never saw anything like it. Nevertheless, after several weeks of partaking in this nonsense, I began to enjoy it and became a baseball player. Several weeks later they recognized that even though this kid who was just learning how to speak the English language was after all a bit of an athlete now that he was using the stick properly and hitting the hell out of that ball they were throwing at him. Many times I hit it squarely and off it went out into what they called "the outfield" and then I ran like a deer from one of these bases to another and sometimes all the way around until I got back to where I started. This was called a home run, as I came into a cheering crowd of all my other players. In fact it was not too long before I really enjoyed doing this nonsense and played it almost on a daily basis.

When not playing "baseball," I had become an avid fan of the Cleveland Indians. This began in the summer of 1937 when Jack Graney and Pinky Hunter, the announcers for WHK Radio in Cleveland announced and described every baseball game that the Cleveland Indians team was playing.

Since I now understood the game, I reveled in every bit of action that I heard on the radio. Jack Graney, who did the actual descriptions, got all excited with every "hit" and every "run" that was made as he screamed into the microphone. It was not long before I learned to love his descriptions and learned all about every player. In fact, I became such an avid fan of this strange game that I knew every player in the American League which was made up of eight cities, each having its own team. As I look back now and recall the past, I doubt if there was a player on any of these eight teams who I did not know by first and last name and what positions they played. As for the Cleveland Indians, I knew everyone of them, by name and their positions. But not only that, I often times learned the names of their wives and learned of all their background information, including where they came from and where they were born. I was a big fan of the Cleveland Indians baseball team. I doubt seriously there was anyone in town who was more smitten with baseball than I was.

I literally lived this odd game. When it wasn't being played, I was thinking about it. At the end of the school year, May 1937, the school gave every child a ticket to attend a Cleveland Indians game on August 27. I savored that ticket and guarded it as though my life depended on it. I looked forward to the event with emotion which I cannot describe. As June came, then July, and then August, I looked at that treasure daily, and spoke of it to anyone who would listen. I would finally get to SEE the players who I knew so well via Jack Graney's daily broadcasts and the sports pages of the newspaper. To finally see a game in person, see the players and be there . . . God, the emotions of it were all too much.

I counted the days twenty-nine, twenty-eight, twenty-seven, and so on until my big day, August 27, one day after my birthday, which was insignificant compared to what was to follow. My mother told me daily not to get so excited, since she was not going to allow me to go the game. How silly I thought, why would she tease me so? This was to be the biggest day of my life. Wasn't her joke cruel?

As the big day neared and I counted down how many days were left, mother kept her not so funny joke up of not letting me go. Why would she do this? Was this not cruel? Why would she tease me by threatening my big day? Five days left, four, three, two, one and her joke persisted. I did not believe it!

The morning of the twenty-seventh arrived, one day after my birthday and I got ready to go. Mother in a stern voice said, "You're not going!" I could not believe! I could not. My pleading and all the tears in my body did no good. She had said no and so it was not to be.

The rest of the day was spent crying and sobbing. I listened to the game on the radio as I wet my surroundings with tears. Was this my mother who loved me? To this day I have no answer, but after sixty-nine years I have not forgiven her.

So went the summer of 1937, with very little activity for me except of course baseball, which was my whole life. In September school started and baseball ended.

The *Cleveland Plain Dealer*, which was a part of my life, was thoroughly read on a daily basis. There was much interest. One of the most exciting and possibly even frightening happenings of early September that year saw Nazi storm troopers in Germany ringing church bells as Adolph Hitler arrived for the opening of the National Socialists Congress in Nuremberg. That event was designed to be the largest display of Nazi power in German history. The size of the gathering was staggering as Hitler reviewed a parade of over 600,000 men. Hundreds of trains were transporting army and paramilitary units to Nuremberg as the men were being housed in thirteen separate cities. An anti-Bolshevik exhibit that linked Communism with Judaism was opened that day. The local Nazi leader, Julius Streicher made the astounding dictum that the town would give people the right to murder Jews. The diplomatic core including the American charge d'affairs was due in a few days. Benito Mussolini was also coming to the gathering. Hitler and Mussolini were expected to exchange high military honors, as Hitler was likely to greet the Duche as an upholder of fascism and one of Europe's leaders against communism. It was interesting to note that the Nazis by this time were taking outlandish nationalistic steps. In Waldenberg Germany, as an example, a court took children away from their parents because they refused to teach them Nazi ideology. The parents were pacifist members of a Christian Sect called the "International Bible Researchers."

The court accused them of creating an environment where children would grow up enemies of the state. The children were delivered into the state's care. A judge delivered a lengthy statement reading in part "the law as a racial and national instrument entrusts German parents with the education of their children only under certain conditions namely, that they educate them in the fashion that the nation and state expect."

Interesting aside from the daily news was the story of Douglas Corrigan, the daredevil aviator who had been forbidden to make a solo trans-Atlantic flight, landed in Dublin, Ireland, explaining with a straight face that his compass misled him into believing that he was flying from New York to Los Angeles. Corrigan said he flew in clouds when he took off from Roosevelt Field, Long Island, and his compass said he was heading west. He added that he realized his mistake only when he cited land at the end of the twenty-eight hour trip. U.S. and Irish officials said they would not punish him although he broke the rules of both countries, earning him the nickname of "Wrong Way Corrigan."

How interesting the *Plain Dealer* was back then. It was to note that Mexico's President, Lazaro Cardenas, had nationalized 350,000 acres of oil lands leased to the Standard Oil

Company of California as part of the nationalization of two million acres. That was the first time in recent nationalization of all potential oil lands in Mexico, in which land had been seized. The move was considered a step toward the gradual elimination of American and British oil companies. Standard oil was capitalized at $400 million in Mexico. It also was seen to endanger all U.S. and British concessions which where mostly organized under Mexican Law in Mexican corporations.

Many of the news items that were read by me at the time were not fully understood, usually not to the depth of their meaning. Nevertheless, there was very little that I did not find interesting.

5

School and the Olympians

Things in Europe were hot and heavy with fear as the Nazi Movement spread like wildfire. Adolph Hitler had become a dictator far beyond what was ever conceived by anyone, with powers which were never ever, ever, ever to be challenged. His words were law in *all* cases. As I had known for quite some time, it was obvious to me that Hitler and his Nazis wanted to annex Austria. In March of 1938, Hitler, the German leader who left Austria in his youth as a penniless artist, was cheered by thousands as he returned to Vienna to pronounce the "Anschluss" of union of that country with Germany. Hitler was driven to the Austrian capital from Linz, where he set up his temporary headquarters.

Forty tanks led the way in. Police cars filled with officers brought up the rear. Along the route, Nazis from all over Austria cheered the man who once pledged that Austria's borders were inviolable. He stood in an open car for most of the drive, wearing his brown storm trooper uniform and returning the nearly hysterical salutes of his ardent supporters. Many of them waved banners emblazoned with swastikas. Some of the Nazis had stitched the symbol into the middle of the Austrian flag. "What we all experience at this moment," Hitler proclaimed in Vienna, "is being experienced also by all other German people. Whatever happens, the German Reich as it stands today shall never be broken by anyone again and shall never be torn apart."

Hitler had signed a decree, making himself commander in chief of the armed forces of Germany and Austria. All soldiers in Austria were to swear allegiance to the Nazi leader who was now the furher of more than seventy million people. Hitler's victory was Kurt Von Schuschnigg's defeat. Since 1934, the Austrian chancellor had tried to prevent the National Socialists from coming to power but the ground was cut out from under him when his benefactor, Benito Mussolini, allied himself with Hitler two years previously.

Kurt Von Schuschnigg, Austria's president, tried to save his government by calling for referendums so that the Austrians could choose between the Nazis and him. The vote was never held. Hitler contacted Austria's Nazi interior minister, Arthur Sseyss-Inquat, and ordered him to have the referendum canceled. Schuschnigg tried to resist but capitulated when he heard that German troops were amassing on his border. Schuschnigg and thousands of his supporters were learning the hard way what happens to opposition of Hitler. They were all placed under arrest.

In the meantime, in the United States, Warner Brothers Studios suspended Bette Davis, the immortal actress, when she refused to rehearse the latest film called for in her contract. Ms. Davis, who had been keeping to her bed for an undisclosed illness, said, "Had it been the life of Sarah Bernhardt or Maximilian and Carlotta, which have both been scheduled for me, I would have attempted to go to the studio, but I did not feel justified in jeopardizing my health on behalf of such an atrocious script." Ms. Davis's last picture was the Oscar-caliber *Jezebel*.

Two weeks after Ms. Davis made her statement, Feodor Chaliapin, the Russian basso considered by many as the greatest singer of all time, died in Paris at age sixty-five. Possibly only Enrico Caruso loomed larger. Chaliapin's reputation was special as no basso had ever achieved such worldwide acclaim.

Also in the news of the baseball world, St. Louis teammates were stunned when the St. Louis Cardinals traded Dizzy Dean to the Chicago Cubs for three players and cash. Just as Dean was about to start his comeback, the right-hander was traded for pitchers Kurt Davis; Clive Sean, an outfielder; and George Stainbeck. It seemed clear that the Cardinals were trying to unload their problem child rather than strengthen their pitching staff. Dean had been voted the National League's most valuable player several years earlier.

Also noteworthy that year was the year the minimum wage law was signed by the Fair Labor Standards Act, which established a minimum wage of forty-cents an hour and a working week of forty-four hours. The new regulations would apply only to those American businesses engaged in interstate commerce.

In the year of 1938 I became heavily involved with sports, which now included a game of basketball of which he had never heard one year earlier. It wasn't too long before I realized that this game was for me. I took to it like a fly to horses, or a kid to peanut butter and jelly. Why hadn't I heard of this sport before? There was much more to the game than merely throwing the ball through that opening ten feet above the ground. A great deal of skill was involved and after graduating from elementary school to junior high school, I found myself on the basketball team, which I enjoyed immensely. Sports, during these years of 1938 and 1939, were in fact my whole being as I looked forward from the time of our playing this "basketball" game in the winter, to the spring when everybody took to baseball and then in the fall to football and then again back to basketball.

All of these sports became a part of me and were surely much more important than anything that I was doing in school at the time. My grades? One really should not ask because there wasn't that much interest in school. We ought to be graded on who was playing what position in the American League of baseball and who was playing for which college football team, or the basketball team of the local high schools and university. I would surely have passed with a 4.0 average. Since this is not how the tests were given, the 4.0 average was not anywhere near which I was to reach. After all, playing was more important by far than studying in school.

I was now in Roosevelt Junior High School on Lee Road in Cleveland Heights. My homeroom teacher, Mr. Miller, although obviously a fine fellow, had the fault of falling asleep during our homeroom period on many occasions. While he nodded off, the kids had a lot of fun such as silently sneaking up to the blackboard and writing some sort of nonsense on it. When Mr. Miller awakened, he would see what was on the blackboard, yet never knew who it was that had played the prank. What was written on the blackboard was usually quite humorous to us all, although he found little humor in it. The giggling and the laughing amongst the kids and the anger of Mr. Miller were almost a daily routine. I believe that the poor chap must have had narcolepsy or something, for his putting his head down signaled that he was about to give off a snore or two. It always told us that it was time to play. We made it our business never to be too loud in fear of waking our sleepy teacher.

Roosevelt Junior High School had much to offer. We played a lot of football with Mr. Cramer, a history teacher from room 113 on the first floor. He had to be very careful not to get too steamed up because even at his young age of the late thirties, he had a rather severe heart condition of which he soon died. Cramer was as popular as one of the kids, an athlete of the eighth and ninth grade. Then there was our principal, Mr. Streeter, who was quite handy with a paddle. When a student at Roosevelt was caught misbehaving, at least in the opinion of the teacher, he was sent to see Mr. Streeter. Mr. Streeter took great joy in having the kid bend over and whacked on the rear end with his paddle.

I am sorry to say that there were many times that I was the victim of a bash on the butt by Streeter and I must confess that yes, indeed, it was very painful and sitting down for the next ten to fifteen minutes was not a pleasure. It seems he had a very special way of whacking you and it was quite effective. Nobody enjoyed being sent to Mr. Streeter. In fact, there were times that I remember when the little boys who were just fourteen years old or so came back from Streeter's office with tears in their eyes after having been so whipped. It was an effective deterrent to our normal behavior.

Promotion to the tenth grade was generally a wonderful experience to which we had to look forward the following September, as we were finally graduating from Roosevelt Junior High School and were about to start in Heights High.

"Heights" had about everything from tennis courts to a baseball diamond, a football field, a swimming pool, gymnasiums, and you name it. It was all there.

I transferred to our new school in 1942, and what followed was an entirely new life. I was assigned to Mr. Dewald's homeroom. He was the physics teacher. He was a little old man who kept his glasses resting squarely on the bridge of his nose and stared over them at the class. He was a no-nonsense guy, and you didn't want to get into trouble with him. It was all business.

In my first semester, I had about five classes, which ranged from just so-so to what I considered quite difficult, and saw it as a definite deterrent to my interests in sports. As a tenth-grader, I was not able to go out for the varsity, and played on what was a freshman team and also in the intramural teams in basketball. I tried out for the swimming team for varsity, and was happy to find that Mr. Uber, the coach, had taken a liking to me. I became a member as a backstroke swimmer. As time went on, I found things more to my liking and scholastically, I was doing well.

After a couple of months of school, the highlight of the past few years occurred as I met a chap by the name of Walter Polachek, who asked if I was interested in joining a fraternity called the Olympians. It excited me, and I immediately accepted the invitation. I was invited to the first meeting on Friday night at a member's house by the name of Alfred Meyers. At the meeting, I was introduced to about fifteen other young fellows who were members of the Olympians and who were students at Shaw High School, Cleveland Heights High School and Shaker Heights High School. There appeared to be an almost immediate bond as I took a tremendous liking to every one of them. I felt at the time that the feelings were mutual and I was made a "pledge."

Arthur Blackman, Morty Coles, Stanlee Fried, Milt Hayman, Bobby Pollack, Leonard Portman, Walter Polachek, Alf Meyers, whose home was where I attended my first meeting, Jerry Matz, Norm Landau, Larry Klein, Ralph Seed, Walter Seidler, Phil Sims, Marty Surad, Harvey Weiss, Fred Bram, Willie Dubick and Kurt Wallach made up the group.

I thought how lucky I was to be with a batch of great guys like these. It was to be the beginning of many, many years of very close friendships. To be exact, as I write these words, I am still very close to all the survivors of that first

The Olympian Club 1944-45

club meeting sixty-six years ago. It has been sixty-six years of brotherhood.

The Olympian Club met every Friday evening at a different boy's home. A business meeting was held which consisted of old business, new business, good and welfare, etc. There was a parliamentarian appointed for a term, and it was his job to see to it that all meetings were held in accordance with Roberts' Rules of Order which every one of the members had to study and learn backwards and forwards. At the end of the master-at-arms' term, another boy was put in charge, and so it went. The friendships were probably closer than I am able to describe. During the week, we had lunch in school and ate together. After school, it was usually sports. We played together, and sometimes we studied together. There was a complete union all week long. Friday evening, of course, was our club meeting and after the meeting, we all went to a sorority meeting.

The sororities at the schools at this time were very much like the fraternities, having meetings as we did. The main difference was that instead of going out to the boys' houses, they just stayed at the club meeting and we, the young men, would come there. We danced, played music, and partied. This was a regular Friday evening event during the school year.

The weekends saw us together doing whatever we wanted to. We had picnics on occasion, and when we went out on a date with the girls, it was almost always a double, triple, or quadruple date, where two or three or four of the Olympians took out two or three or four of the gals. We would go to a movie or whatever and then go to a restaurant and have a bite to eat. And so the school year passed as far as our social life was concerned. It cannot be described in any other manner except wonderful. Should any one of us have a problem with our school-work, every other member was there to see to it that he would get a helping hand. Not enough could possibly be said about our comradery and love for each other.

Every so often a new member was introduced to the club and if he were accepted, he was made a pledge. The member who introduced the new-comer was the pledge master and the pledge was under his control completely. Fun and stupid things were done with this pledge, as we commanded his life. My remembrance most particularly is when my dear friend Freddy Bram became my pledge after I introduced him to the Olympians. The club actually became his family in almost every sense of the word, since Freddy Bram had none. Things I did to Freddy were almost merciless, although always taken in fun, as we all laughed either with or at each other. As an example, I would have him stand at the bus stop apparently waiting for the bus to come. When the bus arrived, the driver opened the door and Fred would have to put his foot on the first rung there, tie his shoelace, thank the bus driver, and walk away. It usually brought many laughs from the passengers. I had given him toilet paper and between all the sheets he was to spread peanut butter. His job was to sell these peanut butter sandwiches on the corner. Needless to say, not many were sold.

One day I had him dress as a girl, gave him a doll, and put him on the streetcar without any money. He was to earn his fare by begging the passengers to give him a little bit of money to feed the baby, which was the doll, of course, and pay for the streetcar ride.

In another little adventure, I had Freddy climb up on a statue of Cosiousko, who was the Polish general hero of the revolutionary war. The statue was large and stood on the public square in downtown Cleveland. Fred had a brush in hand with soap and it was his job to brush the teeth on this statue. The face and teeth were about fifteen to twenty feet high off the ground, and he had to get up there with a ladder to do his brushing. Another bit of nonsense was that he was to measure the width of the Loew's Theater downtown in hot dog lengths.

Prior to his induction into the Olympians, Freddy had to produce a pregnant cat. Now, this took him almost three weeks, but lo and behold, he did find one and as ordered, brought it to a Friday meeting. This was the culmination of the foolishness until the major nonsense of initiation was to take place. On the night of Freddy's initiation there was a blanket of snow of at least six inches on the ground.

It was December and freezing cold as we gathered in Milt Hayman's house for the meeting. Afterwards, Fred's initiation into the Olympian Club took place. Milton produced an ironing board and an iron. Fred was told that after the meeting and during his initiation, he would have to take his shirt off, bend over the ironing board, and we would put the hot iron on his back for a period of not more than three seconds. Needless to say, Freddy turned white as a sheet at the thought of this happening to him. When the meeting ended and the ceremony was about to begin, Freddy was blindfolded and was told to bend over the ironing board with his hands hugging the board itself, and his bare back exposed. Then he was told that the iron would only be put on his back for about three seconds, but not more. As I recall, he shook with fear. We took our time so as not to shorten the ordeal for Fred and after at least four minutes or more, we told him we were ready and that the iron was about to be put on his back. We counted backwards from five to zero, at which point Stanley took a fistful of snow and stuck it onto Fred's back as he was being told that the iron was being placed on him.

As I recall, the bloodcurdling scream which followed could probably be heard a couple of blocks away as we all laughed. Even Fred, once he regained his composure, laughed along with us. This was the type of initiation any new member in the Olympians might expect.

As I look back today, it seems to me to have been a highly unusual situation at our school where we had a number of fraternities such as the Olympians and probably an equal number of sororities that enjoyed the same type of comradery and general friendship that we boys and girls had. As I said a little earlier, it is now sixty-six years later and of the nineteen Olympians that were active when I was in school, there are only eight left. Eleven have passed on.

Most of us attended their funerals. The eight remaining members today are still in touch with each other on a regular basis, although they are located in Steubenville, Ohio; Cleveland, Ohio; Las Vegas, Nevada; St. Louis, Missouri; and Vero Beach, Florida.

I very much enjoyed my high school days, and I look back at them with a great deal of . . .

Members of the Olympian Club at their 40th Year Reunion.

almost reverence. I went on to play baseball and basketball, excelling at both. Although the years were much enjoyed they were also much too short. The comradery and the friendships which ensued over the two years of 1942 through 1944, were never again to be equaled. It seemed I was fortunate in having girlfriend after girlfriend, and although we make fun of the term "puppy love," I must say the emotion of that was very deep. I fell in love twice, almost simultaneously, with a sweetheart and gorgeous little gal called Dolly Koslen, beautiful and feisty she was. Almost simultaneously, I fell in love with another girl called Tami Globus. Her real name was Tamara, but I had nicknamed her Tami and that term stuck for many, many years, although I often felt that she didn't like it too much. I loved them both. Actually, things were easier for me in this regard than might be expected because Tami's family moved to California. That romance was totally put on hold while I was in Cleveland and she was in California writing letters to me, which, of course, I answered immediately. I was almost living out an old saying, "When you're not near the one you love, you love the one you're near." Indeed, it was true here.

6

The Early War Years

The year 1942 was a world disaster punctuated by systematic, efficient, and cold-blooded murder of European Jewry. My paternal family, so very large, in the Ukraine, was slaughtered in genocide through gassings at the Belzec concentration camp, were starved into becoming living corpses, shot in the forests and unmercifully murdered wherever they could be found. My uncles, aunts, cousins, nieces, and nephews, so many in our greater family of over 200 were inhumanely annihilated, worse than cattle in slaughterhouses. The killings did not cease until no one was left except my parents, myself, and two siblings. Only we five survived. The horrors are often described. The United States Holocaust Memorial Museum in Washington, D.C., describes and depicts it all. Countless books have been written. None, no matter how *literally* talented, could begin to describe the agony suffered by so many of the victims. It was more than murder as the Nazi beasts could not be satisfied with murder alone. Only after the most severe torture, amputations without anesthesia, medical experiments of freezing to death, starvation, killing by physical beatings, live burials and babies ripped in half was practiced against the innocent victims were they satisfied. My father wept as he heard the details of it later, as no relatives survived or escaped from these atrocities. As a sixteen-year-old, I could only feel so much. It was so far removed from realities I had ever known and did not even seem to be true, or for that matter real.

The United States had recently entered into two wars. In the Pacific, the Japanese attacked us and were winning as they captured island after island after almost having annihilated our fleet. Grim was the outlook as territories were being captured and thousands killed. We were almost helpless. Could the United States fall next victim to the horrors of this war? Much fear was in our minds daily as the Japanese dominated almost at will. Most frightening to us was the invasion of the Aleutian Islands northwest of Canada where the Japanese invaded our continent and looked forward to marching south.

The European theater of war fared no better. The Nazis had by now conquered or controlled all of mainland Europe. Every country was either under total Nazi military rule or was dominated. The German Wehrmacht stood everywhere as it, the world's mightiest army, was eating up Russian soil and was outside the gates of Moscow. Only England stood free, alone and helpless as the Nazi Luftwaffe was destroying a little more of it daily. London, Leeds, Liverpool, Manchester, and other cities were being bombed daily by thousands of planes. The RAF was putting up strong resistance as dog fights dominated British skies. London was half destroyed. In the Atlantic German submarines operated in wolf packs and were sinking ships to the tune of thousands of tons daily. The United States helped to supply its ally, Russia, with liberty ships sending cargo from the east coast, almost "over the top" to Murmansk. The weekly convoys took off from New York and other East Coast cities and became known as the "Murmansk Run." The German submarines attacked and sent a goodly number, possibly half of them, to the bottom of the sea. It was the most tragic attempt to aid the Russians who had lost and were losing millions of people in the horrible war.

Back in Cleveland we were glued to the radio daily for many hours awaiting news. It seemed almost always to be bad and tragic. The Cleveland *Plain Dealer* was read cover to cover and was always "old news." We had heard it all on the radio before. To a degree, despite my busy schedule, school, part-time jobs, sports, etc., there was always an element of fear. How far would the German and Japanese hordes go? Could they be stopped? This had never occurred. Would we also be overrun? In the not too distant future I also, would have to go to war and fight in the military. Subsequently, there was always a fear present. At least we were no longer in Europe and Hitler did not get to murder Mark Wallach's family as he did my relatives. To a degree we were safe here. But for how long? There was a great amount of uncertainty. Our daily lives in America saw many interesting happenings.

On the West Coast, mostly in California, possibly through a slight bit of paranoia the government passed a law which would literally incarcerate all citizens of Japanese descent. They were to be interned in camps as prisoners not allowed their freedom. Most of them were American citizens; some were even second- or third-generation Americans. We all hated the "Japs" with such hostility and deep inner hatred that no one objected, although it was so basically wrong and unfair as these people lost their homes, their jobs, and their freedom.

Back in Cleveland Mother and Dad decided one day to take a trip to Detroit to visit with my uncle Joe and my aunt Margaret. We had not seen them in months and decided to visit. The drive, about 180 miles, was uneventful as our 1939 Buick hugged the road satisfactorily. Totally, with lunch in Toledo, it took us about five hours before we arrived at Joe and Margaret's house and were greeted by them, Carolyn, now about eleven or twelve years old and their very mean little spitz dog, who couldn't be trusted not to take your arm off. The reunion was wonderful. Dad and his brothers, Joe and A. T. (Adolph) had always been so close and loving to each other. Every meeting appeared to be a joyous rendezvous. Carolyn was the cute little cousin and I always loved her, as I did Claire, A. T.'s daughter, about three years younger than Carolyn.

Joe, after a number of years as a successful factory representative traveling mostly through Michigan and Ohio, had opened his own manufacturing company fabricating back-up lights, battery cables, and other automotive products. He had built a factory in Lavonia outside of Detroit, and another across the river in Windsor, Canada. As a proud and successful corporate entrepreneur he was eager to have my dad see his plants and offered to take him on a tour to each. I asked if I might accompany them and was to be taken along. It was to be an interesting day.

The following morning, quite early, after breakfast, the three of us took off and toured Joe's Lavonia plant being shown how the products were made from raw materials to the finished product. Our visit lasted a couple of hours and Joe took us to lunch. A nice day was being had. It was decided that we would then cross the river and go to Windsor where his other factory was operating. The trip took about an hour. Joe was proud as a peacock being able to show off his success story as I guess a few million dollars must have gone into these factories. They were fully operational producing much-needed products. The early afternoon waned as we spoke to the workers and watched the production line. It was all very interesting and when it was over we headed back to Detroit.

The trip to the river and the bridge took about fifteen minutes. Almost at the middle of the bridge there was a glass house that served as an office. Both Windsor and Detroit police were present in fairly large numbers. There were numerous officials at desks, and the place looked quite governmental. It was here that passports were examined and passage between the countries was permitted or denied. Joe went over the bridge almost daily and always had passport in hand. Mark was made aware of the proceedings and had his passport. Both showed these to the examining official who approved them and then demanded to see mine. I did not have a passport issued to me since I was not yet an American citizen. I, without my dad and Uncle Joe, was taken in for interrogation by a senior official. I gave them my whole background, my German birth, my four years in Holland and now in the United States about five years, etc. There was little they did not find out about me. When all questions were answered and documented I was left (guarded) in a room. The official was to have a meeting with other officers present to determine their course of action and what to do with me at this meeting. It was determined that I was indeed of German birth, did not have an American passport and was therefore adjudicated to be an enemy alien. As such, I would not be allowed into the United States but would be incarcerated.

My uncle and father (not to mention me) were totally panicked as a police cruiser was called and I was taken to a detention center in Detroit where all suspicious German aliens from the state of Michigan and western Ohio were locked up. No amount of pleading on Dad's or Uncle Joe's part made any difference as I was to be kept at the institution until some type of a hearing or trial would be held to determine what would be done with this illegal alien who had tried to come into the United States illegally.

With the new war now raging furiously, our country's Pacific fleet having been mostly destroyed, the Japanese and Germans winning every battle and we, obviously losing the war, paranoia ruled the country. All was feared and much not intelligently managed. Was I to be interned for the duration of the war as were all people of Japanese ancestry? It was surely a possibility. Would they consider that I had been a student in school in Cleveland? Would weight be given to the fact that I was a minor? All these thoughts went through Mother and Dad's scared and panicked minds as they remained at Uncle Joe's and Aunt Margaret's home.

The problem began on Friday and although Joe had many connections in Detroit none could be reached on the weekend. So I rested in detention along with all the other inmates. On Monday Joe was fortunate enough to be able to reach some of his contacts and in another couple of days this dangerous enemy German alien was released.

While incarcerated I made it my business not to let any on the other prisoners know that I spoke German. They all spoke nothing else so I constantly knew what they were saying and what was going on among them. At times in fact they talked about this young prisoner not knowing that I understood every word they were saying. Who they were and whatever happened to them remained unknown to me. I was just happy to know that I was out and once again free.

The next morning Mother, Dad, and I were headed back home to Cleveland, after an interesting and frightening experience never to be forgotten.

7

My Navy Days

Due to the fact that I was not able to speak English in elementary school, I was put back a whole year in school. This year set back was never made up. By the time I reached my eighteenth birthday, I had just completed the eleventh grade. The law of the land in August 1944 was that when a young man turned eighteen years of age, it was mandated that he register at the local post office for the draft. This meant that within one to three weeks thereafter, he would be called upon to leave home and would report to an army base to become a soldier. I detested even the thought of this happening to me, for I did not wish to be cannon fodder in the horrible war that was going on. On the other hand, I had a great penchant for revenge. I enlisted in the United States Navy on August 7. It goes without saying that both of my parents were extremely upset, with mother at times crying as she saw her youngest son about to go off to war and not know whether he would return alive. Within three weeks, I received the twenty-four hour notice to report to Great Lakes Naval Training Station, just outside Chicago, Illinois.

On August 31, 1944, I was officially in the U.S. Navy stationed at "Great Lakes." This was to be boot camp, and it was not easy. Boot camp and ten very concentrated hard weeks of physical education would put us in shape to a point where I could do fifty to seventy-five push-ups. During the next ten weeks, we were indoctrinated into navy life.

Several thousand "boots" were now at Great Lakes for training. The majority of the boys were eighteen years of age. Our particular company was made up of about ninety-five percent Texans. I got along with most of them very well, but I missed the close friendships I had developed over the years. It was not the same with these young fellows. I missed having Jewish acquaintances, of which there were none with the exception of a young boy from Dallas by the name of Irving Roffman. Irving and I seemed to find some type of common ground, possibly due to a similarity in religion and types of folks that we both had known, having been raised in the big city.

One day after about two weeks at Great

Great Lakes Naval Training Station,
November, 1944.

Lakes, we heard that the garbage collectors in nearby Chicago had gone on strike. Thousands of cans filled with garbage lined the curbs on hundreds of streets in Greater Chicago. Northern Illinois stunk. Not only were thousands of tons lining Chicago's streets, but life in the city became unlivable due to the summer heat fermenting the contents of the garbage cans. I think the fetid smell of Chicago permeated most of the Great Lakes that week.

The strikers were holding out for an additional thirty cents an hour. This, in 1944, was an outrageous demand that the city could not—and would not—meet. The days of non collection continued for almost two weeks as more and more of the rotting and stinking stuff piled on the streets daily. Many people left town, unable to bear the stench.

One day, Chicago's mayor placed a call to the captain of Great Lakes Naval Training Station during which time he pleaded for the navy's help. He made his pitch stating that the city had 147 garbage trucks in operating condition. He begged that naval personnel should be assigned to help the city. With four or five men to a truck, Chicago would be cleaned in short order. In the end, the captain gave in and agreed to help salvage Chicago by volunteering several hundred men to do the job.

Chosen for garbage duty were the newest recruits. My barracks with a little under one hundred men was one of a number chosen for "special duty." My presence was requested without formal invitation.

At 6:00 A.M. in early September, a few of us found ourselves at the garbage truck terminal. Four men were assigned to each truck. One man was the designated driver. Two men were to walk alongside the truck, pick up the cans of the stinking stuff, and dump the filled cans into the truck. The fourth man was inside the truck to take the can handed him. He was then to dump it over and give the empty can to the two men on the outside.

With my good fortune, I was assigned to be the inside man. The early morning commenced with my standing on the truck bed floor. After an hour or so, most of my weight was no longer on the steel base. I stood on a foot of smelling debris; an hour or so later, the steel bed of the truck was not to be found as I stood in two feet of stinking refuse. Later yet, I was in it up to my thighs, and by quitting time, 4:00 P.M., I stood in it up to my shoulders.

There was no relief. This was my job and for two weeks, give a day or two, I performed my duty. When coming back to the base, I think even the flies near me didn't want to get too close. I stunk to high heaven and it wasn't until after my shower that anyone on the base came within three feet of me. Weeks three and four of boot camp were spent in this manner, rescuing the city of Chicago.

The camp had many facets such as firefighting, hand-to-hand combat, boxing, training, training, and more training. This would be my life for the ensuing ten weeks. A major focus of my life was the mail. I missed my friends back home enormously. I missed the Olympians, I missed the gals we were running around with, and very much so missed my family, mostly Mother, Dad and my sister, Renée, who at this time was in Michigan, but spent quite a bit of time at home.

October 27 rolled around, approximately seven weeks after my induction. It was Renée's twentieth birthday and although she and Mother and Dad had visited with me at Great Lakes a couple of weeks before, it was a very nostalgic day for me since it was the first time in my eighteen years that I had not been together with Renée on her birthday. I missed her and thought much about her that day. I loved her very much. This has not changed.

The big day to which I looked forward daily was to come on November 11, at which time we terminated boot camp and were given a nine day leave before being sent on our next assignment. Actually, I counted the days until that date rolled around. It was likely one of the happiest ones that I had ever had as I took a train to Cleveland that afternoon, where I was met at the train station by my parents, who took me home to a very happy reunion.

That evening, many of my Olympian friends came over to the house. We had a great big reunion. Although this was an unplanned party, it was, nevertheless, quite a happening as at least ten or twelve came over, along with my uncle Adolph, my aunt Florence, and Claire Louise. Also arriving that evening were my uncle Willie and aunt Regie, who stopped by to see the sailor. I believe I can almost safely say that the next nine days had to have been among the most joyful days of my life until that time. I visited school and was a real big shot there in my fancy uniform. What a marvelous nine days it was! I spent every moment of the precious time either with my Olympian buddies, a little bit of time with the family, evenings with the guys and some of the gals that we hung around with in high school, and so it went.

The nine days went by awfully fast, and it was than about time to go back to the Naval Station at Great Lakes. One of the things that I had missed while in training was caught up on while I was at home. I recall that I had always had great interest in what was happening globally. Such information was totally denied me while I was at Great Lakes, since there were no newspapers and no radio. The world just went on without any of us knowing what was going on. The few days at home gave me a chance to catch up on world events and brought me up to date on what I normally would have read about on a daily basis. Among the happenings were General Bradley's First Army having breached the main Siegfried line east of Aachen to stand less than thirty miles from the outskirts of Cologne on the Rhine.

This had put our infantry close to the industrial Ruhr, one of the principal areas of Germany's armed might. Though this overshadowed all other reports, the offensive to the south also progressed. General George Patton's Third

Army had been moving north as the German lines on the Moselle River were blasted loose. Also of great interest was the Russian capture of Bucharest and the Ploesti oil fields.

The German army was always in dire need of petroleum, which was in very short supply. Most of their gas came from the Ploesti oil fields in Romania. The Russian army had now over-run them. The loss of the largest oil fields in Europe were, I believe, ready to cripple the German war effort.

Romania had changed sides while I was in boot camp and declared war on Germany. Hitler could have prevented the startling development, but he turned down a request from Marshal Antonescu to withdraw Romanian troops from the Russian front. Antonescu thought it was time for the Romanians to start defending Romania. Having been refused by Hitler, the Romanian army rebelled against the Germans and allied itself with the Red Army.

Also, news came to America while I was at boot camp about the concentration camp at Majdanek in Poland. The Poles and the Soviet officials estimated that one and a half-million people were put to death there. Victims were men, women, and children, Jews and Christians alike from every nation in Europe. A six hundred-seventy acre camp carefully laid out with electric barbed wire running around the compound was established. Outside the fence stood fourteen machine-gun turrets. Within the fenced area were automatically sealed gas chambers and crematoriums.

Prisoners were processed efficiently. First, they went to the bathhouse after they were stripped. Their clothes were taken away and shipped to Germany to supplement the people's wardrobes there. The prisoners were then herded into the next room and sealed off, with the exception of holes placed high in the roof. From these, canisters of gas were tossed down. The long showers the people took had opened their pores, allowing the gas to take effect more quickly. Prison guards watched through the glass panes in the ceiling until the people were dead. Bodies were transported to a furnace. Teeth with gold fillings were knocked out to be sold later. Bodies burned in ten to twelve minutes. The crematoriums, when used steadily, could burn nineteen hundred bodies a day. The ashes were then sold to German farmers for fertilizer. This was some of the news that I had missed while at Great Lakes.

On the 28th of November, I stayed up all night on the train and hit Chicago at about 8:00 A.M. I didn't get to Great Lakes until around 10:30 A.M., making me half an hour AOL because of the transportation strike in Chicago. This presented no problem at all. After arriving at Great Lakes, I was put in a new barrack and was told that we'd be leaving the camp the next day headed for Camp Bradford in Virginia for amphibious training. The idea of being assigned to the amphibs frightened me. I don't recall getting a minute's worth of sleep that night. I got on the train on the way to Virginia and stayed in a Pullman car.

After arriving in Norfolk, we were transported to Camp Bradford and, as I recall, it was a horrible assignment. I slept in a tent and wondered what the future for me might be. Apparently, I had been assigned to become a signalman, which I didn't know before my arrival.

Camp Bradford had only tents and the weather was freezing. It seemed that temperatures didn't even reach thirty degrees for days on end and having no heat in the tents made life miserable, to say the least. During the next several weeks I wound up in the sick bay a few times. The duty at Camp Bradford was bad. We were to be up at 5:00 A.M. and until night, it was all amphibious work.

One of my memories of the base was the fact that we had to have water buckets outside of our tents. They had to be filled with water in case of fire. This we tried to do in the morning. The catch here was that it was so cold that the water lasted only a few hours before it turned to ice. By the time we got back from training in the evening, the bucket was frozen solid. For this we were punished with what was called "happy hour."

Happy hour meant just the opposite. In this case it meant that we were to put our seventy-pound seabag on our backs and run with it, as some of the young ensigns sat around and laughed at us. We had to run with this seabag until we literally dropped. I said literally dropped, however, what I really meant was that we ran in a circle until we actually dropped because we could run no more. This was happy hour punishment for the frozen water bucket.

We had no control over the horrible punishment that we received almost every night and it was a matter of several weeks that the ensigns sat around and watched us run around with the seabags on our backs.

One morning, we lined up at 5:00 A.M., and the senior lieutenant came out to a row of approximately one hundred men. In a very pleasant voice, he said something like, "You guys have had it very rough here, I know. However, we have a wonderful opportunity for you. Any man who wants to go to Florida needs to step forward one step." After that statement was made, of the hundred men that were lined up, I think about one hundred and fifty took a step forward. It was a one hundred percent acceptance of the offer for Florida training. We were then told to go back to the barracks. We had the rest of the day off until three o'clock in the afternoon, at which time we would gather for muster again.

At three o'clock, we arrived and were taken to a train station just outside of Camp Bradford, where about eight hundred men boarded a train. The train had a number of small cars which were designed to hold about twenty-five passengers each. With its infinite wisdom, the naval officer in charge had assigned seventy-five men to each car for the trip to Florida. I am sorry to say that I was not one of the fortunate ones who was able to sit, and for the next three and a half days, I found myself either on the floor or standing up while the train chugged along at a very slow pace, stopping at every little town on the way.

The trip appeared almost without end. We were given sandwiches every four or five hours and something to drink. Four days later, we arrived at a whistle-stop, where we saw a metal sign next to the tracks which read FORT PIERCE. Obviously, none of us had ever heard of this place. It was, indeed, a whistle-stop somewhere down in Florida, but we had no idea where. We all disembarked and waited by the tracks for further orders, which came very shortly. We were told that we would be taken to the amphibious base by jitney. Each "jit," as they were called, transported us about four or five miles to the base. The sign as we entered read FORT PIERCE AMPHIBIOUS NAVAL TRAINING CENTER. We checked in and went to sleep. It was now well after midnight. The next few months spent at Fort Pierce meant very heavy amphibious training with attack boats that we commandeered and landed sometimes as many as fifteen to twenty times a day, coming in in Roger formation from five to six miles out in the ocean.

Duty on these LCVPs (Landing Craft Vehicle Personnel) at times was twelve to eighteen hours per day, which shook our kidneys as the small boats were rocked by the waves. Duty on shore

Miami, 1944.

consisted of very heavy physical training. There was really no rest during most of the time at Fort Pierce.

One of our big problems here was the ever-present thought of where we were going, when we were going, and if we would ever come back. We had volunteered, so the Navy could pretty well do with us what they wanted. The training we were undergoing surely reflected that.

During the many weeks in Fort Pierce, I had applied for a job as an interpreter since my Dutch was still pretty much intact and my German was fluent. I also saw to it that I was going to become a signalman. The signalman, of course, was in no less danger than the others on the LCVPs, but this was a job that I felt I could do well.

I had almost daily classes in semaphore and Morse code. After a few weeks, I was reasonably well trained in semaphore and could read at a fairly good speed. My sending sentences was not a problem to me at all since I pretty well had all the letters down and was able to send them speedily. As for Morse code, I had more trouble with that, but came along reasonably well. I was told on a couple of occasions that my application for interpreting had been very seriously considered and that I would hear very shortly.

Nevertheless, this did not happen here. A highlight for me at the amphibious base at Fort Pierce was when Mother wrote, telling me that they would come to Florida to visit. Since the amphibious base was known as Fort Pierce ATB (Amphibious Training Base) and since the "amphibious" had the highest casualty (mortality) rate of the services, certainly the navy, I spared my parents the knowledge that I had volunteered for what by some was known as a suicide outfit. When I wrote home, I had stated that ATB stood for "Aerial Training Base," wishing to spare them fear. This little lie did not last as they found out the truth that, in fact, "A" stood for amphibious rather than aerial. It frightened them half to death to learn their little "Kurtl" might, in fact, get killed. Upon hearing the news, they made arrangements to come and see me for what might be the last time ever.

Their visit lasted only four days and was highly emotional. Tears from Mother, who could not control herself, were ever present. Although I loved them both so completely and was ever so grateful that they had come, I almost looked forward to their leaving, as the constant focus was my possible demise. This was, of course, not meant to be. The caring and love from my family was deep and permeated my entire being. Tears were not shed in front of Mother and Dad. They were, however, there nightly at the barracks after I saw them. I was very grateful that the lieutenant in charge of my immediate outfit allowed me liberty time in Fort Pierce during their visit. This did not necessarily have to be.

On the last day of their visit a professional photograph was taken of the three of us. Did Mother and Dad have the need for it as a possible reminder of the son they once had who was killed in the war? It may have been so. The last day was also memorable when I had to leave them on the bridge in front of the base. I kissed them goodbye and began a mile walk across the bridge. My parents never let me forget that I never waved, nor turned around on that walk over the bridge, which felt like three miles. Tears ran down their faces as they watched their eighteen-year-old son go out of sight, possibly for the last time. I did not wave, I did not turn around. My face was too drenched in tears.

Everything was pretty much secret in our training at Fort Pierce ATB since we knew ab-

Mark, Lena and Kurt, Vero Beach, Florida, 1944.

solutely nothing about our future. Our lights had to be dimmed at night so that one could hardly see, because German submarines were no more than three or four miles offshore and looking for targets. Hardly a week went by that a tanker or some other ship was not sunk right offshore, many times in full view of numerous people on the beach. For one reason or another, I don't know what, none of the men on the base, including myself, were afraid of the submarines. They were sinking ships, but they were not shooting any shells onto the land, so we felt quite safe. The hazard was more in the training than it was in the German submarines offshore. As a matter of fact, one day on the pistol range, during practice, one of the men standing about fifteen feet from me put his gun to his head and blew his brains out. The training here had just been too much for him, and he saw this as the only way out. Duty was tough and the tougher it got, the more it seemed that I was homesick.

One day, we were told we were shipping out. Within a twenty-four-hour period, we were taken back to the train station where we had come in and were not told where it was that we were going. Two days later, we wound up in the city of New Orleans at the Algiers Naval Station.

Many LSTs, many LCIs, many destroyers and amphibious crafts were there, along with regular naval vessels. Algiers was quite a large home for upwards of one hundred and fifty ships. I was billeted on the LST 1040. I was aboard only one day when it took off and we went out to sea. My bunkmate about fifteen feet away was a chap by the name of Anthony Andera, with whom I had become quite friendly.

Anthony was from Indiana and was a very friendly Hoosier with whom I found comradery. About three days out of Algiers, Tony got sick and was allowed to lie down in his bunk. He was running a fever and seemed to be getting worse. Before the 1040 got to Panama, Anthony had died in his bunk. One morning, I noticed that he had not moved.

It never occurred to me that he would never move again. In Colon, Panama, I had asked to accompany his body back to Indiana. This request was denied. He died at the young age of eighteen. We stayed in Colon one night and by midafternoon the next day were in Panama City, which was a city of bars, after bars, after whorehouse, after whorehouse, with a few photograph shops and souvenir stores thrown in to boot.

The LST 1040, though a seagoing vessel, was

really not too seaworthy. Officially, the letters stood for Landing Ship Tank. The vessel had a semi-round bottom and could carry many vehicles, such as trucks, jeeps, tanks, ducks, and various other types of amphibious crafts. Rather than cutting through the water with a pointed bow, the ship bobbled as no other. Crossing oceans in an LST was akin to a fly negotiating in a turbulent bathtub. In battle, it would be an easy target as it totally lacked speed and mobility. Instead of its official name of "Landing Ship Tank," we renamed it "Large Slow Target." The ship listed from side to side at almost all times.

As we headed toward Hawaii, I saw seventy percent of the men heave on a regular basis, being seasick. For some reason, and I don't know why, I did not experience this. The stop in Honolulu was a one-night affair and off we went westward without even a liberty. After a couple more days out, 1040 made one more stop before finally arriving in the Gilbert Islands. There we disembarked and became tent dwellers. Our LST went on, I do not know to where. We stayed on the island, which was loaded with marines and a huge army contingent. It had an airfield which was busy and appeared as though ninety-five percent of the island was swamped with army and marine personnel. It bulged with every bit of military equipment of which I had ever heard—from tanks to trucks to jeeps and ducks. Obviously, something was up and about to happen. At a time like this, scuttlebutt was very common. It passed through the camp and did the rounds on a daily basis. It was very obvious a big, big happening was about to burst.

It appeared that this was the quiet before the storm as equipment kept rolling in by the tons. Everybody was on a ready-to-go-basis. We, as the attack boats, had seen several hundreds of them on the AK ships that were moored just off the island and, obviously, we were to man them in the coming invasion, now apparently only a few days away. Where were we going? What was happening? How big was the venture that we were about to enter? Nobody knew, but there certainly was no shortage of guesswork and scuttlebutt. Something very big was about to explode.

One late afternoon, as I sat in my bunk, a seaman came in and advised me that a lieutenant about a quarter of a mile away had sent for me. I had no idea what was up and hurried lickety-split getting to the lieutenant's tent. I was questioned here about everything under the sun and was advised that they had received orders to send me back stateside. The transfer application made in Fort Pierce for an interpreter's job a couple of months earlier and the order to fill it had now come through, even though I was out here and ready for an invasion.

To say it was a very happy moment would be a euphemism. I was ready within a very short time and about three hours later was on an airplane headed east toward the United States. The flight was uneventful. Ten hours or so after take-off, we landed at France Field, Panama. I was sent directly to a naval office, which was off the base. At that office, I was asked a hundred questions regarding the transfer. I was to go to Washington, D.C., according to my papers, yet no one at France Field where I was to change planes had any records that matched mine. In fact, no records existed as confusion reigned. The decision was made that since no records existed, that my job in Washington was not to be. Likely, the reason was that they didn't know where to send me. It was finally concluded that the interpreting job had been filled and that I was not needed. It was further decided that I would be placed on a flight west to rejoin the invasion fleet. This was an extreme disappointment for me. In my mind, going back was really a matter of life or death. The invasion, which was to come, I did not know where of course, was imminent and would take place at any moment. Did I want to be a part of the attack boats hitting the islands just off the coast of Japan? The answer was a definite no. I was eighteen years old and had hoped that I would live to have a long life. Participation in the invasion was very much not desired.

I asked the officer if I might have liberty to go into town and spend some time there since I wasn't to get on a flight until the next day. The officer thought about it for a moment and then said that he saw no reason why I could not spend a few hours in town, do some sightseeing, visit some of the bars and whatever else there was to be seen. I thanked him, left with my gear, which was placed in the outer office, and headed directly for a building from where buses left for Colon with one pass to get off the base and other one which would allow me to come back in. Many, many ideas went through my mind. Is this going to be my salvation? Am I going back to the Gilberts and on to the invasion? The thoughts never left me. Maybe I can miss it and live. Would I survive?

Colon was a very busy hustling and bustling place with hundreds of sailors on liberty from all the ships that had docked there, along with a number of marines that were stationed permanently in Panama and also hundreds of sailors that had permanent duty at a submarine base. The base had been there since the beginning of the war, and there were more souvenir shops than I could count. The hundreds of girls that sold their bodies were inspected on a regular basis by Navy doctors to see whether they were clear of infection.

If they were, they were given "Certificates of Safety." These were much valued as they were a license to do business. Since Navy doctors examined the girls and the brothels were off limits to civilians, they were considered employees of our government. Many years previously, the United States had committed that a given number (very large) of Panamanians living on the isthmus would be employed by the U.S. government. Since our military supported the ladies, they helped to fill the quota of guaranteed employment.

I spent the evening in Colon and when 10:00 came around, I was with a lovely lady who had been selling her wares. She had come up from

May, 1945, in Colon, Republic of Panama.

Baranquilla, Columbia. We had struck up quite a friendship over about an hour and a half that I had been with her. Our romance was new and all physical, yet there was a certain comradery and respect we had for each other. I found her to be a very bright lady who had nothing in Baranquilla and came to Panama to earn money. Was it right and honorable? No, of course, it was not. Was she another human being in need? I felt she certainly was, and I was not going to judge her.

During our time together, I explained to her what my problem was, and I told her that I was just scared to death to go back to the Gilberts the next day. She was kind and understanding and said that she saw no reason why I should take my life in my hands. She told me that I would be very welcome to stay with her that evening and make up my mind as to what I wanted to do tomorrow morning. This advice was what I was hoping for . . . some love, and a good night's sleep.

In the morning, she and I went to breakfast and got into a very philosophical discussion of life, etc. She told me of the difficulties of exist- ence in Baranquilla, the horrible life she had with an abusive father, and the difficulty she'd

Panama, 1945.

had with life in general. She felt that life was totally unfair and resented very much the fact that she had to do what she did so she could live decently. Could I have judged her? I suppose I might have, but no. It was not for me to judge. Being with her, as another human being with problems and decisions of a grave nature, gave me a feeling of pity and sympathy towards her. She and I had become the best of friends in so short a time span. It was almost love. We rationalized that we were nineteen years old, had a whole lifetime ahead of us in which we could have a family and live a good life in America. Would I challenge life itself by rejoining my old outfit and taking my LCVP on to deadly shores? A final decision was made for life. The decision, of course, was that I would not go back to the base, and I would not die on the shores of a Japanese island by going back to the Gilberts. This was not something to be taken lightly in wartime. I opted, however, to do this and in that manner, saved my life.

I stayed with my new friend for two days. The second morning we came back into town and read in the Colon newspaper that an invasion had taken place in the Pacific. A battle and the landings of thousands of American troops was taking place 300 miles from the Japanese shores on a small island called Okinawa. Lieutenant General Simon Bolivar Buckner, who died of shrapnel wounds early in the invasion, was leading the Fifth and Sixth Marine Divisions. Our LCVP's were in the thick of things, as thousands died. We had landed on the southwest coast and soon ran into the *Shuri* defense line that General Mitsuri Ushijima had constructed across a section on the island's south central sector. Three weeks of bitter cave to cave fighting was killing thousands. The Japanese slipped away after many defeats for a final stand on the southern tip of the island.

Meanwhile, our ships offshore came under desperate attacks by kamikaze pilots. The battles ended after General Ushijima, commander of all Japanese forces, came out of his cave bunker and committed hara-kiri. I will never know how many of my buddies and shipmates died during these few weeks in April of 1945. There were, no doubt, many. I felt my decision was wise, dismissing the cowardly aspect. I was to live, where so many of my Fort Pierce buddies did not. My friend, I have forgotten her name, and I, literally read the words off the newspaper that morning. A decision had now been made that I would go back to France Field and check in, advising the S.P. in charge that I had had too much to drink, got lost, did not know where I was, and had finally found my way back after a couple of days. Would this story fly? I questioned it, nevertheless, I felt a certain amount of peace that I had not felt for several weeks as I said a sad goodbye to a friend I had learned to like very much and almost love. She was my confidante and sweetheart for a few very difficult days.

As planned, I came back to France Field and told the above noted story. I said I had no viable excuses and whatever punishment the navy wished to meet out would be fully understood and accepted. My story was heard. When it was over, I was told they understood my problem but nevertheless, they hauled me off to the brig. I was put in solitary confinement here for about twenty-four hours. A court-martial was surely in the works. Not so, I received a "captain's mast" instead, which could almost compare for trial somewhere between a misdemeanor and a felony. My captain's mast was to be held the next day. I stayed in the brig, of course, that night, and appeared before a naval captain who adju-dicated the proceedings. I told him exactly what

I had told the S.P. in charge. I explained the situation and told him that I would understand what the navy wished to do with me. To say that I was scared is putting it very mildly. I'm sure I must have shaken in my boots with fear as to what was going to happen. Would I be dishonorably discharged? This would have been the horror of all horrors.

Did I deserve it? Maybe so. I felt my life was hanging in limbo. Did I make the right decision? I was alive! Should I have gone back and chanced survival? There were no answers, only fear. I wished my friend were with me. She made so much sense. She was so kind and understanding.

I was alone now, more so than ever in my life. The captain's mast was held early. I was grateful. To my surprise, the charge against me was not as severe as I had feared and I was told that in view of the fact that I did not have my senses about me, having had too much to drink, and in view of the fact that I didn't know the area at all having only been there for one day and having voluntarily come back to France Field, the captain decided that I would get a very minor punishment. The sentence was three days in the marine brig on bread and water. It was now April 11, 1945.

The three days in the brig were not the worst that I had ever spent. I did not so much mind solitary confinement. The bread and water for three days also did not seem like much of a big deal. However, a sailor in a marine brig is not to get off scot-free, I found. There had always been a rivalry between the navy and the marine corp, and this was very much so on the Isthmus of Panama. Being in a marine brig with marine guards was much worse than having been put into a naval penitentiary. The "Gyrenes," as we knew them, were not going to be easy on this sailor-boy that they had locked up. Every so many hours, they took great joy in having me come out of my cell and get on my hands and knees and crawl forward about a hundred yards on the concrete floor. I was to have my pants rolled up over my knees, thus exposing the knee to the concrete as I went. This little maneuver was done every few hours and it was not too long after I had become their ward that the skin on my knees was rubbed raw. By the time the second day came around, it was all bloody and the more blood appeared, the more the marine guards enjoyed watching me do this hundred-yard crawl. This maneuver was carried on a daily basis until the fourteenth, at which time, I think, that bone was visible.

They gave me a great farewell with everybody giving me a slap on the back and telling me how they enjoyed having me as their guest. However, I must say, the slap on the back was not really a tap at all. It was done with the fist and about as hard as they were able to do it. By the time I was free and back on the street, I could hardly walk because my knees were so raw and bloody, and having been hit between the shoulder blades as I was and as often as I was, the upper part of my body ached so much I could hardly breathe.

The marine brig was not too far from our naval barracks and I started to walk back when I noticed the flag was lowered to half-mast. I asked the first sailor that I saw why the flag had been lowered, and I received a very, very dirty look in return, but no answer as he just walked away from me in what was obviously a state of disgust. I did not understand this at all for my question, I thought, was quite civil. I walked a little bit further and saw a boatswain's mate who came in my direction. I stopped him and asked him the same question and got a very similar response of disgusted look and no reply, except to say, "Get out of here," or something

like that in a nasty tone. Once again, I was perplexed at the behavior that I had just been
shown. When I got back to the barracks, I ran
into another chap and asked the same question,
not knowing what kind of response I would get.
In this case, however, it was different. He gave
me a tremendous scolding, pointing out my ig-
norance and wondering how one could be as stupid as I was. He told me the president of the
United States, Franklin Roosevelt, had died. My
immediate response was silence, and a total
state of fear, anger, dismay, and depression all
rolled into one. I stood there gaping, unable to
say a word, not knowing what had hit me. I think
some tears came out of my eyes, but as I look
back now, the only thing that I can remember
was the fear that I felt at that moment, the sadness, and the terribly depressed state in which
I found myself. I went back to my bunk and sat
down. It is not clear in my mind what terror I
felt, however, I do recall that I was totally
speechless probably for the next twenty minutes.

April 1945, was a historic month that will be
remembered for generations. President
Roosevelt, the thirty-first president of the
United States, had died suddenly in Warm
Springs, Georgia. An attending doctor said that

the sixty-three-year-old president died of a cerebral hemorrhage. The president had been at Warm Springs since March 29, resting up from the rigors of trying to bring an end to the war.

His death came at a time of high triumph as the armies and the fleets under his command were at the gates of Berlin and the shores of Japan's homeland. Only hours before his death, he had been posing for a portrait by Elizabeth Shumatoff, commissioned by his longtime friend Lucy Mercer. In the early afternoon, the president had murmured, "I have a terrible headache." He died a short time later. His death was announced by the White House slightly before 6:00 P.M.

While President Roosevelt had appeared to be in declining health in previous months, the rest in Warm Springs seemed to have restored some of his vigor. No members of his family were with him at the end. Mrs. Roosevelt had been attending a Washington meeting of the Thrift Club when told to return to the White House. It was there that she was told of her husband's death. She sent messages to their sons, all of them in the service, saying, "He did his job to the end and as he would want you to do. Bless you all, love, Mother."

President Roosevelt, a New Yorker, was educated at Groton, Harvard, and Columbia, and was considered one of the most remarkable men ever to occupy the White House. He was responsible for initiating the New Deal in the federal effort to bring the nation out of a deep depression after his election in 1932. He was reelected in a landslide in 1936, and in a break with tradition, he sought, and won, an unprecedented third term in 1940, as well as a fourth term just a year before his demise.

His impact on the nation and the war world was perhaps best expressed in the tribute on the senate floor by Senator Robert Taft, an Ohio Republican, and a frequent political adversary, who termed him the greatest figure of our time, one who died a hero of the war for he literally worked himself to death in the service of the American people.

Funeral services were held later in the week in the East Room of the White House with only high officials attending, since the chamber could accommodate only two hundred people. The body then was taken to the late president's hometown in Hyde Park, New York, and he was buried in a plot near the Roosevelt home.

There were times at Coco Solo that were reasonably pleasant. The real war was a few thousand miles away, and the knowledge that we were not directly in the battle gave us both conscious and subconscious comfort. The weekly toll of thousands killed and maimed was only to be read in the papers or heard on the radio. It was in that regard not that different from stateside news, although the knowledge that we could be sent over there any day was never far from the mind. Although "peace" and home were so very much missed, we did have some pleasant times—my love for writing, for instance, and the craving to do it was fed when I was asked to write a weekly column in the Coco Solo newspaper. This occurred early in July 1945.

The editor of the newspaper asked what and how I would be contributing. After my second in-depth discussion, I told him of my plans. My column was called "Sea Breeze," and it was to feature camp humor by, and about, base personnel. Of course, for fear of reprisal, I had made it a point to omit all officers. Only our enlisted personnel, seamen, and petty officers were to become the butt of my jokes. Cynicism often found its way into my writings and it was not too long before almost everyone at Coco Solo looked forward to reading Wallach's "Sea

Breeze." The column was in print over a year and during this time, humor books from the library in Cristobal supplemented my efforts. No one knew whose names would pop up in "Sea Breeze," describing real or fictitious happenings. For instance, Bill Brodsky had a real resemblance to the president of the United States. He appeared in "Sea Breeze" occasionally as "Roosevelt Brodsky." After some time, he was known by this name only. I doubt that most of those who knew him even remembered that his real name was "Bill." It would not surprise me in the least if this moniker did not stay with him the rest of his life. "Roosevelt Brodsky," a fine fellow.

Harry Teitlebaum had a limp. I think a sprained ankle was the cause. I wrote about the fact that Harry had fallen off a forty-foot ladder. Only later was it mentioned that the fall was from the first rung. And so it was with nonsense, humor, and added comradery that I much enjoyed writing the column from July 1945, to August 1946, when I became eligible for discharge. This column was the forerunner of a newspaper column on tennis technique, which I wrote in later years, from 1971 to 2002. I derived much personal gratification from "Sea Breeze."

Near the end of 1945, with the war raging feverishly in both the Atlantic and Pacific theaters of war, large shipping traffic backed up in the canal (the "Big Ditch," as we called it). Ships from destroyers to cruisers, battleships, aircraft carriers, cargo, and the like, parked in the bay for days, waiting their turn to go through. The Colon-Cristobal radio stations HV5K and HOK increased their wattage and broadcasts were made to the ships at sea, on the bay, and the canal on a twenty-four-hour basis. Ships came from many countries with many languages being spoken. English was, by far, the most common. I was asked to broadcast some of my humorous columns. I took great delight in this and at times even gave the stations call letters "Hachee Vi Cinko Ka E achi O Ka." My broadcast career lasted only about four months, but I enjoyed it very much. It is with fond memories that I recall the radio stations and my small contributions.

8

A Kaleidoscope

For the first time in months, the German people, including Adolph Hitler, became extremely joyful. The news of President Roosevelt's death was an elixir to the average German, who was rejoicing. What a great turn of events.

Germany celebrated as it had not done recently. It would now bounce back from its defeats. This was an act of God, and all would tell those who would listen that things would change dramatically. Hitler himself could not publicly partake since he was still holed up in his bunker in Berlin. On one hand, he became elated, on the other, his fifty-sixth birthday was not to be celebrated as he realized that his own days were now numbered. Yet, Hitler was still Hitler. His personal annals were unparalleled.

In the light of history, he may be seen as a demented, yet resolute tyrant. At the height of his unequaled political career, he seemed invincible. He had vanquished nine nations in Europe, repulsed Europe's greatest powers, devised an economic and social fabric based on the deadly subjugation of millions, and hypnotically imposed his will on millions more. Over sixty-five million Germans glorified this demagogue as the savior of Deutschland. In the end, he forced them into an abyss of a nightmarish hell.

The man these millions would salute as Mein Fuhrer was born in Braunau, Austria. His father worked as a customs official, and it was reported that he had beaten Adolph violently on many occasions. Young Adolph grew up to worship the works of Beethoven and Wagner and gained an income in Vienna by painting postcards. He embraced the attitude of the typical Austrian, i.e., intense anti-Semitism and a great fear of Marxism.

At the outbreak of the first World War, Hitler was lifted from an obscure artist to a determined soldier. He recorded in *Mein Kampf* that the war elated him. He went on to say, "I fell on my knees and thanked heaven from an overflowing heart." After the German defeat, Hitler joined the ultra nationalist German Workers' Party, later called the National Socialist German Workers, or Nazi Party. Using his zealous oratory skills, he convinced rich industrialists to back his drive to redeem Germany's humiliation at Versailles.

Hitler also formed a Nazi army, the storm troopers, and tried to oust the government at Munich. He created a *putch* which failed, after which he was jailed. He went to a prison at Lansburg, where he wrote *Mein Kampf* and plotted his path to absolute power, which was to come later.

Following his release from jail, the Nazis and their leaders grew in popularity and on January 30, 1933, Hitler was appointed chancellor of Germany by President Paul Von Hindenburg. With his new authority, the little man with the little mustache crushed all opposition, instituting a totalitarian regime. Hitler's paramount and most dangerous ideological principle was that Germany must develop a pure Arian race. "We must build a master class from elements of a better race," he wrote. This crazed notion and demonic drive to dominate Europe ignited an inferno of horror for millions of Jews and other innocent people who died tragically in his many death camps. Hitler's military victories created in him an overconfidence which eventually derailed the Nazi momentum. The Allies were able to overrun his crumbling defenses.

With the end of Nazism, Hitler—once so mighty—rotted in defeat. Big news of the day during the month of April 1945 were certainly almost a daily happening. Shortly after Roosevelt's demise, Harry Truman became the president of the United States. He had only served a few brief months as vice president and had no inkling of Roosevelt's death when he arrived at the gathering of the so-called Board of Education, an informal group of legislators who met in the capitol office of Speaker Sam Rayburn. As he arrived, he was told to telephone Steve Early, Roosevelt's press secretary, who asked him to come immediately to the White House. When he arrived there, he was told by Mrs. Roosevelt that the president was dead. His inauguration followed very shortly thereafter.

In Italy, the demise of heads of state followed course. A disfigured face and head riddled with bullets caped a corpse atop a pile of twelve male bodies and one female in Milan. The decaying carcass on top belonged to the father of Italian fascism, Benito Mussolini. After a quick and expedient trial, which included cries of "Let me live and I will give you an empire," the once seemingly invincible dictator was shot along with his mistress and eleven others. Certainly history was made during that fateful month of April.

As for me, very shortly after coming out of the brig, I was commanded to appear before Captain Mills, who was the head of the entire Coco Solo complex. The captain was interested mostly in the treatment that I received in the Marine brig while I was their guest. I gave him a brief rundown. He just sat there and nodded. I have no idea what his thoughts were regarding my incarceration or the manner in which I was treated there. The entire interview did not last more than three or four minutes but made a great impression in my mind, having been called before the great Captain Mills.

Major world news continued during this fateful year of 1945. Just seven days after the end of April, Germany surrendered unconditionally, and the war in Europe was over. Germany had capitulated to Allied demands in a ceremony at 2:40 in the morning. All battlefields except those in Czechoslovakia then lay silent. The document of surrender was signed inside a little red schoolhouse at Reims. The unassuming building had been serving as headquarters for General Dwight D. Eisenhower. While Eisenhower did not witness the signing, Chief of Staff Lieutenant General Walter Beatle Smith was present. The USSR, France, and Great Britain were also represented. General Gustav Jodl and General Admiral Hans Friedeburg were the German delegates.

Also of great interest during that fateful spring and summer of 1945 was the fact that German citizens were made to confront reality, being forced to see a form of horrors in Belsen and Buchenwald. Military government officials ordered the townspeople of Burgsteinfurt, Germany, to attend a local theater. There they watched newsreel footage of the scene Allied troops found upon their liberation of concentration camps. Many of the female audience wept openly. Others, even while viewing corpses piled upon each other, expressed doubt that Germans were responsible. However, most could not doubt.

The previous month, healthy, well-fed SS women at Belsen were forced to bury the corpses of prisoners who had starved to death. And so it was in mid-1945 as I served on the pier at the Coco Solo Naval Base on the Isthmus of Panama. A very sad day was had early in May when I was told to take our executive officer out to Cristobal to board the USS *Franklin*, which was so heavily damaged in the Pacific.

The aircraft carrier still contained countless

bodies, and the ship stunk from decay of them. Coming back to the base afterwards, I had some major words with a sailor, Mike Sweeney, whom I disliked immensely. Mike took a swing at me, and we got into a very bad fight during which I think I blackened both his eyes and broke his nose. I did not get hurt too badly. It was not a very nice event. The following day, I had an all-day liberty and went into Colon and then took a train over to Panama City.

A highlight for me during those days was a goodly amount of success on the basketball team. Coco Solo, along with all the other bases throughout Panama, had a camp basketball team. I was fortunate to be a member of eleven men who were on the team. Due to some sharp-shooting and practice for a few weeks, I was the starting right guard. I was in the opening game for about eighty percent of the time and was happy to say we won seventy-six to fifty-nine. My basketball career in Panama was blossoming, and I enjoyed it to no end as this opening game was followed by many, many others over the next few months, during which time I made a bit of a name for myself on the team.

During the following months, I stood duty on watch many times. I likely logged a few hun-

Panama Champion Basketball Team 1945.

dred hours on the docks, mostly uneventful, although on one watch late at night, I caught a civilian prowling. I had to pull my gun on him. I took him into the S.P. station, where he was incarcerated. I have no idea what he was doing or what happened after I arrested him.

The mail during these days was as important to me as ever. Rarely a day went by that I did not receive four or five letters. It is with fond memories that I recall my Olympian friends writing to me from almost all over the world and my doing the same to them. Most particularly correspondence was constant with Walter Polachek, Freddy Bram, and Norm Landau. These were all sailors. The girls from home, and I had many, wrote on a regular basis although I looked forward mainly, and sometimes only, to correspondence from Tami and from Dolly, who made my day or made me unhappy at not having heard from them. It seems that I had lost my heart to them both. The balance of the year was more or less routine with my working on my stripes. Having gotten a petty officer's third class rating earlier in the year, now that the year was drawing to a close, I was working hard toward a new rating of storekeeper second class, which I was hoping to be awarded.

My best friend over a period of time in Panama was a chap by the name of Eddie Ruzinsky. Eddie and I shared much and many times, wound up going on liberty together in Colon, having too much to drink together, going to places where we shouldn't etc. Eddie was a yeoman second class when our relationship ended due to his discharge. By that time, I had become a storekeeper second class, both of us being second class petty officers.

There was an air transport command plane that left Colon on a regular basis going to San José, Costa Rica. For a period of several months, Eddie, when he had a weekend liberty, would hop on the air transport and go to Costa Rica for the full two days, coming back to the base all smiles. One day I asked him what he did in San José since I had not been there. He told me that he had made some friends up there, most particularly, a young lady by the name of Nellie Rogade.

He told me of being with her every time he was in San José. There were not too many American sailors in Costa Rica, so every time he went there, she was able to really show him off as the prize that she had caught, an American sailor. He told me that he was treated like royalty and felt like a big shot every time he came into town and Nellie met him at the airport. Apparently the couple of days that he had with her every time he was on liberty were wild and joyous. He spoke of her many times and one day, I said to him, "Eddie, would you mind if on my next liberty I go to San José? You tell Nellie I'm coming and let me have some time with her."

Being my good friend, he agreed he would share Nellie, and advised her via the mail when I would come into town, and she would meet me at the airport. Recognizing me would, of course, be very simple since there weren't any American sailors that I ever met when I went to San José.

As I got off the plane on my first trip, she headed directly for me and said in perfect English, "My name is Nellie Rogade, and I am a friend of Eddie Ruzinsky. You must be Kurt." This was our formal introduction, then she took me home with her. We wound up the next couple of days walking through downtown San José for hours, sitting on park benches and munching in the lobby and coffee shop of the Grand Hotel. The Grand Hotel was an old-timer. We were very comfortable, having spent several hours there on occasion, just enjoying the atmosphere and lovely surroundings.

San José, Costa Rica, November 17, 1945.

Eddie and I were picked up by Nellie regularly. This went on for months as we both enjoyed downtown San José and sometimes the sites around the city. Thanks to Nellie, these were very much enjoyed liberties in a strange country that neither of us had been to before. Our sleeping quarters, both Eddie and mine, of course, were with Nellie, and the evenings and the nights were raucous. One day, Eddie received a letter from her. I, too, received a very similar letter, telling me that she was carrying my baby. It caused us both great grief since we were fond of her and obviously could not afford to father a child. Problems loomed. The most time that we were able to spend there would have been an occasional weekend, possibly every couple of weeks, sometimes every week either he or I, and that was about it.

To become a father and support a child there was something that neither of us could possibly do. Eddie and I made a terrible decision that we could not ever go back to San José. Both he and I wrote many letters to Nellie and occasionally one of us would receive a reply, although this was a rarity. I think both of us realized we had done wrong, yet were able to do nothing about it. Over a period of time, Nellie, more or less,

Nellie Rogade (a friend in Costa Rica),
February, 1945.

became a bad experience of the past, never again to be revisited. Looking back today, however, I realize how sorry a state of affairs it all was and I have much remorse over our experiences in San José. I wish most sincerely that we could have done something for Nellie, *if*, of course, we were the culprits. It has gone through our minds many times whether or not either Eddie or I did the deed. This I will never know. I have never seen or heard from Nellie Rogade again. The question I have as I write this is whether or not I should document the fact that my sex life in Colon was unbelievable.

As a nineteen-year-old, there were no limits, and for a pack of cigarettes or just plain friendship, the girls in Colon were most happy to be with me as their friend.

The openness of it all was unparalleled prior to my entry into the service and surely totally unfamiliar after my discharge, which occurred in August of 1946.

The beginning of that year, our base began to thin out as men were being discharged. The war was now over by several months and slowly one after another, discharges took place. Men were being sent back to the States and Coco Solo became a much smaller operation than it had been during the war. My basketball career continued quite successfully, and if I am not being too much of a braggard, I might say that I, along with a chap by the name of Don Nelson, who became a fine nationally known college player, were pretty much the stars of the team. Before the season ended for the team, it ended for me. I had broken my big toe. Normally, one can think of a toe as just, oh well, it is just a toe. However, in this case, the break was quite severe. It was very painful, and it was two to three weeks before I was able to put a shoe back on my foot. Actually, the pain was so severe that I still remember it to this day, possibly as much because my Navy basketball career also ended.

World news was showing us that the United States and Russia were at loggerheads, threatening each other as daily newspaper articles spoke of the strain between the two superpowers.

I was not too familiar with the politics, but I must say in looking back that I remember a great amount of fear that we might, once again, go to war, but this time with the Russians. There were major uproars on levels of upper echelon conferences which eventually turned the tide toward peaceful coexistence, although it was extremely tense for months to come.

In February, I was advised that I would be granted a leave for thirty days. The elation of this news is hard to describe here. As I had written previously, I was an extremely homesick kid, and finally after one and a half years overseas, I was going to be shipped back to Cleveland for thirty days. The knowledge that I would see my friends that were not still in the service, all the ladies that wrote to me, and not to mention my family at that time, gave me an emotional high that is hard to describe.

Prior to my departure to Cleveland, I had to break in a new man to manage GSK while I was gone. It was a pleasurable job, knowing that I was breaking him in to replace me. I would no longer be on the docks on guard duty and in the GSK. Jim Hamilton, the chap that I was breaking in, was quite an intelligent young man and adept at almost everything that I was teaching him about the operation. He was a seaman first class and addressed me as sir many times. Surely my petty officer second class rating did not call for that, however, he had respect for my knowledge of the GSK operation and things with him worked out very, very well.

My flight home, which was scheduled for March 22, was cancelled and I had to wait for

In the storeroom, Aug. 1945.

when I might be airborne. The wait was not long but my impatience made it seem like it was forever. Finally on the twenty-fourth of March, I was able to get a flight and hit Cuba late in the afternoon. I had dinner there at Guantanamo Bay (GITMO) and arrived in Miami, Florida, early in the evening. From there I flew directly to Washington.

From Washington I was able to get an ATC flight to Cleveland, where I arrived in the afternoon. I thought I would surprise my parents, and when I got to the corner of Taylor Road and Cedar, which was about half a mile from my house, I made a phone call to my parents, telling them I was still in Panama but expected to be home within a week.

This was a disappointment to my mother and dad because they had expected me almost any time. I was actually playing a dumb joke and after getting off the telephone, I started to walk to my home. The last laugh was on me for when I got home, I found my mother in a wheelchair. This frightened me half to death, not knowing what was wrong with her. She explained that she had broken her left ankle and, therefore, had to be in a wheelchair. For some time I did not know whether I should believe this story, and I thought only the worst. I think it took me twenty-four hours before I finally gave in and realized that she was telling me the truth.

She had been at A. T. and Florence's house, where they had some stepping-stones on the lawn. She had stepped in between the stones, twisted her ankle, and broke it. Here she was in a wheelchair, unable to get around at all. I felt very grateful that this was her problem instead of anything more serious as I had imagined it might have been.

To describe my next thirty days in Cleveland would be very difficult. Although I surely never considered myself any kind of hero, and I must say that I was not, I was treated as such. I had my ribbons on my jersey, was going back to school, being with my friends, hanging around with Dolly, and was spending time with the few Olympians left. I was a hero of the war. I had a little session with my ex-homeroom teacher, Mr. DeWald, who, as usual, was a nasty, frustrated, unkind, lonely old man. We had a chat and he said to me among other things, "Why don't you just stay in the Navy? You'll never amount to anything in civilian life anyway, and at least you'll have some security there." He made it clear to me that I would never be able to earn a

living in civilian life. The navy would give me
my only security. I had a lot of ill feelings towards him, for I had set high goals for myself
after my discharge. I wished to earn a college
degree and become a professional or a successful businessman.

As my memory serves me right, a good part
of my leave in Cleveland was spent with Marty
Surad, Bobby Pollack, Stanlee Fried, and Phil
Simms. Dolly, the love of my life, made me so
happy during this short period back with all the
civilians that I could have walked on air. I spent
many nights with her but just as often had to
pull away to be with Sunny, Margie, and the
boys. An old flame, "Little Audrey," was also on
the agenda, quite often. Although the Olympians were spread around the world, there were
still a number at home, either on leave, having
been discharged, or never having gone, so that
there was usually a quorum for the Friday night
club meeting. I went to every one while I was
home. The thrill of this is rather difficult to describe here. I was really flying high.

During this stay at home, the family came
over quite often and I enjoyed the time spent
with A. T. and Florence, as well as Willie and
Regie, who were regular visitors, usually dur-

ing the day. We had many lengthy talks. To top off all of the visitors from family, Renée and Benno both came into town to see me, now that I was back stateside. Benno had come from Cincinnati, where he was in school, and Renée came from the University of Michigan. We had a complete family together once again and it was enjoyed immensely.

It was May 1 that I got back to Panama and was to spend the next three and a half months there prior to my discharge. On coming back, I found the base had been depleted of personnel considerably and was almost a ghost town compared to what it had been prior to the end of the war. I was counting the days until I would finally be discharged and return to civilian life.

During my almost year and a half on the Isthmus, I did make some civilian friends in town, most particularly a young lady by the name of Sarah Kesselman. The morals in the Jewish community of Colon were so strict that it would be almost sinful to hold a girl's hand, which I did not dare to do. When I spent time with Sarah, it was always as though I was with another young man.

There was no touching of any kind and no sweetness that goes with a male-female relationship. However, just being with a respectable female during that time there was a pleasure for me, so I spent considerable time with her. Sarah's family, of course, saw me as a suitor, and I think I was expected to marry her. Her parents owned a souvenir shop where they both worked. Most of the time, Sarah and her sister were there. Their business by June-July of 1946 had gone almost completely kaput due to the fact that the military had now eased off so much that sales had dropped in half.

By late July, I decided that I would go into town and give my last farewells. I went to the Kesselman souvenir store and spent some time with Sarah saying goodbye to her. I tried to make it clear that I doubted that I would ever see her again. As a final gesture, totally asexually motivated, I felt that I would like to give Sarah a hug and a kiss on the cheek, which I did. Somehow, the word got out that I was guilty of this terrible transgression and it was the talk of the shop and probably others in the Jewish community there as to the sinful action that had taken place. Surely I was expected to be engaged or married to her in very short order. My taking off for America was looked upon as disgraceful.

I was expected to come back to be with her

for the rest of my life. It was surely the costliest kiss I had ever given anybody, and it was done in total innocence. I wished her well, and I would, in fact, never see her again.

In early August, my duties in Coco Solo ceased. I was ready to come back stateside. I took a flight and headed for Miami, Florida, on an ATC airplane. My very dear friend, Gerry Gross, was visiting on Miami Beach and I immediately went to where she and her family were. It was a wonderful reunion. Gerry's brother, Ronnie, was also there, and the three of us spent a few days together. It was a wonderful welcome home to the United States. After two or three days of Miami Beach, I was put on a train at Opa Locka, and headed off to California, where I had chosen to be discharged. I reached Los Angeles after a few days on the train and went immediately to my dear Tami's home.

The reunion with Tami was a wonderful experience. She had moved to California when I was just going into the eleventh grade and, of course, broke my heart doing it. To my great surprise, Morty Coles was in Los Angeles at the same time and we met. I brought him over to Tami's house, and we became a bit of a threesome. We went out to the beaches and spent time there. In addition to Tami, my old friend from Cleveland, Joan Broida, had also moved to California. She came over, and we immediately had a mini-reunion with her. What a change of fortunes I had and how much I appreciated being away from Coco Solo, where I had spent one and a half years, mostly doing labor. I counted the days to my discharge. I was billeted at Terminal Island in San Pedro.

My big day came on August 7, 1946, as I was discharged that morning. Tami, her family, and Morty were at a very colorful ceremony. It was difficult at the time and is still difficult for me today to describe the elation and the feeling of freedom that came over me at finally, once again being a free man and no longer in the military.

The next two weeks were spent in Los Angeles solely with my dear friend, Tami, who I had always loved and learned to love even more during the time that I spent there. I lived at her parents' home and was like a member of the family.

My clothing was still the uniform. I had no civilian clothes and eagerly looked forward to the day that I would be able to buy some and wear clothes like everybody else instead of the uniform which I wore for the last couple of years.

Discharge, Los Angeles, California,
on the biggest day in my life, Wednesday,
August 7, 1946.

A Kaleidoscope

There was nothing that one could do to entertain oneself that Tami and I did not do for the next couple of weeks. It was the beaches during the day or running around, visiting people, enjoying every moment. We went out at night to places like Billie Grays' Band Box, Ziegfield Follies, and all of the big entertainment that was available in Los Angeles and Hollywood. It would be futile to even attempt to describe my emotional high for these next two weeks.

There were times that I thought about the future. My deepest hopes were that I could go to the university and get at least a bachelor's degree, begin to make a living somehow, marry Tami, and be with her for the rest of my life. But these were dreams I had. They were not discussed with her since the subject was really off base in as much as I was unable to do anything about my desires. After a couple of weeks, it was time to go home. The goodbye that I said to my dear girlfriend was very difficult. I did not know when I would ever see her again. Although my intentions were certainly to either come back to Los Angeles, be with her, hopefully to marry her or have her come to Cleveland.

An unwanted goodbye was said to Tami during which we both cried a little bit. It was August 19, 1946. I had made arrangements to drive an elderly couple back to the east. The gentleman must have been close to seventy years old, as was his wife, and they needed someone to drive them to New York. I made arrangements with them that I would go as far as Cleveland, at which time they would have to find someone else to drive the rest of the way if they were unable to do it.

The next morning, the three of us met early and started out towards Las Vegas. The drive was reasonably pleasant, although incessant backseat driving got on my nerves. The elderly gentleman was obviously nervous. We arrived in Las Vegas that evening. I had my first view of this gambling mecca and enjoyed what I saw. It was quite different from anything that I had ever experienced before. At about six o'clock in the morning the following day, we got in the car, drove and drove until close to eight o'clock at night when we hit Salt Lake City. As we came into the outskirts of Salt Lake, we saw a horrible accident in which several people were killed. The accident happened immediately in front of our car and there was very little that we didn't see immediately as it happened. There were bodies lying in the street. It made a very deep, horrible, and not to be forgotten impression. After eating dinner, I sat in my room thinking about what we had just experienced and made up my mind that I was not able to drive any further. I went to the elderly couple's room and advised them that I would be leaving them stranded. Although it was wrong, and I knew it, I had no choice but to do what I did.

The next morning, I went out to Hill Field Air Force Base outside of Salt Lake City in hopes of finding a flight to Cleveland, hopefully on an ATC flight, which as a military man, would have cost me nothing. While at Hill Field, I found that General Wainwright had come into town and was staying there. Due to his presence, there were to be no flights available to any destination in the country.

With this unwanted knowledge, I made arrangements with United Airlines to get a flight to Cleveland, which left in the afternoon of the following day. My arrival at home was very much reminiscent of my coming back in March on leave after being gone for a year and a half. Everyone greeted me. Adolph and Florence, Eddie and Dorothy, and Willie and Regie came over. In addition to the family, Olympians, possibly seven or eight of them, came over to the house and it was a homecoming long to be remembered.

There was love here. I was home, home, home. Again, the thrill of arrival in Cleveland permeated me. I soon enrolled at Western Reserve University and became a college-boy freshman, even though I had not finished high school. Arrangements were available to a discharged veteran who had not finished high school that admission could be had on a probationary period. If, at the end of the freshman year, a reasonable grade point average was attained, the student would then be eligible to receive his high school diploma. It was under these conditions that I was fortunate enough to be allowed to enroll at Western Reserve University and begin my studies there very shortly after my arrival home. My initial goal of moving forward with my life had now been met.

9

Life after the War

In November of 1946, my sister, Renée, was married. While at the University of Michigan, she had met and was courted by an almost-neighbor from University Heights. His name was Harvey Harris, a fine looking redhead. Renée and Harvey made a good-looking young couple. Harvey had recently been discharged from the army. He was a Case Institute of Technology graduate with a new degree in engineering.

He and I had met for the first time after I came home, a newly discharged veteran of the Navy. Harvey and I hit it off very well. I was fond of him and felt I was not only gaining a new brother, but a good friend as well. Our friendship and close relationship has now lasted for the better part of sixty-two years. I could not have chosen anyone better. Renée and Harvey are a big plus in my life, as they have been for years, although I don't get to see enough of them, nor have I ever.

Sister Renée, 1944.

That year I bought a broken-down 1938 Desoto and became a big shot with my buddies, as I now had wheels. Occasionally, my friends and I would go down to the Red Cross and donate a pint of blood. They paid fifty dollars for it. It was "happy money" for a college kid. Also that year, I had my tonsils taken out. I made everyone happy, as I couldn't talk for three days. Thinking back about it now, it still hurts.

Freddy Bram's mother had leukemia and was slowly dying. At the time, he was still in the Navy, stationed in Saipan. Walter Polacheck, who had changed his name to Page, and I sat with her for hours. She needed blood transfusions, and Walter and I donated the blood as well.

I enjoyed school and I studied hard. The thought of obtaining a college degree motivated me. Along with much studying, I spent hours playing bridge. I also made the varsity in basketball and had some great games.

The big news in 1947 was the nightmarish letter that I received from Tami advising me that she had gotten married. I was totally destroyed. Another event during the year was that I finally received my Victory Medal from the Navy, which came to me a year after I was discharged.

On December 21, 1947, my brother, Benno, married a lady by the name of Madelyn Harris in Cincinnati. Madelyn's family was quite large and there were many social to-dos, which I and the rest of the family attended. Freddie Bram had come home from Saipan on an emergency discharge, due to his mother's serious illness. Freddie had no family whatsoever. He was the only person with her until Walter Page and I decided that we would, more or less, become "family" and begin to spend considerable time with Fred and with his mother in the hospital. Gisella Bram was in need of nursing care aside from what the hospital would provide. Walter, Freddie and I took shifts of eight hours and up as Gisella was unable to eat anything at all for what appeared to be weeks. The only thing that she was able to take in was ginger ale. Walter, Freddie, and I went through one or two bottles of ginger ale on all of our shifts.

After many weeks of nursing Gisella, she passed away, and Freddie was left with no family and no job. He had remained in the home where he and his mother lived, but was now unable to pay the rent or support himself at all. Mrs. Page, Walter's mother, was an extremely kind person who saw Freddie's plight and offered him living quarters on the third floor in their large home. For the next few years, this is where Fred resided. The Pages housed and fed him, as though he were their own son.

My passion, most of that year, was bridge, tennis, and basketball, at which I spent many, many hours. I did well in school keeping up a decent grade average, despite the fact that I believe I played more bridge than I attended classes. It had almost become an addiction. Life was good.

A frightening event during 1948 was the continuing struggle that our government had with Russia. At times, it appeared that our country might go to war once again—this time, with the former ally. This frightened me no end and was on my mind at all times. A highlight of the year included a Russian blockade of the city of Berlin. The Russian commanders had tightened the blockade around the Allied sector of Berlin. The Western powers said they were determined to fly in enough supplies to keep the population from starving. This was to become quite an effort. The Allies estimated that they would have to fly in twenty-five hundred tons of food a day to satisfy requirements in the Western zone. At that time, only six tons were flown in daily.

The Soviet military administration had announced that it would ban all food shipments from Soviet areas into Berlin. The Russians also intercepted six barges that were bound for Berlin from Hamburg. The crackdown on canal traffic followed earlier blockades of roads and raillines. Just previously, the Soviets had stopped all coal shipments and they had reduced the supply of electricity to the allied sector of Berlin.

In response to all this, the Allies outlawed food shipments to the Russians. This was not expected to hurt them too much, but it was believed that interruption of coal and steel shipments would have an effect. Morale in the Western sector of Berlin remained high.

Later on in the year, the Republicans chose New York Governor Thomas E. Dewey as their presidential candidate and Governor Earl Warren of California as his vice presidential running mate. In framing what could be called the tale of two coasts, the Republicans' meeting in Philadelphia had hoped to wrest control of the White House from the Democrats, who had reigned since the days of Herbert Hoover. This would be Dewey's second presidential bid. He was defeated in 1944 by President Roosevelt.

While the Republicans had named Dewey and Warren, President Truman, in a fighting mood, accepted the Democratic presidential nomination predicting victory in the fall and saying he would call Congress back into session to deal with housing, education, civil rights, and other matters.

The Democratic Convention that year was held in Philadelphia, and they named Senator Alben Barkley of Kentucky as the vice presidential candidate. Late in the year, campaigning in New York City, President Truman made a strong pro-Israel pitch in his speech to the Liberal Party at Madison Square Garden, vowing that Israel must be large enough and strong enough to make its people self-supporting and secure. Hideki Tojo, the man who promised to establish a new order in Asia, was sentenced to hang by the International Tribunal. Through assassinations and staged incidents, Tojo and his generals whipped Japan into militaristic fervor and plunged the country into World War II, predicting that Democracy, such as in the United States, was soft and lacked the will to fight back. Of twenty-three other defendants on trial with Tojo, seven were sentenced to hang and sixteen were given sentences of life in prison.

Despite Truman's support, Israel's bid for a seat in the United Nations was rejected by the Security Council because of the abstention of France and Canada. The vote was five in favor, one opposed. Five abstained, which included Britain, China, and Belgium. Since the majority of seven was needed, abstention amounted to a vote against.

On August 25, 1948, mother, Harvey, and I took Renée to the hospital to give birth to what would be mother's first grandchild and my new nephew or niece. The four of us arrived at Mount Sinai Hospital a little bit after 6:00, and Renée was checked in. Harvey, mother, and I sat in the lobby, and we waited and waited until the three of us became so fidgety and anxious about what was happening in the other room that we could not handle it anymore. Harvey and I decided that the three of us sitting in the waiting room wasn't going to make things go any quicker and suggested that he and mother would go to Clark's Restaurant on 105th and Euclid and that I should stay there and wait to see what would happen. When they returned, I would be able to report to them on Renée's progress in giving birth.

Mother and he left on their way to Clark's,

where they remained for forty-five minutes. Upon returning, some more waiting was in store for the three of us. Although we tried to practice at least some patience, after a time this wore thin. The situation was no different now than it was when the two of them left.

I decided that I was going to go to Clark's and have something to eat also, and convinced my mother that she should come with me again, and this time, we would leave Harvey in the waiting room. We went and had a leisure dinner at Clark's, while mother fidgeted and Harvey stayed back at the waiting room.

After an hour and a half, we came back. Harvey's report was again, that there was no progress and Renée was not giving birth yet. The doctor told us there was really no telling when the baby might come and that we would just have to be patient. This was not to be. Here was Harvey, chewing his nails and scared, mother an anxious and unwilling bystander along with me, all in a dither awaiting the arrival of what would be the first of a new generation.

Clark's restaurant once again saw us. This time all three, as we stayed there until almost 11:30 that night. Again, we trudged back, and there was nothing going on. This scene played out the rest of the night with usually two out of the three leaving for the restaurant and one at the hospital to report when the other two would come back.

At seven o'clock in the morning, with the three of us nearly asleep, the nurse came out and informed us that Renée had given birth to a six-pound eight-ounce little girl. We were all jubilant. Both mother and daughter were doing well. The jubilation carried on for forty-eight hours. We all celebrated our new member, to be named Judith.

In the next couple of days, I visited the hospital daily and spent hours with Sis. What thrilling days these were. Renée and baby Judy finally came home. It took some time before "normal" would once again enter our lives, or at least a new type of "normal," whatever this meant. It was now time for the new daddy to get to work and support the family he created. A short-lived job as an engineer had not worked out and serious thought was given to earning a living. Harvey took a job as a small dealer selling redwood storm windows and doors. It took a lot of drive and salesmanship. Although I was not always around, I knew that Harvey took to the task. This was no soft job. Possibly making a few extra bucks here could be accomplished brainlessly. Making a good living, supporting a home and family on the other hand, was a different matter. The stakes were high. The family needed to be supported, and Harvey worked hard. I often worried for my sis and Harvey. Were they going to make it? Would they be OK? The weeks went by and happily, financial well-being was attained. I really believe that I thrived on it as much as they did, and possibly more. A whole new dimension was developing.

While working diligently, Harvey and my dad drew up plans to build a house. Much thought and happy moments filled their minds as they anticipated ownership of their new home. Dad and Harvey had joined up to build Harvey and Renée's first home. The project was ambitious and love laden.

The home was soon completed and the little family nested in. Harvey continued working hard, and windows were being sold by the hundreds. The little factory for which Harvey was working thrived, much to the credit of Harvey's labor. Sales were such that the number of window orders from Harvey to be filled made the factory busy and kept it going. A very short period of time later, other small dealers were hired and the small factory Harvey worked for grew.

One day, Harvey came to me and said that I could work for him to sell windows also and make some money. I took him up on his offer and took the job. I was grateful to him and looked forward to working together with him.

In the ensuing weeks, I was given a sample and papers that I had to learn how to fill out for the bank to finance the storm windows that I would sell to homeowners. The job at first was really quite difficult, inasmuch as I had never done anything like this before. I could not make it at all. I canvassed with my sample for days and weeks, scouring neighborhoods where new homes were being built. If I saw prospective buyers looking at their new homes, I made hard sales pitches. My main hours for working in the summer were from about 5:00 in the evening until it got dark, and then I came home. Saturday and Sunday were to be my big days, and I started out at eight o'clock on Saturday and worked till 6:00 or so in the evening. The same thing was done every Sunday. The job proved to be quite unsuccessful for me, since I just could not score at all. In total I had spent eight weeks putting in a few hundred hours out on the road, spending my gas money in attempting to succeed as a storm window salesman. It was to no avail. I saw so many redwood windows and doors on houses, and wondered who it was that sold them. I knew that since they were there, somebody actually profited by thirty-five, forty, and as high as fifty dollars on each job.

I realized one day that maybe I was canvassing in the wrong neighborhoods. I was trying to sell in relatively well-to-do areas. These buyers of homes all seemed to have connections. I couldn't compete somehow, and I was not about to be the guy from whom they would purchase their storm windows and doors. In about the tenth week of this failing endeavor, I decided that I would go to the south and west end of town near where the Chevrolet and Ford factories were. I would sell to the factory workers. There, I figured, I would find customers, who, most likely, would not have good connections to purchase things such as storm windows. I also went to Garfield Heights, Maple Heights, and Bedford to find cheaper homes. My first sale resulted. It was actually the genesis of a very fine run, because after the first sale, within the next few weeks, I succeeded again, and again.

Sale after sale came. I had found my niche and was beginning to make some real nice profits. I was proud of having created a business for myself. At the factory, I became known, as the owner Jack Lashkow always said, as "pretty boy." Jack would say, "Pretty boy is dumb." He would follow this by saying "like a fox." I enjoyed my time with Jack and Harvey and became a little bit like the fairhaired boy who was helping to keep the factory rolling with my orders.

The weeks and months that followed saw me growing by leaps and bounds, working with builders, canvassing harder and harder than ever. I was now making many hundreds of dollars, sometimes thousands, weekly. I was making six and seven hundred dollars on weekends. In 1948 and 1949, this perpetuated great buying power. Were I to compare my income from the storm window business during the very late 1940s, it could easily have placed me in a very high-income bracket today. It represented wealth in today's money. I had become a big shot and purchased a new convertible, as well as a brand-new Hudson automobile.

Indeed, as 1949 rolled around, I was a big man with income far beyond anything I had ever dreamed of. All this was an almost part-time business, since I was a full-time student at Western Reserve University. Though my inordinate business success meant much to me, working for my bachelor's degree and beyond was more important. Tennis and basketball on the varsity team meant much also. There was no magna cum laude or anything like that. My grade average was set fairly steadily, at OK, but no honors. Were I to have devoted full time to studies, no basketball, no tennis, and no business, a magna cum laude could have been possible.

But this was not to be. Somehow, I was able to keep my basketball career going and played varsity for a couple of years missing many practices, but nevertheless, staying on the team. The highlight of my career at Western Reserve was playing against Kent State on the first team and scoring twenty-one points, highest on the team. Basketball, along with the storm window business and the finishing of my education, was very gratifying. I received my bachelor of arts degree in 1949. As you can read here, my life was very full, with no time to spare.

My social life while at Western Reserve University had been spread out amongst various ladies since Tami was in California and married and Dolly and I had broken up. There was

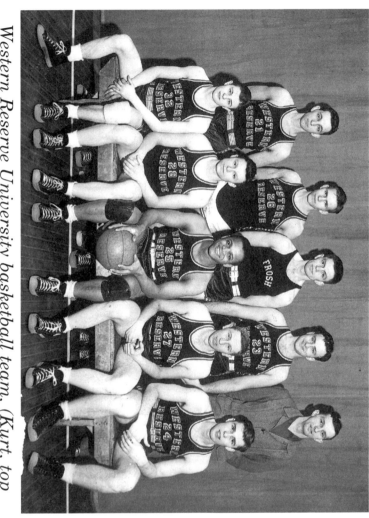

Western Reserve University basketball team, (Kurt, top row second from right).

no real love in my life with the possible exception of a very lovely lady by the name of Elaine Reich. Elaine and I had studied together at school and became a bit involved with each other. Many times I wondered whether it was a real romance, or if she were only my "buddy." Also, I met a very beautiful lady, who fit all my dreams. She was five feet, eleven inches in height, gorgeous, and super bright. Her name was June Dietz, a dream not to be realized. June was of a different religion and lived very near Lakewood on the west side of town. With the schedule that I kept, and the thirty-mile distance between homes, I often regret that she and I went nowhere. June and I spent a few months together, but not any more than that. It was not too long before we split, and I only saw her occasionally after that.

As an aside, during my years at "Reserve," as the school was called, I was perfecting my skills as a hypnotist. About three years after I was discharged from the Navy, I regularly dabbled in hypnosis. After numerous sessions working with willing volunteers, I began perfecting this art to a degree that even surprised me, let alone my subjects and my audiences. By the time I had reached my senior year, proficiency had set in to a point where I was putting on show after show at the university. "Kurt, the hypnotist," became sought after and performances were given monthly and oftentimes more.

I was sticking needles into fingers and having the subjects smile with glee as they often laughed and many times wanted the other fingers treated. Frequently, I turned my subjects into barking dogs and meowing cats. I often placed two chairs four feet apart, and turned my subjects into stiff boards who had their heads resting on one chair, with feet and ankles on the other. I never had anyone sit on the prone still human board, although I felt I could sufficiently have the body stiffened to hold such weight. When my acts were finished and the audience was either hilarious with laughter over some of the antics I had my subjects perform, or were in awe at the performances, I awakened my subjects after instilling them with posthypnotic suggestions, which became the highlight of the show. One such antic was to posthypnotically suggest (order) that upon hearing me say "cracker jack," they would faint away into a deep third-stage hypnotic trance. This was an easy accomplishment for me but a bit on the dangerous side as the subject could fall to the ground and hurt him or herself. I always saw to it that two people would stand very close to the subject to catch him or her. I was always successful in having them caught. Although the shows were successful, and my posthypnotic suggestions often highlighted the shows, I never turned my performances into ventures of monetary gain. Sororities and fraternities of the late-1940s had little money. In fact, were it not for the GI Bill, most of the students could not possibly have afforded even the books, let alone the tuition to attend school. Tuition was twelve dollars per semester hour. The GI Bill paid it for us veterans, and we were given fifty dollars per month for living expenses. This was not much, even for those days. Almost all of my performances were pro bono. I received much gratitude instead of financial rewards, but everyone was happy.

After receiving my degree, I just felt that I needed to attend more classes. I wanted to earn a master's degree. There was no comfort out of school, and I enrolled in a hearing and speech program, which would get me a master's degree as a hearing and speech pathologist in one and a half year's time. Basketball was pretty much history now and good tennis rare as my window business grew and studies were hard. My life now was almost total concentration on studies and my now-growing window company.

Many hours of student teaching were mandated with much audiology testing of children. All my work toward my master's degree was completed, and I began working on my thesis, "The workings of the human cochlea," along with anatomical drawings to accompany the thesis. This, and the business, totally consumed me. While academically involved, I applied for a teaching position in my field at Michigan State University in Lansing, Michigan. After much paperwork, I was favorably looked upon as a teaching candidate, if I should get my degree with the proper grade point average. The salary was to be $4,500.00 annually. Tenure could be had in five years. With tenure, the salary would go to $5,000.00 and professor designation might follow.

As "Kurt Wasco" (Wallach Aluminum Sash Company) grew, and my responsibilities with it, the decision to stay with the aluminum window business was made and all work on the thesis and the cochlea ceased. I was now to be a full-time aluminum window dealer. The time was 1950. Harvey, by this time, dropped out of the business and began building homes, which he did successfully. I had no need to worry anymore about his and Renée's livelihood.

After the conclusion of my studies at Western Reserve University, I spent my full time selling storm windows. Business did not always entirely monopolize my time, and I, once again, turned to tennis as my number one sport. Since being out of school, basketball was now over. I played tennis regularly at Cain Park as well as Cumberland. An interesting note here that I would like to interject is that my financial reward for having spent two years in the military, mostly overseas, finally arrived a few years after my discharge.

The bonus from the Veteran's Administration was one hundred and forty-seven dollars. Was this worth two years of fear and agony? The hundred and forty-seven dollars was not much more than a token to me, and it really didn't matter since my window business was now going along at full speed. I was averaging at least two sales per day, and the average sale was netting me somewhere between forty-five and sixty dollars. Since I was just three or four years out of service and recently graduated from the university, this kind of money in the late 1940s and early 1950s was big bucks.

I bought myself another brand-new automobile, my third. A black beauty. The car had about everything on it that the dealer was able to add to it. I was very proud to be the owner of the new automobile. This was an accomplishment in the late 1940s which was not common and surely not so amongst a kid in his early twenties. The car cost me six hundred ninety-five dollars. At the time, that was pricey. It was to become my work vehicle. I also had many short romances in it in the evenings with some of my dear friends.

As I look in my diary here, which has been guiding me through many memories and helping me put on paper what comes to mind, I noticed that I said something to the effect that I felt like I was turning into a deck of cards. It seems by September I was playing bridge almost on a daily basis, and sometimes at night, when I taught it.

I regretted the days that I did not make any sales and I was quite hard on myself, for I was planning to save my money to build a house for cash when I found the right girl. At twenty-three years of age, it was a big ambition, which I found easy to accomplish. Averaging almost a hundred dollars a day on my own sales and having no cost of living to speak of, since I was living at home, the dollars piled up. It was a fortune of money at the time. I was a huge success.

The year 1950 had snuck up on us, and we were in a new decade. I was now out of graduate school at the Garfield House at Western Reserve University and enjoying the business world. I found much of it very interesting, and I looked forward to being a wealthy man. My window business continued more successfully than ever. I had opened a showroom on Carnegie Avenue, which was about eighty feet in width, and had a lower level for storage. We enjoyed our new quarters. The showroom was magnificent, built with aluminum siding and storm windows throughout, including a large picture window behind which I had a young artist by the name of Victor Cord paint a beautiful mural. The move to the Carnegie Avenue showroom perked up business tremendously. More trucks were leased and I took on a few more installers. At that time, I also hired more salespeople, who turned out to be more of a problem than they were an asset. The year was spent playing a lot of tennis and working a full-time window business.

The news of the day worldwide politically, was disastrous. North Korean forces had crossed the

thirty-eighth parallel, and invaded South Korea. A declaration of war was broadcast by Pyong
Yang radio. Within hours, the North Koreans
were forcing the South Korean guards to retreat
across a broad front. Communist units faced
little resistance as they headed towards Seoul.
The United States seemed surprised by the attack, which they blamed on the Soviet Union.

President Truman, traveling in Kansas City,
said he was not aware of a formal declaration of
war by the North Koreans. The United States
Ambassador to Seoul said there was no reason
for alarm. He was unaware of whether the North
Koreans wished to precipitate all-out warfare.
Actually, that was precisely what they had intended, according to the report prepared for the
United Nations' secretary at Lake Success. The
secretary, Trygve Lie, received reports and called
the Security Council into an emergency meeting that afternoon. In one of the sharpest reso-
lutions that ever passed, the council accused
North Korea of breaching the peace and demanded that the Communists withdraw their
troops immediately.

North Korea and the Soviet Union both said
that the vote was illegal because China was not
represented by council. The invasion there put

the fear of God into me and most young people in the country, as we all felt that we were going to be going back to war. I had just been discharged four years previously and men were being called up now by the thousands to cope with a potential war. President Truman started the powerful American war machine engine as he authorized broad military buildups for fighting in Korea and granted the military the power to wage war.

The president ordered mobilization of the Marine Corps and National Guard, bringing into service one hundred and fourteen thousand American men with a hundred thousand soon to swell the military ranks via the selective service system. Now all branches of the armed forces were activated. Plans also included bolstering the American army with two hundred and forty thousand additional men, bringing it to eight hundred and thirty-four thousand.

While increasing manpower, Truman also boosted funding to meet the challenge of the Communist aggression. Congress approved his request for $1.2 billion dollars to continue the neutral Defense Assistance Program, a program that aided nations combating Communism. The mobilization of money and men followed. The

United Nations Security Council voted in July to give the United States full command of the UN troops defending South Korea. The seven to nothing vote with Egypt, India, and Yugoslavia abstaining and the Soviet Union continuing its boycott, placed special responsibilities on America. Truman accepted the burden and appointed General Douglas McArthur chief of the United Nations' forces. By now, I was extremely happy that when discharged four years earlier, I had opted to get out of the reserves, although the Navy put a tremendous amount of pressure on me to remain in it. Had I remained in the reserves, as so many guys did, I would likely have been called back in. The fact that I did not agree to remain in the reserves did not give them the right to call me up into the military forces, which were now being built up. My fear of being called up, however, was not small, as we thought surely that the conflict would escalate resulting in, most likely, war with Russia, which scared the hell out of me. I'd had enough. Two years was more than I wanted to handle, and at this stage of the game with a career ahead of me, I was not interested in the least of being back in the military, going out to sea, or whatever the Navy would have in store for me.

Many of my colleagues and friends were not quite so lucky and were called back into the service to prepare them for the war, which appeared imminent. The United States, at that time, had gone into South Korea with a large number of troops and the conflict was on. I continued on with one eye on my window business, and one eye watching the daily news to see what was happening overseas. It was like déjà vu of several years earlier and very, very frightening.

10

The Marriage

I was playing tennis at the Shaker Heights High School tennis courts one day, when I was introduced to a young lady by the name of Bubbles Wolpaw. Bubbles was not the prettiest girl, but seemed to be nice enough. Although she was not a tennis player, she was on the tennis court with a racquet, which did not get very much action.

I was not in the least interested in her tennis. Because she was a lovely young person of the opposite sex, she was of interest to me, and we struck up a friendship. Prior to leaving the courts that day, I asked her for a date, and she and I went out. I don't really recall where we went or what we did, but we spent an evening together. I think I impressed her immensely with my new Hudson automobile, which was quite the thing in those days. The evening ended with a very light and short kiss on the cheek. I went home wondering whether I had met somebody of importance.

Bubbles and I had a second date a couple of

weeks later, at which time she told me that she was leaving for Wheaton College in Norton, Massachusetts, the following week. Our second date was nice. I was extremely impressed with her background. She lived in a mansion. Her parents and I took to each other. I believe this very much influenced Bubbles to be interested in me. I did not know what her real name was. Her father called her "Bubs," but everyone else that knew her called her Bubbles. In fact, I don't know if there was anybody that knew what her real name was except her parents and maybe some other members of her family. It seems when she was two or three years old, she had wallpaper in her bedroom with bubbles on it. This brought on the name.

Bubbles left for college that week. Was I interested in her? I believe that I was, and as the old saying goes, "Absence makes the heart grow fonder." I had visions and illusions about this new lady that I had met. She was now absent and away at school. She told me she would be coming home on a week or two-weeks, and asked if I would see her during this period of time. She was, as I recall, very interested in me, and my interest in her may not have been much less.

Bubbles came home at Thanksgiving time,

and I had a date with her to go out. Thanksgiving time in 1950 showed us the heaviest snowfall that Cleveland had had in its history. It had been snowing all afternoon the day I took her out, and by the time we got back to her house, the snow was so high the car actually could not negotiate the road. We were stuck in her home. Lucy, her mother, was a personable gal, who obviously liked me very much. Her father was a nice guy, and there we were, the four of us, sitting around talking about . . . gosh, I don't know what.

After a while, Lucy looked outside and saw that the snow had now piled up somewhere around four feet and said to me, "Kurt, there's no way that you can go home." The car probably could not travel the road. We had turned the radio on and heard that no one was allowed out on the streets. There was a curfew on. I called my parents and told them the situation. They were very understanding and told me to stay over at the Wolpaws' if I wished, and to call them in the morning to keep in touch with them. They, of course, were also checking on the snowfall.

The following morning, I awakened in my room and looked outside to see that there were at least another six or eight inches of snow on the ground that had fallen during the night. My car was barely visible under piles and piles of snow, which in places, I believe were five feet high. That morning we met in the dining room almost at the same time.

The maid had made a very nice breakfast consisting of . . . I don't remember what, but it was quite sumptuous. This must have been around nine o'clock and we sat in the dining room, not the breakfast room, I don't know why that was, for at least an hour and a half to two hours. During that time, we discussed my career, my business, and very much so Bubbles' school, Wheaton College, what she was doing there, her studies, and her life in the northeast. There was a bit of formality about the whole morning. I was not very much at home with the three of them and the maid standing around ready to serve more coffee. I wondered, where does this go from here?

Lucy, as the minutes went by, became more and more friendly. She was almost like a girlfriend to me. She carried the conversation on and was quite complimentary to me. Harry was a rather quiet gentleman who had stayed home, for he, too, could not go to the office. Their cars were in the garage. Had they opened their garage door they would have been met with five feet of snow. There was no way the automobile could have gone on its way out into the street. Everyone was confined to their homes.

Passing the rest of that day was interesting being with Lucy, Bubbles, and Harry. I must say that I very much enjoyed them. Harry, although rather quiet, was a very sharp gentleman. He questioned me about many, many things, and I had an idea that he was much more interested than just on a casual basis. I told him all about Kurt Wasco, which was my company, and very proudly boasted of the company's progress for these past couple of years and how we were established as likely the second largest aluminum window company in Cuyahoga County. I believe I must have impressed him, for after all, here I was, just a twenty-four-year-old kid. I had gotten my college degree, I had spent a couple of years in the military, and as I look back now, I suppose was a little bit above the average fellow having accomplished what I did since I had left high school back in 1944.

I was on the telephone with my mother and dad two or three times that day, the last call being around 9:30 in the evening, when I announced, and they realized also, that there was no way that I could come home. The curfew was still on, and the snow had not abated. The next morning was not very much different as we all met in the dining room, where, once again, a sumptuous meal was served, and then we got into very deep philosophical conversations. Harry's great interest in me frightened me, for he was more analytical than Lucy, who was just a very friendly, lovely lady, who had established a rapport with me as contrasted to Harry's deep interest in just about everything that I had done and experienced, and was experiencing. In many ways, that day was a bit frightening for me also, for I realized these lovely people had much more than just a passing interest in me.

What Bubbles did was obvious, and if I may analyze, I would have to say that Lucy's interest in me was even greater. She had a real feeling for me. I was scared silly. I called my parents at about eight o'clock in the evening, for I certainly did not wish to spend another night with Harry, Lucy, and Bubbles. At that time, I boldly announced that I was going home and would brave the hazards of the four feet of snow. There was a little bit of objection, however, not too much, and I headed out to my car, which did start, and in half an hour, I was back at home with my parents. I told them about my two-day visit at the Wolpaw house. My mother's feelings were that surely I had met some very, very fine people, and I could, of course, do much worse, if you wished to be serious. Bubbles could easily have been my friend, but to be romantically entangled with her, possibly with serious intentions, was out of the question. She just did not turn me on at all. I spoke to her a couple of times before she took off for Wheaton again as her little vacation ended.

Over the next few weeks, she wrote me on a regular basis and I answered her. During the time between Thanksgiving and the early part of January, Lucy called me on at least four or five occasions to speak with me. She would tell me about "Bubs" at school and what was going on in her life, etc. On one of these discussions on the telephone, she told me that Bubbles would be coming home from school in January, and asked if I would see her. I told Lucy that it would be my pleasure, and I left it at that.

A few days before Bubbles was to come home, there was another telephone call from Lucy, asking me if I would come over for dinner with the family. They had invited a Dr. Newman, a very close friend of theirs, and his wife for dinner, also their daughter. They wanted me to be there as well. I was too timid to say no to the invitation, which I likely should have done. I was beginning to fear the total entanglement I found myself in. Something told me that I had lost all control. It was all like becoming a member of that family. The manner in which Lucy spoke to me was scary. I was being tied to Bubbles

Kurt's first wife, Bubbles, at her graduation, in 1954.

and I had no interest in that. My feelings for Bubbles were not romantic but friendly and warm only. Was there even an ounce of romance in the back of my mind? The answer to that was a very definite no.

The following week, Bubbles came home and I telephoned her with a friendly welcome home call, telling her that I had accepted her mother's invitation to dinner for the following evening. We spoke on the phone for about five minutes, not much longer. The following day, I came over to their house as a dinner guest.

Dr. Newman and his wife, Ella, were at the house before I arrived and when I came, I was introduced to them and their daughter by Harry. They were also very fine people. Actually, very much like Harry and Lucy. The butler served drinks in the living room, and after half an hour of hors d'oeuvres and small talk, we went into the dining room where the maid served dinner. It was almost like a formal affair, with the help and the manner in which everything was set. We had gotten through the main course when Lucy took a fork and banged it on an empty wine glass, saying that she had an announcement to make. I sat there, probably shivering in fear, for I had no idea what was coming, when Lucy said, "Please, all of you raise your glasses to congratulate the newly engaged couple." To try to explain my emotions at that point would be almost impossible. The only words that I can come up with were severe fright. This was possibly one of the most shocking moments of my life. I just sat there frozen in my chair. I had no idea what to say, and was likely like an inanimate object. I was totally speechless.

The evening progressed with much small talk

and constant congratulations and plans for the future, which I actually did not have the nerve to deny. Would it have been possible for me to say, "No, this isn't right; no, I'm not interested," or "No, I'm not going to marry your daughter"?

I did not have the strength to do anything of the sort and went along with the entire charade. Finally, much to my relief, the evening ended. I drove home about as quickly as I could. Upon arriving there, I found that my mother and dad were in bed, about to go to sleep. I must have jolted them as I came in and screeched out the news of what had happened to me that evening. My father, being very calm and logical, said, "Well, Kurt, do you love this girl?" My answer of course was that I certainly had no intentions whatsoever of marrying her, nor looked forward to spending the rest of my life with her. I protested, "No way, no way."

My mother, on the other hand, had an entirely different approach. She said, "You know the Wolpaws are an outstanding social family, and possibly extremely wealthy."

My rebuttal to that was that "I don't give a damn about either their wealth or their social standing, and I do not have any thoughts at all of tying in with them as Harry and Lucy's son-in-law, being married to Bubbles."

My protests went on and on, and finally, my dad said to me, "Well, Kurt, what are you going to do about it?" The question stumped me altogether for I knew that I did not have the strength, the nerve, or the ability to go back to that fine family and say to them, "No, I'm not interested in your daughter, I'm not going to marry her." There's no question in my mind, then or now, that I did not have the ability to do that. I had hoped that time might change the calamity that had set upon me. Bubbles, a few days later, went back to school and Kurt Wasco of Cleveland, which was at this time a very successful business, began to take up 100 percent of my time. Many builders looked to my company for their windows. We were very active in seeking out prospective buyers of homes to sell them our products and this was quite intense. As for the Wolpaws, Lucy had started to plan parties.

There were to be showers given for Bubbles when she came home from school, and these were planned on an almost weekly or semi-weekly basis when she came home in April, at the end of the semester, which now was about the middle of the month. I just stuck it out and corresponded with Bubbles, never, ever mentioning the fact that the family had planned this marriage.

April came, and so did the showers. One after the other, one fancier than the next, sometimes twenty girls, sometimes more, always a big outstanding event. Guessing now, as I look back from the time of April when Bubbles came home until the wedding date—that they had planned for August 15—which I was unable to deny, there must have been minimally ten fancy showers. I never had the strength to say no, and when that fateful day came on August 15, Cleveland saw one of its finest, most ornate weddings in its history. There were twelve bridesmaids, I believe, and I probably had ten to twelve ushers that were involved in the ceremony. Both families were well attended, and most of my Olympian fraternity brothers were present. Lord knows how many friends of Bubbles were there making this a gala evening, not to be forgotten. By the late night of August 15, Bubbles and I were husband and wife. The *Cleveland Plain Dealer,* had never in its history carried a full-page picture of a Jewish bride in its social section. That Sunday, they ran a full-page picture in color of Mrs. Kurt Wallach.

11

Cleveland to Miami

Harry, Bubbles' father, had given us, among other things, a wedding gift to take a cruise to Caracas, Venezuela, leaving from New York. He had purchased a Pullman car berth on a train leaving from the Terminal Tower for New York that evening, a couple of hours after the wedding ceremony ended. Walter Page, my Olympian buddy, had found out which Pullman car had been reserved for us on the train leaving Cleveland about twelve thirty. He boarded the train well before we did, unbeknownst to anyone, and with a very dark green paint, painted the toilet seat. After this little bit of shenanigans, he quickly left the train and was not to be seen any longer. We boarded the train about midnight, and needless to say, huge embarrassment followed. The paint was not to be easily removed from Bubbles' rear end.

The following morning, we were in New York and boarded the ship headed for South America. Not remembering the incident of the evening before, Bubbles decided that we should take a dip in the swimming pool on the top deck. We went topside and it was not too long before she became the laughing stock, as people saw the ring which extended from slightly above the back of her knee to the bottom of her bathing suit. It was difficult to remove that paint. We enlisted the help of the little hospital they had on the ship. Getting that ring off Bubbles' back end was an almost impossible job. We stayed on the ship until we came to South America and spent some time in Laguirra and Caracas before going on to Baranquilla and Cali in Columbia, as well as Bogata and Medeline. The cruise back to the United States was uneventful.

Upon arrival in New York, we got a train, which took us back to Cleveland, where we settled into a beautiful apartment that was a unit of a building that Harry and his brothers owned. The building was in the finest part of Shaker Heights. We were obviously the youngest people in it.

The news of the day was still the war in Korea, which frightened me no less than it had previously. It had blown up into a full-scale conflict, as the North Koreans were being supplied and helped by the Chinese, and the South Koreans were getting help from America and the United Nations. The war was one of major consequence. The question in my mind, on a daily basis was, was I going to be called back into the military. The thought of that frightened me, most particularly, when we learned that the Chinese had entered the conflict in Korea, and the United States was on the verge of a full-fledged war with China.

A spokesman for the Eighth Army said that two Chinese divisions had thrown themselves into the fighting in the northwestern part of the country. Five divisions were amassed in Manchuria on the other side of the Yalu River. Three hundred thousand combat-proven Communist troops were ready to move. Chinese troops crossed the Yalu near Supungmn and threatened to cut off a British brigade. Allied planes struck back against the communists. Another American unit was threatened. The Chinese attacked ferociously along the Chong Chon River.

Another interesting tidbit of news this day in nineteen fifty-one, was the fact that Americans averaged an income of fourteen hundred, thirty six dollars for each man, woman, and child annually. This report came from the Commerce

Department. Total individual income payments were divided by the population, which meant that the averages were pulled up by large incomes of the very rich.

The figure represented a gain of one hundred sixteen dollars or nine percent over the nineteen forty-nine figures, and represented the highest dollar total in history, though a rise in the tax burden cut down the net in nineteen fifty. The average incomes ranged from six hundred and ninety-eight dollars a year in Mississippi to nineteen hundred eighty-six dollars in New York.

In the world of tennis, Maureen Connolly, a golden haired girl of sixteen, upset the veteran Shirley Frye in three sets in the finals of the United States Tennis Championships and became the youngest ever to win the title at Forest Hills. Ms. Connolly, affectionately known as little Mo, hit the ball with amazing velocity in capturing the Forest Hills match by a 6–3, 1–6, 6–4 score. The San Diego shotmaker did not go to the net until the final game and the match was not settled until the final stroke. It was so nerveracking, that Ms. Connolly's coach was near collapse at the end. Ms. Frye's game was predicated on her defense.

The outcome might have been different had she gone to the net much earlier. Ms. Connolly netted the ball only three times in the set and made only eleven errors to Ms. Frye's thirty.

Bubbles and I had now, after the return from our honeymoon, settled into our apartment at 15820 South Moreland Boulevard. The address at the time was one of great prestige. At the young age of twenty-four, we lived as millionaires in this beautiful apartment. We had two brand-new automobiles, one for each, and I went to my office daily, which was a beehive of activities with orders being written and installers filling their trucks with windows. Kurt Wasco, the young company I had started two years earlier was now the second largest aluminum window distributor in northern Ohio. At age twenty-four, almost twenty-five, I seemed to many to have arrived at a pinnacle not reached by many at so young an age, or for that matter, at all.

Bubbles enjoyed her social life with many friends. There were many parties and many lunches. In addition to these activities, she enrolled at Western Reserve University since she had not finished at Wheaton prior to our marriage, and was busy studying for her bachelor's degree. She obtained that the following year as

I carried on with the company. There was talk of making a family.

My dad convinced me that it was high time that I leave the apartment building on South Moreland and build a home in Shaker Heights. Dad, at that time, had numerous building lots on Rye Road, Hazelmere, Wimbledon, South Woodland, etc., and offered me any lot I wished to purchase from him. I agreed that this was a venture worth undertaking. I purchased a lot from him on Wimbledon about half a block from a new elementary school that was just being finished.

I attempted to find financing for the construction of this home which was quite large. It would be a beautiful edifice. It turned out after going to several banks that there were deed restrictions placed on all the property in this area by the founders and original developers known as the Van Sweringen Company. The Van Sweringens were prejudicial and placed articles in the deed restrictions that no families of first-generation Italians may live in this area, which was known as Duffield Downs, and no families of the Jewish faith were allowed to live in Duffield Downs, etc. It was as highly prejudiced as could conceivably be placed into deed restrictions. The bottom line was, there was no way that any bank would agree to place a mortgage on a home that my dad and I had decided we would build for my wife and me.

Since I had purchased the lot from my father and took great offense at these deed restrictions, I was more determined than ever that I was not going to let these so-and-so's keep me from building a home that dad and I had decided I would have for myself and a future family. Since my business was good and the lot was paid for free and clear, I told my father one day that it didn't frighten me one bit to go ahead and start construction without a mortgage. Dad originally objected to this idea since it was a little bit foreign to him that a home of this size should be built without a mortgage.

I made my case to him and we began to build. It took us about ten months from the time we broke ground until the home was completed. I was proud, and I suppose I can be to this day, to write that during this ten-month period, I paid all the labor bills, as well as all the material bills in the construction of the home, and never at any time dug into my savings account. My earnings from Kurt Wasco of Cleveland paid all invoices. The home was paid or in full. My bank account at that time had not been diminished, but, in fact, had grown by quite a sum. The company's flourishing was by no means accidental. I was now pretty much out of the game of tennis, basketball, studies, etc., and devoted all my time to the business of aluminum storm windows and doors. The harder I worked, it seemed, the faster the company grew and became more and more successful. I was as proud as a peacock at the accomplishments.

Inasmuch as we were now twenty-five and twenty years of age, Bubbles and I decided that we should have a family. Our plans came into fruition on January 30, 1954. We were blessed with a beautiful little girl, whom I wanted to call Loralei. Bubbles objected, finally agreeing with me that the name Laurie Kay would be chosen. We were the proud parents of a beautiful little girl. It was the third granddaughter that my mother and father had and the first grandchild for Harry and Lucy. The baby was healthy, and we took great pleasure in seeing her early development.

We decided she was not to be an only child and planned to have a second one shortly thereafter. In June of 1956, another beautiful little girl with great big eyes was born to us. We

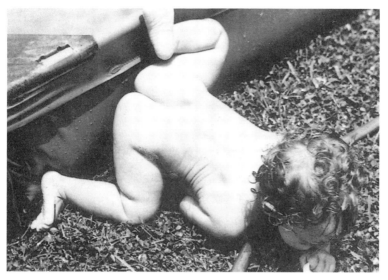

Daughter Penny, age six months, falling out of our backyard pool, 1957.

Penny, 1960.

named her Penny Lyn. I was now almost thirty years of age and Bubbles was twenty-five.

Kurt Wasco of Cleveland was thriving. However, looking into the future, I saw that there was going to be a decline of major proportion in the aluminum storm window and door business since builders were now beginning to include these along with the primary windows, and this would cut the storm window and door dealer out altogether.

In anticipation of this, I had made plans that were not exactly to Bubbles' liking. I had my heart set on moving to the sunny South. One evening, as I was leaving a customer's house rather late at night, my car was stuck in about a foot and a half of snow. The wheels went round and round and somehow this automobile just refused to go forward. As I recall, it took me about forty-five minutes before I was finally able to get the car moving again. I did not arrive home until after 10 P.M. I was extremely upset and said to my wife, "This is it. We are going to move to Florida."

Bubbles' reaction to this news was one hundred percent negative. She had definite ideas that she did not want to live in Florida. All my pleading and telling her of the advantages of

Older daughter Laurie, age seven, in 1961.

twelve months of sunshine that would far out-weigh what we had in Cleveland did not make an impression on her at all. The discussions of my moving the family to Miami Beach, where I had wanted to go, were at a standstill.

In time, as more discussions took place, Bubbles agreed and I put the house that we had built on the market, as well as the business. It did not take long for both house and business to be sold. Still shy of thirty years of age, I moved my little family from Cleveland to Golden Beach, Florida, a suburb slightly north of Miami Beach.

Golden Beach became our new home in 1957. I had rented a waterfront house which backed onto the Intracoastal Waterway. It was by all measure a fine little residence with three bed-rooms and two baths on a beautifully landscaped lot. A terrazzo floor throughout coupled with ocean breezes made it a cool haven that we hoped would be much enjoyed. Our optimism was not long-lived.

On the other side of the Intracoastal was empty, low-lying land, a few hundred undevel-oped and marshy acres. Not knowing the local problems, Bubbles and I were unaware of the fact that countless thousands, maybe millions, of mosquitoes inhabited these marshes. When the wind blew from the west, hundreds of thousands of these little bloodsuckers were blown over to Golden Beach, where they feasted on the human inhabitants. In short, our lovely home was not fit for us to live in.

My days and evenings were spent swatting and spraying. One evening I decided to count my victims. After 167 of these menaces were killed, I lost count. Laurie and Penny spent considerable time crying. Their bodies had bites on them from head to toe. It was pathetic to view their agony. I considered moving to a nearby hotel on the ocean but refrained from doing so due to the insecurity of not having any income. There was no business and no job. Money had to be preserved.

My early days in Miami were spent studying for the real estate exam I would be taking in order to become licensed as a salesman. When studies were completed, I became eligible to take the much-awaited exam at the Angebilt Hotel in Orlando. To my happy surprise, I received a ninety-four percent, which was the third highest among more than one hundred and twenty people taking the exam. I was now a licensed real estate salesman.

License in hand, I applied for a job at

numerous real estate brokerages and was hired by Feiner Real Estate on Washington Avenue in downtown Miami Beach. "Pop" Feiner, a fine old gentleman of seventy, was retiring and had turned daily operations over to his son, an obese, lazy, malcontent who could no more run a real estate company than I could cure diseased chickens. As the business faltered, so did my career as a real estate salesman. In short, my career ended in failure along with that of Feiner Real Estate.

Again unemployed, I decided to go into business. After considerable searching, I found and then purchased twenty-six building lots in northeast Miami. A corporation called "Penny Homes" was formed and I commenced with construction of lovely homes. Two models, the "Laurie" and the "Barbara" were built. I began a career as a home builder.

Penny Homes Corporation built twenty-six homes in a part of north Miami called "Ives Estates." In 1957, a 1,500-square-foot house, three bedrooms, two baths, terrazzo floors, tile roof and amenities sold for $14,000 to $16,000. Most homes were on seventy-five-foot lots and for an additional $1,000, a thirty-foot by fifteen-foot swimming pool (sometimes screened in) could be had. When building these homes, I watched every dollar that went into them, for the competition in the building business was more than merely keen. A two hundred dollar difference in the price of a home often meant a sale or no sale. Construction materials or labor costs were measured by ten dollars more or less at times.

Sales at Penny Homes were slow as a very overbuilt market caused large problems to builders, many of whom went under. As a neophyte, rookie tenderfoot having recently graduated from a six-month contractor course, I followed the spending rules closely, watched every outgoing buck and thus, survived. Profit margins were minimal. A 1,500-square-foot house built over a five month period could show a $1,000 profit. This was very little, even in those days. My superintendent did all rough and finish carpentry work with his men. He hired and fully supervised roofing, electrical, plumbing, concrete, and all other work on a home, including hiring labor and landscaping. Cost for his services was one dollar per square foot of construction.

Having a nice home, two small daughters, and a wife to feed was a hard task. To maximize income, I bought a pair of huge heavy boots and worked a few hours daily at manual labor. Not having the skills of a plumber, carpenter, electrician, or other labor, all I could contribute was expended by my digging footings. Cleaning up of trash was an occasional job, along with other nonskilled efforts.

Though it was demeaning, that is how I spent a part of my early building business career. It did enable me to purchase some small luxuries for my family at the time. For the most part, however, it was digging footing. The normal $1,000 profit on the sale of a home was often stretched to $1,100 or $1,200.

In addition to becoming the developer/builder of Penny Homes, I found and purchased an apartment site on the Broad Causeway leading to Miami Beach. It was a beautiful property backing onto the water where a first-class seawall and a 250-foot-long dock stood. The purchase was an exceptionally good buy. I decided to build a twenty-two unit apartment building on the property. Plans were drawn for a beautiful building, a true one-of-a-kind, to be named "Keystone Park."

One day I ran across a newspaper article which discussed buildings in Latin America and Puerto Rico. One project caught my eye. The article spoke of building what they called "condominium units," numerous units in a building, each having its own deed in fee simple ownership.

Until now, I had only known of these things being "cooperatives," where every owner of an apartment had a share of the building. For example, in a fifty-unit building, a corporation was formed having fifty shares of stock. Each owner would receive one share per apartment. The "co-ops," as they were known, worked fine except for the fact that each shareholder was responsible for every other. Should one unit fail to meet its obligation (mortgage, taxes, insurance, etc.), all others would have to pick up the responsibility.

Many times problems arose. With the South American advent of "condominium," each owner has the fee title to his/her unit, plus common area share with no responsibilities for others. Obviously, it was a far better investment than the "co-op."

I made up my mind that I would build such a building although none had ever been built in Florida before. My problem was to find financing for it. A problem it was, indeed. Inasmuch as no lending institution had ever been involved in anything like this, none wished to be the first. I hunted and scoured every banking institution, insurance company, mortgage broker, and mortgage banker in Florida. None would lend. Finally, before giving up and considering the effort futile, I got a call from a Mr. Phil Fruitstone of Florida Bond and Mortgage Company. He was interested in my concept and had contacted many sources, finally landing a foreign bank willing to place the mortgage. I was overjoyed and after several weeks and mountains of paperwork, the mortgage was placed and construction commenced.

During the construction phase, thousands were spent advertising the coming of this new residential investment opportunity. Even one full-page picture ad was placed in the *Miami Herald*. No sales were made. I didn't even come close. Surely when the building was completed it would sell out I thought. But no, I did not come close to anything resembling a sale. The empty building, beautiful as it was, just stood. Financial disaster loomed. No one was willing to make a large purchase of something they did not understand. All my literature describing and teaching what a "condominium" was failed. They didn't understand, and they didn't buy.

Keystone Park condominium apartment.

I finally gave up on my failing venture and turned the building into a regular apartment building. Economic times were slow, and it took months before I finally rented out half the building. It was then placed on the market for sale. One day, a jeweler and his wife, Muriel Egizi, came by, loved the building and made a fair offer for its purchase.

I agreed to the offer and a contract for sale was written. We were both happy, and Muriel looked forward to the closing. Later, Mrs. Egizi told me that they planned on moving into one of the units. I advised her very sternly against her decision. I pushed hard to avoid this, as I knew the tenants would drive her crazy if she lived in the building. A burned-out lightbulb, a lost key, a drip in a faucet, a leaky window, or any of a hundred little maladies would send the tenant running for the owner/occupant. No matter how hard I urged her, it was to no avail. Shortly after the closing, the Egizis moved in. As I had predicted, the poor lady had no peace as the tenants' demands continued daily. They were literally driving poor Muriel crazy as knocks on the door were heard as late as 11:00 or 11:30 at night.

One day, I got a phone call from the Egizis. They wanted me to come over. Upon my arrival, they told me that I had cheated them with this monstrous investment. They were so angry with me. They all but questioned my ancestry as they insisted I must buy the building back. I had no intention of doing so but finally agreed to offer them a ridiculously low price for the building. This made them even angrier. They felt it was like adding insult to injury. I left their home definitely not as a friend. The situation was finished—so I thought. Two weeks later, Muriel phoned and asked me to come by. I did not know what to expect this time. A very friendly Mrs. Egizi met me at the door, asked me in, and offered me a cup of coffee. I accepted, anxiously wondering what was next. She told me that she and her husband had thought my offer over and would accept it.

I was once more to be the owner of the Keystone Park, this time at an extremely advantageous price. I was happy because I made a second, even larger profit this time. However, I did not want to own this building. Building a small subdivision of homes now kept me extremely busy. I had no interest in being a landlord with the petty grievances and other problems that go with such ownership. An aggressive campaign was launched, hoping to find a buyer.

In a matter of six weeks, Joshua Levy, a young Israeli gentleman, showed great interest in the building. After some lengthy negotiations and a final meeting of the minds, a sales agreement was drafted. Levy paid a hefty price for this fine edifice and became its third owner. Remembering Muriel Egizi's problems, I very sternly advised Joshua not to move into the building. To be sure he got the full message, I repeated almost in direct quotes and verbatim Muriel's problems, 11:00 P.M. callers at the door, and all. I thought for sure my full message had penetrated. A short time later, I found out that I was wrong since Levy moved into one of the units lock, stock, and barrel, less than one week after the closing.

A repeat performance, as expected, was taking place as tenants rang his doorbell at will. A replay of the previous drama unfolded. As if following a script, Levy called me weeks later and asked if I would buy the building back. As before, I made a ridiculously low offer to my new adversary, like my previous customer. Again, as before, I was recontacted and once more, I bought the building back several months later. By now, I was able to pay off the mortgage and the building was free and clear.

Once again, the Keystone Park was placed on the market. It sold in three months, and I financed the building for the new buyer. Twenty years later, the mortgage was paid off, writing a closure to the saga of Florida's first condominium, which never was. It was almost like the call girl who sold it, yet still had it to sell again.

The mosquito situation in Golden Beach had not abated. The children were miserable, and we all bore welts from hundreds of bites. Although now a builder of homes, we spent a few Sundays looking at model homes from other builders and purchased a lovely four-bedroom house in North Miami Beach. A new life was about to begin as we finally escaped the dreaded mosquitoes of Golden Beach.

It was now 1958. My business took me to building homes for people in different locations from my lots. I built all over, including apartment buildings as far away as Pompano. The work was hard, the gamble great, and the rewards small. With these facts established, by 1962, I finished my last project and chose to leave the business which had afforded us a good lifestyle, eventually allowing us to live in a luxurious waterfront home, with a pool, air conditioning, and many other desirable amenities. Though not rich, my family was well-off beyond the reach of the average family's income. A new business was going to be chosen a month or two later.

One day, I read an ad in the *Miami Herald* from Washington Federal Savings and Loan Association. They announced the opening of a new branch office and a contest in which any new depositor could partake if they would open an account. The bank had placed a clear glass barrel in the lobby of the branch. This was filled with half dollars, quarters, dimes, and nickels. A picture of this appeared in the ad, along with a statement that the filled barrel weighed over 2,000 pounds. I do not recall the exact figure. Further, it stated that a new depositor could record a guess as to how much money the barrel contained. The winner of the contest would win a new car and won second place, a large TV set. I pondered about this and concluded that if I weighed each coin of different denominations, and could know the ratio of all coins to each other with the knowledge of the total weight of coins in the barrel, I could make a very educated guess as to how much money the barrel contained.

The next day I went to the bank branch, stood

in front of the barrel for five minutes (exact, to the second) and counted all the half dollars I could record. Following this, the same was done for the quarters, then again the same for the dimes, and then for the nickels. Thus, I created a reasonable ratio between the coins.

Now having all information documented, I sat down to figure this out as it related to the total weight in the barrel. My conclusion was that the barrel contained $38,760.00. I registered this number with the bank under my name. Ten days after the close of the contest, the *Miami Herald* ran an ad showing a picture of the car and below it appeared my name and address as the contest winner. I had won a new automobile.

Bubbles, the children and I, lived well, each with their own activities. One day, Bubbles announced that she and one Ralph Robbins had decided to bowl in a temple couples league as partners from October to April. This was 1962 to 1963. They would have dinner together and an evening of bowling every Tuesday for about twenty-two weeks. My objections were vehement and very verbal. Selma Robbins, Ralph's wife, also fought with Ralph, objecting likely equally vociferously about the weekly dates the two had planned for the many weeks ahead. Bubbles then suggested a "switch," stating there would be no objections were Selma and I to be together on Tuesday nights. Neither Mrs. Robbins nor I would hear of such goings-on. The situation worsened as neither Ralph nor Bubbles abated and starting in October for over twenty weeks, they had their dinner and bowling dates.

Being a temple-sponsored bowling league with only temple member couples participating, it need not be described what this scandal caused, most particularly since I was the rabbi's brother and Bubbles his sister-in-law. The winter season saw much more scandal than bowling.

While the Tuesday night debacle continued, Selma Robbins was at home sometimes crying and I was babysitter for my two daughters. My neighbor, whose business I helped finance, would call and ask if I would come over and visit with her and her two sons. Their porch was twenty feet from Laurie's room. Should she or Penny have wanted me, I was right there. This later became an issue.

After bowling season ended and Tuesday nights became normal again, I came home from the office one day to a complete surprise. Laurie and Penny were not at home. Bubbles confronted me and asked that we go to the library where she said, "I want a divorce." Jokingly, totally in disbelief, I said, "Sure, I'll hire Stan and you use Lew. It'll be a great trial." She replied, "I'm serious." I kept joking and finally said something to the effect that I thought her sense of humor was stilted. She replied that she was serious and not kidding. It was the first time that I grasped what I saw as an outrageous situation. When I then asked where the children were, she told me she had dropped them off at Ralph's house so that they should not be involved.

I got on the phone and called Harry (Bubbles' father) and relayed the news to him. He and Lucy, who had gotten on the extension line, asked me what I had done. Dumbfounded, I replied I had just come home. I could think of no more. Her parents got on the phone with Bubbles, who advised them she was too young when she got married and hadn't had the opportunity to "see the bright lights and to date." Harry suggested that he and Lucy would fly down to talk to her. Bubbles replied she wouldn't see them. Her protests and her parents' back-and-forth debate finally ended with an agreement that they could stay only a short time should they come to Miami. They arrived within forty-eight hours.

For the next couple of days, Bubbles made it quite clear to her parents that she fully intended to go through with this divorce no matter what they had to say. She told them that she wanted to see the bright lights, she wanted to go out, she was too young when she got married and didn't have the chance to see the world, etc. It was almost a silly scene for a lady with a family, a husband, and nine- and seven-year-old daughters to all of a sudden come to the conclusion that she'd missed out in her younger years and wanted to party or whatever was on her mind. Although Harry and Lucy were Bubbles' parents, there was very little question during their stay here that they were one hundred percent on my side and not hers. It seems that Bubbles, in the previous six to eight months while she was dating Ralph, had dropped about twelve to fifteen pounds, fixed her hair very nicely with a new beautician, and all of a sudden was flexing her glamour muscles. I have always surmised that in the finding of this newly found glamour, she found a motivation for her to wanting to be single again, family be damned.

Harry and Lucy left Miami after a few days, totally brokenhearted. Bubbles already had an attorney draw the divorce complaint and that was in the lawyers' office, waiting to be filed. Harry had convinced the lawyer or Bubbles, I don't recall who, to hold off on this and let us have a trial period during which time, possibly, she would simmer down and come to her senses. Bubbles finally agreed that this is what we would do. We all hoped for the possibility of salvaging this fractured marriage. Harry, Lucy, and I were all wrong. There was no salvaging the situation. She had made up her mind this was what she wanted, and neither her parents nor her husband could convince her otherwise.

What happened over the next several weeks was a shameful display of behavior. Every time she and I had even the slightest difference, she would scream something, such as "One more word from you and I am going to see my lawyer." I guess one day she'd said that too often and I screamed back at her, "Go see your damn lawyer. See him right now and if you like, I'll drive you there, but by all means get over there because I don't want any part of you anymore." That pretty much sealed the fate of our marriage.

Shortly thereafter, when we were convinced this marriage was not going to be salvaged, I moved out of the house and took an apartment on the top floor of the Caribbean Towers on Seventy-ninth Street in Miami Beach. The top floor of the building was mine. It was a gorgeous place to be. My wife gave me a sendoff of several plastic plates, a few plastic forks and knives, and some picnic equipment that we had in our closet and it was with this that I left for good.

Afterwards, she went to Cleveland and I said to myself all the things collected over the years did not belong solely to her. I went back to the house and took all my belongings and a couple of pieces of furniture that I needed. The split was still ninety percent for her and ten percent for me. It was not much longer thereafter that the divorce was finalized.

During the divorce trial, my attorney made a motion asking the court to prevent Bubbles from taking my children out of Miami since she had spoken of moving back to Cleveland. The judge turned that motion down and said she can go anywhere she wants, take the children with her, and that I would have to go wherever she is if I wanted to see them.

My life was now shattered. I had lost everything I

had left. My two little girls were my whole life, and I was going to lose them. Bubbles did not leave Miami at that time as I thought she would, but stayed another couple of years.

12

Business to Business

The building business at this time had pretty well run its course for profitability and after several months of struggling in it, I decided I would end my building career and start something anew. I purchased a total of 1,400 acres of land in South Dade and Monroe County. The land was rather marginal, not wet in the winter and spring. It did stand about an inch of water during the summer. I formed a corporation and called it Sunny Palm Acres. I divided my land into one and a quarter-acre parcels and made fancy literature featuring advantages to land investments. Daily ads and color pictures showing the property appeared in the newspaper. The method of sales was quite simple. I placed a small ad in the *Miami Herald,* which stated investment acreage for sale, fifteen dollars down, fifteen dollars per month in Sunny Palm Acres, and I put the telephone number in. On an average day, I'd get one or two calls and sometimes as many as three or four from people interested in buying land. I made appointments at the homes of the people who inquired and sold them an acre and a quarter, two and a half, or sometimes five acres.

The one and a quarter-acre parcel would cost nine hundred and ninety dollars and would have to be paid out at fifteen dollars down and fifteen dollars per month. The two and a half acres cost eighteen ninety-five and that was twenty-five dollars a month with a twenty-five dollar downpayment. The five-acre parcels went for thirty-five hundred dollars, which called for a thirty-five dollar down payment at thirty-five dollars per month. I had worked out an excellent program. We were getting sufficient telephone calls and wrote quite a bit of business. I felt I had really hit a home run and would be coming in for some very big dollars. Since I had only paid fifty or seventy-five dollars an acre for the land, it was a huge spread from purchase price to sale price. However, there was no cash up front since all the buyers paid was fifteen, twenty-five or thirty-five dollars.

For the next couple of years, Sunny Palm Acres did exceptionally well. I attempted at all times to push our customers for a five-acre purchase. I was quite successful at this on at least fifty percent of the sales that were made. If a customer, after having purchased the land, ever complained that it was swampland, that it was not a good deal, or if he were dissatisfied, it was my policy to ask them to come into the office and discuss it. When the customer came in, I greeted them and immediately offered to give them all of their money back, a one hundred percent refund right on the spot if they would bring me their title. Customers saying they felt they had bought swampland and felt cheated called occasionally. After being asked to come in to receive their money back, most were highly surprised at the offer. I do not recall ever having a customer leave with a refund on the land that he had purchased. They left our office happy. Our integrity left them with the title to their land.

Sunny Palm Acres Corporation was a healthy little company, which produced far beyond expectations for approximately three years. After three years of running the company, a syndicated columnist by the name of Sylvia Porter ran a series of articles in national newspapers exposing "land swindles and sales of swampland in Florida." Although Sunny Palm was not guilty, it was painted with the same brush as the swindlers. The business was destroyed. Where I was getting two and three telephone calls daily, the Sylvia Porter articles reduced these to zero. The business had died a quick and painful death. I was left with three hundred and fifty acres of unsold land. Realizing the business was dead, I sold it all in bulk.

A short time after closing Sunny Palm Acres, I met a con man by the name of Herbert Cooper. Cooper befriended me and appeared like a constant companion on a daily basis having me over to his home, in fact, having the children and me to dinner at his house, etc. He said he was involved in an interesting business and wanted to know whether I would join him. Inasmuch as Sunny Palm Acres was now closed, I told him yes that I would certainly be interested to see what he was doing and joining him since I could classify myself among the unemployed. Cooper said that he was in the bowling alley business. The maple pins used in bowling were encased in plastic. He explained to me that a set of ten pins cost the bowling alley operator about a hundred and twenty-five dollars, which he had to spend regularly to keep his bowling alleys in top-notch condition. He said that he can replasticize used bowling pins at a small cost of thirty-five dollars per set and explained to me that the only difficulty in this business was buying the used pins since they had to be purchased to send to the company plasticizing them and renewing them.

The proposition sounded like an excellent situation. One day he advised me that he found many sets available in Detroit and would I purchase them. I said yes. The pins were to be sent to the factory to have them replasticized. In order to buy the pins, I had to give him eight thousand dollars. I would have to wait until the pins were picked up, replasticized, and then sold. This, he stated, might take a matter of four or five weeks. I purchased my first batch of pins and waited. In a matter of three weeks, I was told that the pins had been replasticized and had been sold for fourteen thousand five hundred dollars. I was given a check in that amount. Soon more pins were bought. Many times, deals that look too good to be true, are.

This was the case with the bowling pin business. It looked too good to be real. There was no work to be done by me and apparently a sufficient amount of pins could be bought and then a handsome amount of money would be made. A second purchase was made and about four weeks thereafter, I received another check with a forty-two hundred dollar profit. This was the last. The scenario of the bowling pins continued with many, many orders being placed.

We finally reached the point where Cooper owed me close to a hundred and fifty thousand dollars. It was not too long before I knew I had been taken for a ride as not another cent was to be received. No pins had ever been bought. No pins had ever been plasticized, and no pins had ever been sold. There was no such business. And so the scam ended.

My loss represented a small fortune to me. I had pretty well split what I owned with my ex-wife and here I was out over a hundred and fifty thousand dollars, which I could surely not afford to lose. I had all my receipts and all the paperwork that was involved with each transaction and filed a claim with the court. There was a lot of shady politics in North Miami Beach at that time, and a crooked attorney with solid connections got Cooper off scot-free in court. The judge, obviously bought off, said "there was lack of proper evidence." There is no doubt that there was a hefty payoff to a judge, who was setting a criminal free. I was now in rather deep financial trouble. My money was mostly gone, and I had no income of any kind. The child support and the alimony continued, and somehow, I managed to pay every dime that was owed every month, which squeezed me to a point where if this kept up much longer, I would not have enough money for food or sustenance. The situation was tragic.

After several months of unemployment, I had a luncheon date with an old friend, a former neighbor. She had taken a piece of cork and put some bobby pins into it from the back end and stuck them upwards into her bouffant hairdo. Ladies' styles in the mid-nineteen sixties had the hair poofed up and many times, two or three inches of hair were kept up high, eventually to fall due to the law of gravity.

When I saw the crazy homemade tool used, I asked why she didn't buy something to keep her hair up. She told me that nothing like it was available. I took an immediate interest in the possibility of manufacturing and marketing such an item and began to look around for a plastic extrusion company that could manufacture a similar tool.

I met a young chap by the name of Leonard Marquez. Leonard had a plastic molding shop where he created all types of small products. I showed him a little prototype that I had made and asked if he could create a similar tool for me. I wanted a professional tool rather than bobby pins stuck backwards into a piece of cork. He stated that he would try.

After a couple of weeks, Leonard created an instrument with a plastic handle and metal tines inserted therein. The tool looked professional to me, and I decided that I would go into the business of manufacturing it. Much time was spent creating literature, packaging, and advertising, etc., until a complete set of materials was created. All this included a plastic box that served as a fancy container for the tool. Twelve such boxes could be placed into a larger display box, which was also created. The product was complete with all materials for promotion and marketing.

I then set out to find factory representatives in the beauty supply industry to look at my product. I requested their input as to whether they felt that it would sell. To my surprise, the various representatives that I contacted and showed my product to were quite interested and felt that this tool would be used by operators and could also be sold.

I opened an office on Lincoln Road in Miami Beach and began promotions of this newfangled product, which I named Glamour Lift. To my surprise and joy, "Glamour Lift" became an almost instant success. Beauty shops not only throughout Florida, but also nationally, were gobbling it up. Distributors ordered by the gross and I couldn't keep them in stock. The orders were so plentiful that my friend Lenny Marquez hired a complete second shift for the shop.

Boxes and literature were being bought and printed far and beyond my ability to pay for them. Three bank loans were obtained to fund the company, which I had named Kurtell (for Kurt Leo). I looked forward to supplying the demand that had become a Herculean task as I hired new personnel almost daily. A new office and warehouse building was built, which soon employed thirty-five people. Factory representatives were hired to cover the country from coast to coast. Glamour Lift spread over the land like a rash. Orders came from as far away as Japan. Orders came in from major drugstore chains for many, many gross at a time, and when the mail was opened in my office daily, there were orders to the tune of many thousands of dollars. This was to be the beginning of a very profitable, large manufacturing and importing business.

Over the period of the next year or two, Kurtell and Company distributed its products from California to England. By the mid-1960s, possibly 1967 or s'68, I had more than a hundred sales representatives covering every drugstore and variety store chain as well as the entire beauty supply industry, which encompassed all the beauty shops in the country. On a survey created by *Beauty Shop* magazine in 1968, it showed that of the three hundred and twenty-five thousand beauty shops in the country, almost three hundred thousand sold or used Kurtell and Company products. I was extremely aggressive at marketing at the industry shows, which were held almost monthly in one part of the country or another. I was successful in running a business far beyond anything that I had thought would become under my ownership. The company grew faster than I was able to control it.

One day after a lengthy session with our banker and accountant, we reached the conclusion that our bank account was too small to fund the business that was developing. Accounts receivable were running sixty-days on average, and the amount of expenses that we had during that time, i.e., normal overhead, salaries, commissions, products, advertising, etc., could not carry the load. I was advised that we would be best off to merge the company or do an outright sale in order not to fall into a cash flow shortage trap, which could have destroyed the company. Immediately upon coming to the conclusion that these findings were correct, I searched for a company which could be a suitor to us to merge with my company and, thus, create something which was large enough to be either on the American Stock Exchange or the New York Stock Exchange.

Shortly thereafter, I found a company called Richford Industries, which happened to be located in South Florida. Richford and Kurtell, via principals, executives, accountants, and a banker, spent uncountable hours scanning a merger route, which was eventually found and accepted by both companies. The surviving name of the merged company was to be Richford Industries. We were now on the American Stock Exchange. When the merger of Kurtell and Richford finally became public, the stock rose by almost thirty percent. Jointly, our assets were well up in nine figures, and we were healthy. Lines of credit to the new company were strong enough to allow almost limitless expansion.

With this luxury, I expanded our line of products to where eventually Kurtell manufactured, imported, and marketed over sixty-five proprietary items. I took an employment contract that supplied me with a hefty annual salary and various insurance policies, which made my life easier. Richford-Kurtell should have made me a wealthy man.

The situation looked quite good for some time, however, there was a major problem which developed and continued to worsen over several months. The problem was that I, as president of this division of the company, and a chap by the name of Steve Kneapler, who was president of Richford Industries and chairman of the board, did not get along at all. We were like water and fire, never having a meeting of the minds about anything at all. As the months went by, animosity developed to a point where we could not even talk to each other. To continue operating the company under these circumstances was not possible. Through our separate attorneys with little personal contact, we agreed for the company to buy me out. This buyout gave a five-year salary contract and sufficient additional stock to make a very satisfactory solution to the problem of personalities. It was 1969 when I left Richford-Kurtell as a very well-to-do man.

13

Marital Intranquility

During the time I was with Richford-Kurtell, I was a lonely single man. My makeup was such that I was a very poor bachelor who lived very sadly without a companion, preferably a wife. Searching for one was a difficult task. It had now been some time since the divorce from Bubbles and the loneliness was, at times, more than I could bear.

I met with good fortune one day when I decided to go to a meeting of the "Sky Liners," as they were called. This was a social club consisting of single people who had to meet the following requirements. Any female wishing to belong to this social club had to be five feet eleven inches in height or more and any male had to be six feet two inches in height. When I went to the first meeting I felt like a shrimp since I did not stand more than six feet. In fact, as I recall, I don't believe I was anything over six feet and barely met that number. In order to allow my presence, I had to put wedges on the insides of my shoes. They added about an inch and a half to my stature. Even with this, I was still a shorty in the group and should, by all rights, have been turned down for membership in the club. However, they allowed me in and even asked me if I would come to the next meeting. I was extremely pleased with this because I found that the group of people that I had met that evening were very fine folks with whom I would like to be acquainted and where I felt I would find friendships.

The following month, the anticipated meetings took place in Bay Harbor. It was with great pleasure that I found that the club had decided to allow me to not only come, but also become a member. I do not believe such membership could have been possible without the little wedges inside of my shoes. Six feet was not six feet two, as required for males, and had they known of my exact height, even the friendships that I had made with these very lovely people would not have gotten me into the club. The height standards were strictly enforced. Nevertheless, here I was, a member now in good standing. Obviously, tennis shoes or some kind of flat footwear were out for me. I had to be extremely careful and be sure that I never left my wedges at home.

I met an unusually nice lady by the name of Miriam Kowalsky on the second meeting. Miriam was Jewish, a nice looking lady with a marvelous personality. I took to her, and we became very friendly. It did not take too long before I felt a kinship with her, which could possibly be described as love. Although her name was Miriam, she was never called that. Mimi was the moniker by which she went, and Mimi and I spent the meetings sitting with each other and afterwards, going out together for something to eat. I began to date her and found that my initial impressions were certainly correct. I would love to have married Mimi, but was hesitant since she had two teenage sons and a four-year-old daughter. To take on a family of three at this stage of my life was something that I did not wish to do, and this stood between us. The subject of marriage came up on occasion, and finally I decided one day that I would never find anybody as wonderful to be my life's companion and decided that I would propose marriage to her. She accepted, and we became engaged.

About two months after Mimi and I became so close, she became sick. Her face doubled in size with edema. It happened all of a sudden and was awful to see. She suffered terribly and when all the blood tests were in, she was diagnosed as having lupus erythematosus. Her body gained twenty-five pounds in a matter of three or four days, and her face looked very much like a balloon. After I had taken her to the hospital, the doctors explained to me that her future was very uncertain. I questioned whether I should go through with the marriage plans we made. My problem at this point was huge. Should I abandon someone that I loved in her time of need? I was not the type of person capable of doing that, yet, on the other hand, to marry a lady with three young children who would likely not survive very long was not an option either.

Mimi and I did not discuss the problem at hand, for we both knew what we were facing. I think that she felt that it might be unfair to me to enter into a marriage where she would not survive, leaving me with three children. I, on the other hand, felt that I'd be willing to take it on if I had some kind of assurance, or at least thoughts in my mind, that she could survive this horrible illness. No answers were forthcoming. When we were together, the subject had become almost taboo, although we both had it on our minds and rarely on our tongues. Marriage plans were now on the back burner. As days and weeks passed, both our brains kept it away from our tongues as we avoided the harsh realities that lay ahead. The children felt it as much as Mimi and I. No questions were verbalized by them, although their lives hung on a string.

About eight weeks after the original diagnosis of lupus, the doctor said that he erred in his diagnosis and that the sickness was, in fact, chronic glomerulonephritis. I was at first elated to hear this. But I found out later that this disease was as dangerous as lupus. The glomeruli in the kidneys closed up, causing the kidneys to malfunction. The prognosis was probably fatality. The joy of the misdiagnosis was very short-lived. The kidney ailment had an equally bad assessment with little chance of a cure.

My life was in total disarray. I could under no circumstances abandon the lady I loved, nor could I marry her. There were no answers. It was about August or September that I finally told Mimi that I could not go through with our plans under the circumstances. I hurt her to a point that I cannot begin to describe and suffered greatly from what I had done. Yet I knew that in the long run, my decision was likely the correct one.

Mimi's future on earth was medically diagnosed

as short. My decision broke Mimi's heart. She now insisted that all contact cease. This demand was adhered to, and we broke up completely. I became the loneliest of men once again. The year wore on, and it was now about the beginning of December. I had no social life, did not date, and all but rotted in what was almost like a period of mourning. The guilt at times was more than I could bear. One day I phoned Mimi and asked if I might come over. Her answer was a stern no. I told her I only wanted to stop in for a moment to deliver some Christmas gifts for the children and not to see her. Hearing this, she allowed me to stop by. When I arrived, I got a wonderful welcome from the three kids with whom I had built a great rapport. Inside the house, we opened about ten presents. It was not too long before the tears began to flow from both Mimi's eyes and mine. The children left us alone in the living room as Mimi and I literally melted into one. How cruel life could be. The sparks of love ignited as I swore that I'd see the illness through as Mimi's husband. I didn't care what the future might dictate. We were to be in this together and see it through together. After a while, the children came back into the room. Everyone, all five of us, cried as they were told of our plans for the future. I believe the kids knew how ill their mother was and had now found an anchor of strength in me. No literary ability can adequately portray the emotions of that evening. We had created a family.

Mimi and I were married the next month. I had a very lovely home at the time on Bay Harbor Island in Miami Beach, a very uppity high-class neighborhood. The home had been featured in a magazine at one time. It was absolutely beautiful and spacious. I had lived in it by myself for some time.

To describe my new family would be an interesting thing. Mimi enjoyed wearing heels, and I encouraged her not to give that up because she was always beautiful when she put on her shoes and stood six feet three and a half inches. She had a gorgeous figure, a wonderful smile, and a way about her that made everybody love her at first sight.

She would tell me that if people asked her the silly question "How's the weather up there?" she would say she felt like spitting on them and telling them it was raining. But this was Mimi in her classic beauty and marvelous personality. Two of the children were boys and one a girl, Lynn, a bright, sweet four year old. Michael, the oldest, grew up finally to be six feet nine inches in height. He was a real good-looking kid and extremely bright. His grades in school were always straight A's. Michael stood at the head of the class. He, very much like Mimi, had a wonderful personality, was magnetic, and just as sweet as a human being could be. We got along famously. In our own way, we loved each other.

A problem came into our lives which seemed to grow by the month. His name was Stephen. Stephen was not really the most masculine of boys, not to say that he was effeminate but surely not very much male. He enjoyed playing with little girls that were much younger than he.

Although never admitting it, Mimi showed clearly that she understood that this boy had some problems. I could not get along with Stephen at all. We had a situation where if I put my arms around Mimi when he was near, he, in one way or another, would see to it that it did not last very long. My handling of the matter of Stephen and his mother, who was like a mama bear with her cub, never went well. To say I was jealous would probably have been partially true.

Stephen constantly did things that annoyed

me, and when he realized that I was annoyed by whatever specific action, he would repeat it to get under my nerves. As an example of this behavior pattern, he always played out in the street in his socks. The size fifteen socks wore out playing on the concrete street daily. When he realized how I objected to this, he went out onto the street every free moment with his socks on, but no shoes. My pleading to his mother to interfere in this behavior pattern did no good. The practice continued to aggravate me.

On Saturdays and Sundays when not in school, Stephen would not get dressed and would just wear his pajamas. When I objected to the boy wearing pajamas all day long, the practice continued, never missing a day. Not a weekend went by that he didn't stay in his pajamas, never putting clothes on. Mimi never cooperated with me to oppose Stephen's behavior. She was always on Stephen's side, protecting him from this horrible husband who she said abused him. The relationship was sad. Mimi and I were married about five years. He succeeded in coming between two people who were in love with each other. I don't recall ever admiring or respecting any human being more than Mimi, but we could not endure the battles over her son.

By the early seventies, our lives had taken a tremendous hit. There was such strain that we were totally removed from one another. An example were our dinners every evening. Mimi would make dinner for herself and for the three children, and they sat together at one table discussing the happenings in school that day. I sat at another table eating alone. The family was in shambles.

Fortunately, Mimi's illness had gone into complete remission. She was like a healthy person. The marriage, with Stephen's help, had deteriorated to a point of no return. Mimi was surviving her illness, but the marriage died, ending in a very sad divorce.

14

Tennis and More

During my years of marriage to Mimi there was really not too much in the way of business to which I was attached. There was quite a bit of unemployment time during a lengthy period. I was not sure which direction I was headed, and I had no plan of any kind for some time. My time was spent at the Jockey Club playing tennis almost daily. I continued playing in some of the local tournaments, in which I was doing quite well, and continued as head umpire at the Orange Bowl Tennis Tournament, which I had been doing for many years. The Orange Bowl tournament under Eddie Herr invited the top fifty or so young players in the country to compete in what turned out to be like a junior "U.S. Open" as more than half of the invitees wound up to be professionals, and many of them became ranked in the top ten. This took a little bit of my time. The playing of tournaments and the daily practice at the Jockey Club had perfected my game to its highest standards since I began playing.

One day it was suggested to me that since this is what I seemed to be enjoying most and this is what I was doing all the time, why didn't I try to become a sanctioned tennis professional by becoming a member of the USPTA (United States Professional Tennis Association). I decided to try this suggestion and made my contacts. After a while, I received a very thorough testing from the powers that be at the USPTA and was quite happy when I was accepted and was now considered a professional by that organization.

I continued playing daily and had built a bit of a name for myself in the local tennis world. My name appeared in the sports pages on many occasions. I was invited by the Carriage House to talk to the owners about becoming the tennis pro at that fine institution on the beach. I met with the owners of the Carriage House one day, and we agreed that I would become head pro for their tennis complex. This was a real feather in my cap. I did not realize how difficult a job this would become, but I took to it with great fervor and enjoyed every moment of teaching during the ensuing number of weeks and months. The job after a while wore thin as the fancy ladies at the Carriage House, who were paying a few hundred dollars a night in their hotel rooms, would address me as "hey, you" and much of the time treated me as though I were just one of the lowly hired help. I resented that immensely since I certainly considered myself at least on an even par with most of them and did not take well to being talked down to, as was the case so many times. I stayed on the job for over a year and although not as enjoyable as it was the first several months, I continued on making a living at teaching. The tournament play continued, but no money was to be made there.

In 1971 I was fortunate to be invited by the directors of the U.S. Open in Forest Hills, New York, to become an umpire at the U.S. Open tournament for that year. The honor was a great one. The pay was zero. I spent two weeks in New York, during which time I was a linesman or a chair umpire on probably close to thirty matches. I also warmed up and rallied with some of the players. It was extremely pleasurable since I made friends with many of the top players in the world. The matches that I umpired were in the daily newspapers throughout the world. Many times pictures of matches that I was umpiring appeared in magazines and newspapers nationwide. The two weeks spent there, al-

Kurt wins tennis championship.

though nonproductive monetarily, were a great experience and I made many contacts of which I had never dreamed.

I came back to Miami and several months later, received a similar invitation to umpire at Wimbledon in London. The referee in charge was Alan Mills, who had been on the job for possibly as long as twenty years. I am sorry that I was unable to accept that invitation since the time off from the Carriage House job did not allow that. The expenses involved, and not being paid for the work, were more than I was willing to get involved with. Therefore, I skipped Wimbledon.

Tennis had become my whole life for a period of several years. I was eventually appointed as head umpire for eleven southeastern states by the Umpiring Association for a new tennis league that had been formed. This league played its matches with "tennis teams," whereby one city would play against another city in similar fashion as we see in football, baseball, and basketball, with cities being represented.

Umpiring these matches took a goodly amount of time and, once again, I became friendly with the top players in the world who had been recruited to play on these teams. There were times that I had the opportunity to play with them, not competitively, but to rally with them, warm them up, and have our fun matches when they were not on the court for serious play. This amount of time on the tennis court with the top ten to twenty players in the world was a great thrill, to say the least. Most of those five years had me doing the tennis route and enjoying it to a great degree, although as I wrote previously, it had its downside with the manner in which I was treated by some of the "students" whom I was teaching.

One day, I decided that I would build my own tennis club and not be an employee of the Carriage House any longer. I found a piece of land on 149th Street and Sixth Avenue in Miami, had plans drawn, and within the next few months, possibly eight or nine from beginning to completion, built the Miami Racquet Club. The Miami Racquet Club had eight tennis courts, which were all lit. They were clay courts with hardtrue surfaces. There was a lovely clubhouse, a pro shop, a little snack shop, etc. When the club initially started in business, we had as high as two hundred and thirty members who played regularly. We were open from eight o'clock in the morning until ten o'clock at night. These actually became my hours for some time, very much to my consternation, because I was overworked, to say the least.

I was the pro at the club along with another pro who I had hired by the name of Fernando Guarrachi from Chili. Fernando was a well-known tournament player, and he and I both took over all the lessons that had to be given at the Miami Racquet Club. After about six months, I developed a malady in my right wrist. After visiting a number of doctors, I was told that it was a subluxation of the lunate and nav-

The six best tennis pros in Florida.
Kurt is third from right.

icular bones and that I needed surgery. The surgery was successful, and I was in a cast for almost nine months, which put me out of the game of tennis altogether. The nine months saw me working at the club. Since I was divorced, there was no other life for me except the Miami Racquet Club, and to say I put in eighty hours a week at the job would not be an exaggeration.

My whole life was work, work, and work. There was really very little else, very little in the way of social life, and this was the way it was for a couple of more years. There were times I became philosophical about my tennis life. What was this all about? I was devoting my time and efforts to a game, a sport, and an activity that should have been an avocation. Was this really what my life should be? I was, after all, overage and undertalented to play on the big tour, the big time, and the big money of the tennis game. Should I devote my "overage talent" to be a second-rate professional on the local scene? On the other hand, I had been through so much, maybe it was time to coast for a few years.

After a catharsis or two, some soul searching, and a few compromises, I decided to stay with this game I so loved. I could surely contribute my share and then some on the local level to augment income and to maintain the lifestyle to which I had become accustomed. I decided to write a book on tennis humor. I had witnessed so many really funny happenings on the courts over the years, sharing them might be a good idea. How about calling it *Tennis is a Funny Racquet*. The book must be extra good and reach the national tennis scene. It must be sufficiently well done to make publishers look up and take notice. It could become a best seller. Why not?

One day I sat down, pen in hand, all prepared to begin. I didn't get far as frustration took over. Putting my poor work aside, I decided to wait a day or two and then start over. My second attempt failed. I came to realize it just couldn't be done in prose but needed to be shown in pictures.

The humor I wished to share via my book really needed to be illustrated rather than written in words. I was surely not a talented artist and couldn't do the job alone. I needed an illustrator.

After a thorough search of Miami, I came upon a young chap of great talent. His name was Bill Aaron. He was pleased and said "honored" to be my illustrator. His talent was unchallenged and I was more than merely happy to have found him. After considerable time spent and research here and there, Bill and I came up with over 150 fitting cartoons that were to be used for the book.

My next step was finding a publisher. Inasmuch as a very fine job had been done, publishers were not too hard to find. I wound up with Seeman Publishing Company, a medium-sized house with a fine reputation. They loved my book and were more then ready to start. Seeman's felt many thousands of copies would be sold and a profitable venture was forecast. I, too, was anxious but decided before publishing, I wished to share what I had created with the world's top professionals, to get their thoughts and possibly written comments. After having umpired a hundred or more matches as head umpire for eleven southern states, rallied in practice with most of the world's best, my reaching them and getting their endorsement would not be difficult.

Because the U.S. Open would be held in New York in August and because I would, once again, be working there as a chair umpire, I waited for this tournament to see my old friends and ask for their help. This turned out not to be very difficult, as friendships had long been established. Most of the top players heartily endorsed my work, including my old friend Arthur Ashe. I took my endorsements to Seeman's. Unfor-

Chair umpire, U.S. Open, Forest Hills, New York.

tunately, for reasons unknown, they slashed my 150 cartoons to fewer than 120. I had nothing to say about this, although I was greatly disappointed. Furthermore, Seeman, whom I later discovered to be a bigot, refused to publish some very nice words written to me by Ashe. They had considered him "inferior."

When the book finally came out, it was to be

classified as a successful publish. It did not make any best-seller lists but sold very satisfactorily, most particularly within the tennis industry, where it appeared in most pro shops nationally. Indeed, it turned out to be a very happy endeavor.

Tennis remained my life. It was the food I ate and the air I breathed. When not playing, I was teaching. When not teaching, I was busy with the United States Tennis Association, of which I was a member. I was ranked at my highest, twenty-fourth in the state of Florida.

The success of my tennis book, a literary simplicity at best, brought back memories of my newspaper column "Sea Breeze," which I wrote weekly for over a year while in the Navy in Panama. I pondered, why not write a column on "Tennis Technique" that might be published. Surely I knew my subject well enough. Over a period of six or seven weeks, I authored a teaching column almost every night. These were carefully thought-out in detail. I was pleased with my creations.

An appointment was made with the editor of the *North Dade Journal* to get his thoughts on my work. I left copies in his office and awaited a phone call. To my pleasant surprise, he called and told me that he loved the columns and, as a player himself, had benefited from them. He then discussed terms with me for the regular publications of the columns in the paper and so the popular "Tennis Technique" column was born. The *Journal* had no exclusive on my work and over the next thirty years, "Tennis Technique" was published in countless newspapers and magazines. In 2003, I retired from the column writing business. I felt "enough was enough." I had given my best to the world of tennis.

Worldwide events were interesting. World news during these years had many exciting things happening. A third of the United States' students, it was reported, were using pot. A federal survey of marijuana use on college campuses had revealed that thirty one percent of students have tried the drug and fourteen percent were regular users. The figures released by the National Institute of Mental Health were based on questionnaires distributed to ten thousand students at fifty colleges. The report concluded that the percentages showed a substantial increase among college students from previous surveys. In some areas such as California, use of the drug might have crested a trend, which the report predicted, would eventually spread elsewhere. The report did not record whether use of other drugs was increasing.

There were many other happenings of interest. Rolls-Royce in 1971 had declared bankruptcy in what politicians described as a major national tragedy for England. The company said it had been driven to the action by the huge losses incurred at developing a new jet engine for Lockheed Aircraft Corporation's new Tri-Star Airliner.

The British government quickly announced that it would take over Rolls jet engine activities for national defense projects, including development of the engines for the British-French Concorde supersonic jetliner. It was not to interfere with the manufacturing of Rolls-Royce automobiles, which set a world standard for luxury but accounted for only five percent of the company's sales. Rolls-Royce made only two thousand automobiles a year, most of which were sold in the United States. Its more important role was as the centerpiece to the British aircraft industry. Rolls engines powered most of Britain's military and commercial aircraft. With Rolls-Royce's downfall, it was agreed to produce the new jet engine for Lockheed at a price that turned out to be much too low.

The months went on with many interesting happenings throughout the world. Washington had ten thousand marchers come into the city who called themselves the Mayday Tribe, trying to shut down the government. They disrupted the capital for several hours as they battled with police and littered the streets with garbage. Thousands of demonstrators, including Chicago's seven and defendant Rennie Davis, were arrested. They were herded in temporary detention centers near Robert F. Kennedy Stadium.

About half of them were being held overnight. The others were treated like traffic offenders and released. Federal government managers asked employees to come to work early in the morning to avoid the protest. Many government workers obliged but got caught in the traffic for up to three hours as the marchers objected to the Vietnam War.

In California, sounding as good as he ever had, Frank Sinatra charmed the audience gathered to hear his farewell appearance at the Los Angeles Music Center as he wandered down memory lane with "I've Got You Under My Skin," "Angel Eyes," "My Way," and other songs he had made during his thirty years on stage. Once the idol of bobby-soxers, the fifty-five-year-old singer said he was serious about his retirement. "There are a lot of things I want to do that I haven't done," he stated.

During these years, so many things took place worldwide. It was July in 1971, when the Apollo 15 astronauts David Scott and James Irving took mankind's first ride on the moon, steering their four-wheeled moon rover for several miles through craters and boulders on the rough lunar surface. Scott and Irving became the seventh and eighth men to walk on the moon and the first to ride in a vehicle. They landed on the moon's Sea of Rains and left their lunar modular falcon at nine o'clock in the morning. A few minutes later, they detached the rover from the spacecraft and set off on their exploratory trip. The rover's front steering did not function, but the vehicle was designed to be maneuvered with the rear wheels only and worked well. When the astronauts made their first stop at the rim of Elbow Crater, a mile from the lunar module, mission control in Houston turned on the rover's television camera which transmitted color pictures of remarkable sharpness to Earth. Viewers could watch the astronauts evaluate and collect rock samples. At one point, they exclaimed, "There's some beautiful geology out here." Their ride lasted two hours and took them five miles before they returned to the lunar module. Scott and Irving were scheduled to make more trips on the lunar rover. They would join the third Apollo 15 astronaut, Alfred Warden, in the command ship for the return trip home.

Also during this time in 1971, past President Nikita Khrushchev died in Moscow. The Russians didn't know about his death until they heard the news on their shortwave radios. Hours had passed before the Kremlin made an official announcement. The former head of the Soviet Communist Party had been a nonperson since he was purged seven years earlier. Only Khrushchev's wife, Nina, and one of his daughters were at his side as he succumbed to a heart attack. It was considered unlikely that the once-powerful Soviet party boss was to be given a state funeral. This did not happen. The Russians will remember Khrushchev as the man who vilified Stalin and tried to rehabilitate his enemies. In the United States, Americans remember the man who banged his shoe on the table at the United Nations. These were the happenings of the early 1970s, interesting as they were.

In mid-1975, I finally sold the Miami Racquet Club. I had made an exchange for a shopping center in Plattsburg, New York. The racquet club was not doing well since so many tennis courts were being built in the Miami area that there was actually a glut. The club had begun to lose membership and the sale of it in exchange for the shopping center in Plattsburg turned out to be a very good one. I was, once again, unemployed, this time as a semi-investor since I now had a shopping center in Plattsburg, which I named the "Wallach Plaza." It was almost always full and provided a rather reasonable income. It was, in fact, about the only income of consequence that I had. There were fifteen stores in addition to the Greyhound Bus Station and Terminal, a very busy place. The buses were in and out all day, which afforded the merchants considerable business but tore up my tarmac to a point where resurfacing the blacktop, driveways, and parking spaces became almost a semi-monthly event. The plaza was a good business for me, however, it did not afford the kind of income I desired. Visits there during my ownership were few and far between. "Wallach Plaza" was the major shopping center in Plattsburg, a place so cold and northern that even Santa Claus had to go north to get there. I was told even Mrs. Claus wore long johns.

I was very unsatisfied with life since I was, once again, unproductive in my daily endeavors. I had been dating a lovely lady by the name of Judy Strauss, who had many problems of her own. Judy had just gone through a very difficult divorce and had, through this divorce, lost her eleven-year-old son to her ex-husband, an attorney who turned the boy against her totally. It was extremely hard for Judy, who suffered immensely with pangs of guilt and great sorrow. There were many times that she and I actually stood each other up, both suffering loneliness. Judy was a teacher in Carol City and was quite busy with her work. I, on the other hand, was, once again, a loner, an unemployed tennis bum after the sale of the club. We carried on for sometime with no future ahead.

It was not my intention to marry Judy since I saw many problems that existed between us. This was much to her consternation as she felt that we would lead a good life together, which never materialized. I did love her. Of this there was no doubt.

It was at this time that I thought my life had ended as I began to get phone calls and mail from my daughters, Laurie and Penny, demanding in no uncertain terms that they be allowed to be adopted by my ex-wife's new husband. My answer week after week was an emphatic no. My ex-wife, Bubbles, made it clear to me that should I refuse the request/demand that I would never again see my daughters in my lifetime. The children, now sixteen and fourteen years old, were likely heavily coached with this message and made it equally clear to me that they had seen the last of me should I refuse. Refuse I did. To change the threats made was not possible. The three of them had totally and irrevocably made up their mind that I would eternally be out of their lives should I not agree to the adoption they demanded.

My life was in shambles. I was alone in all ways, sans family. My nearest blood relatives, my children, wanted me completely out of their lives via adoption by a stranger I had never met. I never forgave them. The demand, though unalterable, lay dormant for some time. My agony did not. One day, I spoke with my older daughter, Laurie, on the phone. A new wrinkle was developing. Laurie, the good salesman that she was, advised me that should she get her way and be allowed to be adopted that she and Penny would again see me on a regular basis. This had not been the case for the past two years, during which time they had allowed almost no contact at all. "Let us be adopted and we will be like your real daughters again" was the theme.

The discussion led to plans to be made for Florida visits, possible vacations together and more. Relations with each other would again be formed. It all sounded great. Could I trust them? Did I have a choice? After weeks of agony, I concluded that there was no choice, for to never again see my girls would be more than I could bear. The following month, my daughters, Laurie and Penny, dropped the name of Wallach and were no longer legally my children. It was, although I had previously gone through so much, the darkest day of my life. I was forty-four years old. Suicide was planned.

What followed this tragedy made life worse yet. Now that I was no longer the legal father, my ex-wife was teaching a new moniker for me. I was to be known as "only the biological father." I believe there was an accent on the world "only." Would the promise of our once more being together should I grant the adoption request be honored? Sadly, it was not. It was not kept to a degree that I was not to see my children again for the next twenty years. Contact was not allowed, nor was it possible. This was made clear to me. My life was over. Suicide? How was it to be done?

My daughter, Laurie, moved to Israel. Times were hard for her there. I repeatedly wrote to her and told her I would come and visit her there. I felt that despite hurt and rebuke, I could help her out. Maybe some money left behind after my visit would make life a bit easier for her. The answer was an emphatic no. I was told that were I to come, she would see to it that I wouldn't find her. The flight tickets I purchased were turned in for a refund. I wondered if I survived, if I would ever be able to forgive them. Animosity was not in order, agony and pain overshadowed that. To end my life was on my mind daily. I was a coward. I was not able to go through with it, although I felt my life had ended. I was far beyond hatred for my ex-wife and animosity for my two children who had destroyed me. It didn't matter anymore. My life was over.

15

Florida, Texas, Florida

One day, I was approached by a gentleman from Houston, who wanted very much to move to Miami and wanted to make an exchange for twenty-six building lots that he had in Texas. The building lots were in a rather expensive neighborhood and were offered to me on an exchange for various assets that I had. The bottom line of the exchange, which eventually took place, was that I traded him a commercial lot I owned on Biscayne Boulevard, a piece of property I had in Pompano, my home in Bay Harbor, and a sports car which I drove around town. The exchange was made, and I felt that the move to Houston might start a new life for me. I had hoped that with a brother in Houston, at least the loneliness and lack of family of any kind in Miami might be relieved through living in the same city with him. This turned out to be a tremendous disappointment as he was hardly a worthwhile human being with whom I wished to relate. He masqueraded as a rabbi with a doctor's degree, which was never earned, and lived a life about as phony as a three dollar bill. It did not take long before I had nothing to do with him.

I bought a house in Houston, which turned out to be a good buy. It was a beautiful home in Afton Oaks, inside the Houston loop. After moving into it, I became quite active in the local tennis circles once again spending considerable time on the tennis courts. I began to build a subdivision of expensive homes on the twenty-six lots for which I had traded.

The homes were approximately twenty-five miles from downtown Houston. They were beautiful three- and four thousand square-foot edifices, which should, in normal times, have sold reasonably well. However, the times in the mid- to late 1970s were not exactly normal as the country was suffering a severe gasoline shortage.

The day of our official opening saw a full-page story in the *Houston Chronicle*. On the front page with large headlines and much prose it was suggested that people should not move more than three or four miles away from their jobs, nor certainly five miles further from downtown. This was suggested, almost dictated, due to the terrible shortage of gasoline. People were unable to buy it in sufficient quantities to travel where they wanted to go. In fact, the shortage was so severe that one could only buy gasoline on even or odd days. One could only purchase gasoline three or four days per week and on the other days, your license number on the automobile prohibited you from buying.

Due to this problem, people did not consider purchasing homes twenty-five to thirty miles outside of town, which is where Wallach's Glen was located. This was the name I had given the project. Although I ran full-page ads in the *Houston Chronicle*, promoted and advertised through all the Realtors, sales were meager and the company which I had formed for Wallach's Glen, was doing no business at all. For a period of many months, no houses were sold. We had a considerable amount of vandalism, which caused us constant repair problems. I felt construction of the project was a huge mistake, but I was stuck with it. For the next twelve to fifteen months, I suffered with this subdivision and finally built my last home, which was the twelfth house and sold it. I concluded that there was no profit to be seen here, stopped any further plans for construction, and put the rest of the lots up for sale.

My social life in Houston was extremely slim. As a new bachelor in town, I did meet many people but for the most part, there was no contact of any kind that I could say was a worthwhile endeavor. I joined the temple and made one good friend who was not female, but a chap by the name of Aaron Adler. Aaron and I became close friends, a friendship that lasted for years until his demise from liver failure. He also had suffered divorce recently and was going through many problems. He had problems with his business, with two bad sons, and an ex-wife who made life miserable for him. Aaron and I commiserated with each other and went to many events together. Neither of us found any satisfaction in life. His severe health problems made our relationship even more difficult. Aaron's business went belly-up and I helped him out by buying the building that he owned. He was no longer able to make the mortgage payments. After buying the property, I eventually sold it for a profit.

While I was involved with these various endeavors of different nature, I purchased a shopping center in San Antonio in a very fine new district. The shopping center was a twenty-four-store complex, which did quite well. I felt that being a couple of hundred miles away from it would not allow me to manage it properly. Due to this, I put it on the market and in short order had a reasonably good sale which made up a little bit for the losses that I had had in the building business, which had gone bad. This was my life in Houston for about a year and a half.

I was now, once again, inactive with very few targets at which to aim. A lot of tennis was certainly not sufficient to satisfy the psyche. I was lonely and extremely homesick for Miami. One day, I decided that remaining in Houston was not an option for me. I just wanted to go home. Home was Miami, Florida, where I had spent just shy of the past twenty years. What I would go home to was a bit of a mystery due to the fact that I really did not have anyone waiting for me there. It would be like starting over again, but at least it was what I had known as home. There would be no family and likely no close friends, but this is where I thought I might go.

The thought of Miami ran around my brain for a long time and one day, I decided possibly I should go to Sarasota. At least in Sarasota, my sister and brother-in-law had a condominium which they visited on a regular basis. The downside of Sarasota was that it was a new city to me. I knew absolutely no one. It was a totally strange place to me. Although I had visited there, it was unfamiliar territory. Renée and Harvey would come down for a period of three or four weeks once a year, possibly even twice, and I said to myself, "That is not sufficient." The choice between Miami or Sarasota loomed for a long time. It was difficult to make up my mind, and therefore, I stayed put in Houston.

One day, I decided that this indecision of mine as to where my future would be could no longer continue and that a choice had to be made. It might just as well have been a toss of a coin that would be the deciding factor. Intellectually, I could not make a choice—neither Miami or Sarasota were answers for me. To go back to Cleveland was out of the question. It had entered my mind for I had so many contacts in Cleveland. Were I to go there, I would have my family, mother, father, Renée, and many friends. The climate in Cleveland, being what it was, is what had me leave there to begin with. To go back to that was not something that I relished and I ruled that out.

Finally, a decision was made, and I opted to go to Sarasota, Florida. I took a flight there one weekend, contacted a couple of Realtors, and had them show me around the Greater Sarasota area. I had made known that I wanted a waterfront home, which would have been likely on Tampa Bay, and I wanted a large piece of land. I did not want a seventy-five or hundred-foot lot.

The Realtors showed me around and I was introduced to a two-acre parcel on Westmoreland Drive in north Sarasota. The positives of it were the facts that it was quite large, the home adequate, not great, but certainly acceptable, and it did have wonderful waterfront with about an eight-mile view across the bay. The downside was that the neighborhood was not the nicest, and it was, in fact, too close to the airport, with airplanes flying overhead every hour making huge noises. I stayed in Sarasota about four days, a little bit more than I had planned. I chose to purchase the home on Westmoreland, made a contract which was to be closed in a matter of ninety days. I then headed back to Houston and settled down in my home at 4602 Banning.

Almost immediately upon coming back to Houston, I decided that I should call a number of Realtors, list my house on the market, and hope that it would sell prior to my leaving for Florida. I decided to call many Realtors instead of just one and have them bring their sales personnel out in what is called a caravan. The home would thus be exposed to many salespeople. With my having this advantage, surely one of these folks would find me a buyer. I made appointments for the Realtors to bring their people. One real estate company per day.

The third day of my showing the home to Realtors saw Century 21 bringing about eight or ten salespeople to the house. There were two steps down into the living room from the foyer and as I was standing in the living room, a lovely looking lady came in and stood at the head of these two steps.

Our eyes met, and I immediately knew that this was somebody that I wanted to meet. It seemed there was immediate chemistry. Some excitement followed when I noticed there was no ring on her left finger and I asked if she was a single lady or if she was married or attached at all. She said to me that she had been dating someone on a regular basis but there was no permanent relationship. I immediately asked her if she would consider going out to dinner with me. She replied, "Why don't you call me tonight." That evening, her card in hand, I phoned her and began what turned out to be the beginning of about a one-and-a half-hour conversation. Her name was Marilyn Oakes. It appeared that we clicked instantly.

She was easy to talk to, and I was really very comfortable speaking with her. I felt as though I had known her for years. I asked her if she would come to dinner with me tomorrow night, which would have been a Wednesday. I chose a very fine theater restaurant. She agreed. I picked her up and we went to the restaurant.

Almost immediately upon being seated the play started, and we both were uneasy with the fact that here we were wanting to get acquainted, wanting to speak to each other, and we were compelled to watch this play, which was of little interest to either of us. At this point, I said to her, "I would like to leave. I don't want to watch the play, I would like to get to know you." These words were in complete accord with Marilyn's thinking, and she and I left the theater and headed toward the nearest Denny's restaurant.

We got to Denny's at probably close to seven o'clock in the evening after having been at the theater restaurant. We sat down and started to talk as we did the evening before, with speech flowing very freely from me to her and from her to me. It appeared there was an immediate rapport. The lady was beautiful, and it was obvious to me that she was as bright, personable, and sharp as she was lovely.

The dinner stretched on, eight o'clock, nine o'clock, ten o'clock and by a quarter to eleven, after probably a dozen cups of coffee after dinner, she said that she had to go to the hospital where she worked at night on the eleven to seven shift as a radiologic technologist. I drove her to the hospital and prior to letting her off, asked if she would have dinner with me tomorrow night. She said she would.

The following evening, I picked Marilyn up at about six o'clock and we went back to Denny's. The dinner and the coffee went on again from probably about six to a quarter to eleven, with speech flowing very freely. Here were two people who just met who were like a couple of folks who had been together for the last twenty years. We were that comfortable with each other. I dropped Marilyn off at the hospital, and we agreed that I would pick her up the following night, which would have been Friday evening, and that we would go back to Denny's. The next evening, I picked her up and again we went to Denny's as was agreed, and again we sat there and we talked, and talked, and talked. The hours went by. Neither of us realized how fast the time had flown.

When it came time to take Marilyn to the hospital, or back to her car that was at the real estate office, I drove in the wrong direction. Her car at her real estate office was south of Denny's, and I turned out of the parking lot and headed due north to my home. Marilyn screamed at me, yelled, and carried on, "You can't do this, I've got to get to work." I said to her, "You're not going to work, you're coming home with me." One can not imagine the battle that ensued as she insisted that she was not coming to my house and I insisted that there's no way I was going to take her back to her car.

She wasn't going anywhere else except to my home. When we got to the house, we parked in the driveway for a couple of minutes, still arguing, screaming, and yelling. I finally said "I'm taking the keys to the car, and I'm going inside the house. You're coming in, or you can stay in here."

It did not take too long before Marilyn came in to continue the fight. I explained my action by telling her that I wanted to marry her. Her reply a few times over was "No way! I don't even know you." The battle lasted with no winner declared for quite some time. I could make no headway it seemed. The answer appeared to be no, and she meant it. There was to be no backing off, yet she agreed to stay overnight.

The next morning when we awakened, I asked Marilyn if she would come with me to San Jacinto, which is a small community some miles from Houston. I wanted to see the battleship *Texas,* which was moored there, or it may have been mothballed there, I'm not sure which. She agreed, and we took a ride which was quite lengthy, during which time we had pretty well made up our differences and were laughing and smiling at each other. There were obvious feelings for one another that one could not escape. I had fallen in love; there was no question about it. In retrospect, as I look back, I feel that the same could be said for Marilyn for we were like a couple of kids, just plain happy and jolly.

When we got to San Jacinto, we saw the battleship, paid not too much attention to it, and went out for lunch. Our discussions of the evening before continued, and I explained to Marilyn the advantages of her becoming Mrs. Kurt Wallach. This time it did not take too long when she said that she would enjoy being my wife and that we should get engaged right then and there. This we did. I was now to be married to the finest person in the world. It had taken only three days.

The next couple of weeks were spent being with each other. I had gone out shopping for a diamond ring. What I bought was beautiful, and I placed it on her finger. There was much glee as we looked forward to our new life together.

I told Marilyn of the home that I had purchased in Sarasota. She was quite eager to see what that was like. I told her the only way that could happen was if we hopped on an airplane and then she would see for herself what I had been describing. This we did approximately two and a half weeks after our engagement.

Our short trip to Sarasota from Houston gave Marilyn an idea as to what her new home would be and an introduction to the community of Sarasota. I had felt right along that she had all the confidence in the world in me, but truth be known, I still was more or less a stranger to her. Our trip was short and I thought successful since she loved the new house.

We had now returned from Sarasota to Houston. Marilyn had moved into my home, and we were both enjoying the constant companionship and total lack of loneliness that she probably suffered as well as I during the years.

I was absolutely thrilled with this wonderful lady who was now living with me and would soon be my wife. There was not too much work at hand for me. I had prepared the house for sale and saw to it that it was one hundred percent neat and uncluttered at all times so that possible buyers, prospects, or "suspects" could be shown through.

Prospects for the sale of the house were not to be found for several weeks. There was practically no one. One day, one of the salespeople who had come with his broker a number of weeks earlier to preview the house came over and wanted to know what the best price I would take for the it. He and another sales representative were going to be married and needed a home. They both loved my house and became our number one prospect. I was wrong in my initial assessment that they were just nosing around without any serious intentions and was soon presented a contract for them to purchase. The contract was quite satisfactory, and I had no problem in signing it. Thus, the sale of the house at 4602 Banning in Houston commenced. This freed my mind to look forward to what lay ahead for us.

With the sale of the house now completed, I looked forward to the move back to my beloved Florida. Prior to doing that, however, we were going to make a concerted effort to sell Marilyn's town house, which she had bought several months previously. It was a lovely town house in the southwest end of town. We kept open house, advertised, used brokers, etc., but were not fortunate enough to make a sale while we were still in Houston. I picked up the mortgage payments and all other expenses involved with it and put it into "the portfolio," so to speak. No sale was to be effected.

Our other activity was to prepare Frances, Marilyn's mother, and her grandmother, Grace, to move to Sarasota with us. Yes, they were baggage, but quite well behaved. Marilyn spent considerable time preparing them both, packing up their belongings and generally getting them ready to move out of Houston. Wherever Marilyn went, there went Frances and Grace and so it had been for some time. When all was readied and the closing took place on the home on Banning, we started on our journey to Sarasota.

At the time, I was collecting vintage automobiles. In order not to have to drive them all to Florida, I sold four of them. The fifth one was a

1938 Plymouth in excellent condition. I loaded that up with belongings and had it transported to Sarasota while Marilyn, Frances, and Grandma Grace got into our car. The journey had begun. The trip was uneventful in many ways. It was not easy, yet three days later, the four of us arrived in Sarasota. We had made arrangements for Frances and Grace to live in assisted living homes in Sarasota. We took care of that business, depositing them both and seeing to it that they were comfortable and taken care of. Now we began the housekeeping job at our new address on Westmoreland Boulevard in Sarasota. The home I had purchased was on two and a half acres on the bay with about an eight- or nine-mile view across the bay. To say the least, it was a gorgeous site. The home was not large, but quite acceptable. When our furniture came, we were like busy little bees for a week or so turning "the house" into "a home." About a week after this was done, it looked like we had lived there for years.

Marilyn and I chose to be married on September 12, which was a couple of months after we arrived in Sarasota. My mother and dad flew in from Cleveland and were to spend some time in Sarasota with Harvey and Renée, who had

Marilyn, 2006.

also come down. Since Marilyn didn't know any of my family, her meeting Mother, Dad, Renée, and Harvey was an experience every time a new introduction was made. My mother, after we were married, took to Marilyn and loved her dearly. She could not possibly have had a better daughter-in-law for Marilyn took care of her in a fashion that was almost beyond description. She catered to my dad, who loved her with all his heart, and to my mother, taking care of them probably better than any daughter could take care of her own parents. My seeing this was a real pleasure.

Since we were going to be living in Sarasota and since Harvey and Renée were going to spend some time there, Mother and Dad decided to sell their home in Cleveland.

We helped them purchase a lovely place in the Bradenton area, where they settled in shortly after we had come to Sarasota. It was actually the first time in some time that I had family. This was very important to me and a wonderful feeling to know that I, once again, had some sort of roots with my mother and father there and now with my new and wonderful wife at my side. Our life together was great. As for Marilyn and my relationship, during all this time, I can only say that I absolutely worshipped her in every way. My initial impressions of her being as bright as I thought she was and as wonderful a human being as I initially saw, were proven to be correct. I considered myself to be a very, very lucky man to have a wife such as she.

It is difficult to describe the feeling of the roots that I now felt around me with my wife, my mother, my father, and occasionally Harvey and Renée also in the same geographic area. Sarasota proved to be a wonderful move.

16

Family

While we had settled down in Sarasota, we thought permanently, our life was only with and for each other. My daughters were estranged from me. I had not seen either one for many, many years. They were on my mind regularly, and I longed for the old days when I had my two little girls. By this time, there was no contact, no knowledge of them at all. I knew that Laurie had left Israel, where she had spent a few years. Penny, I had heard, lived in California, where she had gone to school. Since Mother and Dad in Cleveland spoke to no one who knew about them, they were totally lost to me.

One day, I heard that Laurie was to marry a young English fellow she had met in Israel. The news came from one of my Olympian friends. For the first time, on what seemed to me to be a millennium, and out of the blue, I received a phone call from her. It was not a friendly conversation. She told me in a very matter-of-fact way that she was being married tomorrow and wanted to be sure that I was not coming to Cleveland and that I was not welcome.

She was relieved to hear that no such thought was on my mind. To have driven a spike through my heart could not have been more awful. How could I, totally innocent of any wrongdoing, be treated in such a manner? My emotions boiled over with more hatred for Bubbles then had ever before existed. My daughter was being married. Her wish was that her father would be nowhere near. God, how does one forgive? There was no more contact after this as the status quo of so many years continued on its ugly path.

Possibly a year or more later I received a phone call from my dear friend Walter Page. We had spoken often over the years, but this time he called to congratulate me on the fact that I had become a grandfather. Laurie had given birth to a little girl. Feelings of joy, sorrow, anger, disappointment, and more were all rolled into one. How could life be so cruel? Yet it was what it was, and there was no rationalizing. The child likely was to grow up a stranger to her grandfather as her daughter had chosen to be a stranger to her father. I later learned that she had been named Shira. In my own unexplainable way, I had learned to love this Shira, my unknown granddaughter, and my blood.

Life has so many strange twists that one cannot grasp. The separation from my daughter and grandchild was finally to come to an end, totally unpredictably and unexpected. I received a phone call from a young man by the name of Harvey Mitchell, who promptly introduced himself to me as my son-in-law. It was almost unbelievable. He and I had a very lengthy conversation from which I learned a lot.

All the no contact over the years had left me in the dark about my daughter, her life, and her marriage. I learned that I was no less persona non grata then ever before. The horrible lies told to Laurie by her mother were still believed by her. I learned so much from a young man who did not know me but had been convinced by the family that I was no good. I felt his conception of me was as bad as one human could have for another. I do not know if I was right.

After the lengthy call was almost over, he told me he was a sales manager for a local company, that he traveled extensively, and that he expected to be in Tampa in a couple of weeks. I immediately invited him to spend a day with me so that he and I could become acquainted. The invitation was very welcome.

A couple of weeks later, the two strangers, father-in-law and son-in-law, met at the Tampa airport. It was still early morning. For the next ten hours, breakfast, lunch, and dinner, there wasn't a moment of quiet between us. I learned his history, he learned mine, and most important, he learned all about my daughter, his wife. No doubt this was a great revelation. A nice comradery evolved and there was respect. Could this fellow, his wife's father, possibly be the same rogue, scoundrel, cheat, and adulterer that he had been led to believe? In his mind, he had met a decent person, a good guy. It was no doubt a conundrum.

Before we left each other, Harvey took a vow that he would bring father and daughter together, along with and as a bonus, my new granddaughter. After we parted and I returned home, tears covered my face.

A short time after Harvey left and went back to Cleveland, a phone call emanated from my daughter Laurie. To the best of my memory, it was a bit cold and very guarded.

I believe Harvey had told her that he spent a day with a pretty good guy and a gentleman. I think, although I don't know, that he expressed severe doubts about the general conception of this father-in-law. Thanks to Harvey, our discussion led to plans once again after so many years to meet and get to know each other. The emotions ran high. Plans were soon crafted for a visit to my sister, Renée, and her Harvey's condo in Sarasota. This took place not too long thereafter.

Marilyn and I were at the airport with Renée and Harvey as Laurie and Harvey's plane arrived. Their deplaning and our seeing each other again for the first time in so many years brought tears to all of us. I did not recognize Laurie at all—couldn't have picked her out of a crowd. I knew only that it was Laurie since I recognized her husband, Harvey. Otherwise, I would not have known. Hugs, tears, and sobs became the order of the day as we greeted. The emotions were almost too much for all us.

The next few days were spent on the beach behind the condo. The heavy air had lifted and every passing hour got us a bit more acquainted and comfortable. Father and daughter had finally, after so many years, been reunited. Laurie's reacquaintance now gave me motivation and desire to once again see Penny.

No doubt upon returning to Cleveland, the full impact of father and daughter having gotten back together must have been told to Bubbles. The reaction, though I believe it to have been negative and likely not well received, must have shaken her nest. Within a short time, surely it would all find its way to Penny in California. I felt it was time to strike while the iron was hot and phoned Penny myself. Possibly hearing from me after all these years was not a surprise, since our conversation flowed freely. It had been so many years and again, as with Laurie, emotions ran high and the goose bumps grew as we communicated for about an hour. I proposed that I would come out to Los Angeles and spend a few days with her.

Arrangements were made and within a month, I flew west to meet my daughter. Penny had been totally indoctrinated by her mother. The reunion was greatly anticipated. My flight to Los Angeles seemed endless, and my mind was filled with anticipation about the reunion. What would it be like? Would I, as with Laurie, not recognize this lady who I had not seen for so many years?

Penny met me at the airport. I did not recognize her although she saw who I was almost immediately. After a few minutes, those big eyes of hers, which resembled headlights, brought back the memory of years gone by. Although the years had changed her and she now appeared so mature, Penny was Penny and could not be mistaken.

The next few days were spent wandering and meeting some of her friends, to whom she was now introducing me as the long lost father. Being with her bore a little less pressure than with Laurie. Nevertheless, most words were very carefully weighed before being uttered. Neither of us was totally sure of ourselves. One day, the two of us drove out to Long Beach where the ship, the *Queen Mary*, was docked.

It had been fifty years, more or less, since I crossed the Atlantic Ocean to the United States on the beautiful new liner, which at the time was the world's largest. Penny and I spent almost the whole day aboard the magnificent ship. It was a great venue and brought back many memories of years gone by and a different era. I recalled many rooms and cabins. It was in 1936 when I first boarded her.

Time was up all too quickly and I had to get back to Florida, which I did after my fifth day in Los Angeles. The reunions, so long overdue, of daughter and father, had finally been accomplished. What would the future hold?

17

Business and Mark's Demise

Now that we were settled in Sarasota, it was time to buckle down and get back to work. I had retained my Florida real estate broker's license and began to use it. Instead of opening a normal real estate broker's office as all the other brokers did, I opened one that specialized in discounted commissions for sellers. The usual way real estate is sold is that the seller contracts with the broker to sell their home. The normal commission is six percent, in Sarasota, at times, seven percent. The listing broker advertises the property, attempts to sell it, and puts it into the multiple listing service of the Board of Realtors. The multiple listing service is open to all real estate agents belonging to it in the area and someone, hopefully, would then sell the home. When the home sold, there would be a fifty-fifty split of the commission between the selling broker and the listing broker. This was the normal real estate business throughout the country.

Although this is the manner in which real estate was generally sold, I did not wish to become a part of the "dog-eat-dog" scene. There were hundreds of salespeople around. If you look at Florida, the state in its entirety, there were three hundred and sixty-seven thousand licensed real estate agents and brokers. To get in on this rat race and attempt to make a living at it would have been extremely difficult.

I had decided on a new method of selling houses. The program that I had set forth advertised to people that they did not need to spend six or seven percent on a commission. The name of my new company was Thrift Way Home Sales, and Thrift Way Home Sales would see to it that the house was sold with a three percent commission. The manner in which that was done was that a seller, almost always living in the home for sale, would be given a Thrift Way Open House sign, and a THRIFT WAY HOME SALES FOR SALE SIGN, literature, and an education on selling a house.

The program was such that Thrift Way Home Sales demanded that the house seller, the owner of the property, would keep open house on Saturday and/or Sunday or both. The open house sign would be put out, and the homeowner would act as salesperson. The homeowner was instructed that if a prospect looking at the house seemed serious, that they should call the office immediately and I would then go out and help close the sale. I had the contract forms and I would write the contract for the sale of the house. In this manner, there was only one broker, and this broker only took three percent, as opposed to the six or seven percent that the house seller would otherwise have to pay.

I began the program with a very heavy advertising campaign, including a huge billboard showing three percent commission to sell your home. It was not too long before the telephone at the office started ringing with people owning homes and wishing to sell them calling us to see if we could do the job for them. I employed no salespeople. When the calls came in, I would visit the home, give them nice literature that Thrift Way Home Sales had made up, and sold them on the idea of a partnership of themselves and Thrift Way selling their home without outside help and without six or seven percent to be paid out. Thus, I listed the home for sale, usually for a period of a hundred and twenty days, on an exclusive basis. A FOR SALE sign of Thrift Way Homes Sales appeared in front of every home so listed.

The business was extremely difficult inasmuch as it required a seven day week for me and many days, ten or twelve hours of work. The people would call in at all hours and I had to be available. If somebody called at seven o'clock at night, and many times there were such evening calls due to the fact that men were not working after seven o'clock, I would go out to that home and write a listing agreement that we could sell on an exclusive basis.

This, many times, took me an hour or two at the house where I so often met the seller at night, not getting home until ten-thirty or eleven. This went on seven days a week. Saturdays and Sundays became my busiest days, often ten to twelve hours of work.

The weeks and months went by. Listings had amounted up to almost a hundred homes exclusively handled by Thrift Way. I was the only "salesman." I handled all the listings and all the sales. Marilyn was a help in the office, but could do nothing else since she was not licensed at the time and could not participate in talking to prospects at all under Florida law. Therefore, I was the listing person and the seller. The business thrived. The city of Sarasota real estate industry was convinced that Thrift Way Home Sales had twenty or twenty-five salespeople from the looks of the advertising that I did and from the number of for sale signs by Thrift Way that appeared all throughout the city of Sarasota and surrounding counties. Thrift Way had become a major player. I think possibly the second largest in Sarasota. I doubt if any had 100 exclusive listings at one time.

I kept the company going for a year and a half or so and then one day I said to Marilyn, "This isn't the type of life I would like to lead. I quit." She was angry at my phrasing it in so strong a manner, but I knew that although the company was successful, and we were making good money, I was not going to burn myself out and continue to work in the manner that I had. To slow it down was really not possible. In many ways, the company owned me more than I owned it, and thus, Thrift Way Home Sales was closed down. Once again, I was without a job and without a business. The Sarasota real estate industry was much relieved.

Marilyn and I had become very much disturbed with the home in which we were living. The airport, about a half mile to the east of us, became more active by the week, it seemed, and huge airplanes were flying overhead, drowning us out with their noise fourteen hours per day. Also, there was a considerable amount of soot that came down on our beautifully painted white roof, which after a number of months turned gray and then almost a blackish color from the soot of the airplanes. We literally had tire tracks on the roof. Aside from this kind of dirt pollution, the noise pollution was even worse. At all hours there was this loud noise overhead. We could not hear ourselves think, and we put the home on the market.

A short time after the house was put on the market, a gentleman by the name of Jim Goss appeared and said he was interested in the home. He made us a crazy proposition. He proposed that I take a second mortgage on a mobile home park, which he owned, and he would purchase the home from me at our asking price. He would repay me out of the proceeds from his income, which was primarily from the ownership of numerous mobile home parks which he owned. In view of the fact that this particular mobile home park, which he described, had a very small mortgage and a large value, I saw no reason why I could not accept a second mortgage as payment. I felt quite safe with it, for had he forfeited, I would have wound up with a four million dollar piece of property that only had about five hundred thousand dollars standing out against it in the way of a mortgage lien. The deal was made.

Jim and I became good friends. He was a jolly, bright, nice guy that you could not help but like. He asked me what I had in mind in business. I explained to him that I had closed up Thrift Way Home Sales, and then I told him that what I had in mind was to buy an apartment building or two and convert them into condominiums after fixing them up, and then sell the condominium units. I already had my eye on several projects that I might have purchased and would convert from apartments to condos.

He listened to the program that I had in mind and when I explained the whole plan to him, he stated he had something much better for me to do. Jim was exclusively in the mobile home park business and told me that he would like to introduce me to his industry and have me purchase a mobile home park to see if I liked the business. Buying a park was extremely difficult. They were good investments and hard to find, but Jim said that he could probably find one for me. I agreed to his proposal and told him I was interested. "Let's look around."

A short time later, Jim called me and told me that he had found a hundred and thirty-six space mobile home park in St. Petersburg. It was a good buy, and he proposed that I purchase it. Inasmuch as we had sold our house to him, we were free to move to St. Petersburg, where the community was. In reasonably short order, this is exactly what happened.

Once again, we picked up Frances, once again, we picked up Grace, and off we went to St. Petersburg, where we bought another lovely home. This, also on Tampa Bay. We found a nice retirement community for Frances and another for Grace. These were assisted living facilities. We put both of the elderly ladies into them and, once again, repeated our experience of Sarasota, fixing up the home and settling down into it. Now being in St. Petersburg, I had a business.

Although normally an owner does not spend too much time in a mobile home park, I did not know the industry and made it my business to be there daily. After a while, I began to purchase and sell houses in the park, which was known as Hidden Village. I had an office there and enjoyed being able to partake in commerce on a daily basis. It was a wonderful feeling to have breakfast in the morning and have someplace to go for the rest of the day and then come home to a loving wife at night.

The mobile home park Hidden Village was an excellent purchase. It produced good income, which I actually doubled by my sales program. I would take options on homes, sell them, exercise my option, and in this manner having sold the home prior to even purchasing it, I had a very profitable business for quite some time. We were happy like pigs in mud in St. Petersburg. After being there for about a year, an opportunity to buy a second mobile home park came up, and I purchased a park in the city of Largo, which is a suburb of St. Petersburg. This park also had a little shopping center in front of it and, once again, proved to be an excellent purchase. I again instituted the sales program there. I took options on houses, sold them even though I didn't own them, and after the sale was made, I would purchase them prior to closing and everybody was happy. We made good deals for buyer and seller and were well remunerated for the work.

Although Marilyn and I were happy in St. Petersburg, it was only to a degree. I missed my hometown, which was Miami, and many times we visited there, driving down from St. Petersburg. Every time I came home to Miami, I had goose bumps. In fact, my goose bumps had goose bumps. It was my city, and I loved it. I wanted in the worst way to live there.

One day, I got up in the morning and Marilyn said to me, "I am going to purchase a testing kit at the drugstore to see if I am pregnant." This took me by great surprise. I was fifty-five years of age, Marilyn was thirty-eight, and it certainly was not the time at this stage of our lives to begin a family. That evening, Marilyn did her little test with the kit she had purchased and, sure enough, it showed positive, that, in fact, she was pregnant. To say that I was in a state of shock would be the understatement of the year. To be a father at the age of fifty-five, with two grown daughters, was about the furthest thing from my mind. Did I want to become a father? The answer was emphatically no. On the other hand, to have a child with my loving wife, Marilyn, whom I adored, was something that could not be denied either.

Dad had now been ill with what was likely Alzheimer's or senility. Many times his senses and demeanor were absurd and often led to frightening behavior. It was obvious that he was on a downhill slide. Mother, now eighty-seven years old, was not able to manage any longer. Their quality of life had deteriorated to a point where it could not continue in its status quo.

After discussions with Renée and my brother, we decided that dad should be placed in a nursing home in Houston. The decision greatly saddened me although there was no other choice. Dad's condition had, by this time, deteriorated to a degree where a commercial flight was no longer possible. It just wasn't an option anymore. I hired a private plane with pilot and a nurse to transport him. The flight to Houston was made with the pilot, the nurse, Mother, Dad, myself, and a six-month pregnant Marilyn aboard.

Flying conditions due to extremely turbulent weather likely should have dictated that the plane should not have taken off and that the flight should have been postponed. However, this was not the case as we took off from the Sarasota airport on a rainy morning. I believe all passengers, and likely the pilot, had trepidations, nevertheless, we were airborne at 10:00 A.M. one June day in 1981. Weather conditions worsened as we flew over the Gulf of Mexico, and as we got over the panhandle, the storm was so severe that a landing was mandated. By this time, the pilot appeared to be shaking in fear as sweat ran off his forehead. He was looking for a place for an emergency landing, but found difficulty in locating one. When a field was finally located and he attempted to land, the storm was so severe that landing the little plane was not possible. By the time he brought the plane to higher altitude, he had made three unsuccessful attempts.

The weather did not abate nor did the fear we all had. Our pilot was wringing wet from perspiration caused by alarm and fright. Two more potential landing fields were found, with similar failure to land. The gas tank was now about empty, so he switched over to an auxiliary tank, giving the plane sufficient fuel to continue. An hour later, he spotted a field and successfully made an emergency landing. We sighed with relief, all having endured a most fearful experience not to be soon forgotten.

After two hours on the ground and a needed refueling, we, once again, took off, likely a bit scared but with no more panic. We landed in Houston, to be met by my brother's family, and went directly to the chosen nursing home where Dad was checked in despite his many protests. Mother stayed with him the rest of the day and well into the evening, eventually going to a hotel room that had been arranged for her. Marilyn and I stayed only long enough to take a flight back to Florida. These were sad times indeed as the future for Dad had become all too clear. He did not have too much life left. There were tears in my eyes as we arrived back home.

I was in daily touch with Mother for the next several disastrous weeks. Dad had fallen out of bed and broken his hip. Mother suffered, living in panic over the situation and becoming verbally abused by my brother, who made matters worse. Although mother's mind was sharp and she lacked nothing mentally, he had threatened to have her declared incompetent. Renée and I would, of course, hear of no such thing, and the matter became a nonissue.

Mother suffered in Houston horribly as one dreadful day after another saw Dad's condition decline, as my brother's behavior added to the agony. On August 6, 1981, my mother phoned and said, "Your father is no more." It was, for sure, the saddest day of my life. Dad's body was brought back to Cleveland, where he was buried in Mayfield Cemetery after close to 150 friends and relatives attended the service. A great man, never fully appreciated in life had passed away.

One day we received a call from our real estate agent in Sarasota, who was in charge of my parents' home, which had not yet been sold. We were told that my brother had come to Florida, hired a truck, and had all the valuables, TV sets, etc., loaded up and half emptied the home. My parents' belongings, heisted, made their way to Houston. Although this pilfering came as a surprise, possibly it should not have, since past shady and dishonest dealings had taken place previously. It was likely the "nature of the beast." The man has no morals or decency. I saw him only as a small-time thief.

On October the 9, our baby was born. There was no question as to naming the little boy. We named him Mark, after my father, and a middle name of Joseph, after my father's brother, Joe. We were now a family. Kurt, Marilyn, and Mark. We went from one, to two, and then to three, and life was good, life was normal, and we lived it to the fullest.

My son, Mark, 1994.

18

Life's Problems

Marilyn understood my desire to move to Miami and one day said to me, "If you really want to sell the parks here and move south, I would not object. We can find something on the lower east coast. There have to be some mobile home parks there." I had learned to like the business and this is what I wanted to do. Finding a park was not easy, but I would be very aggressive in a hunt and felt that I would find what I was looking for. The two parks in St. Petersburg were sold, and Marilyn and I, once again, took off, carrying with us her mother, Frances, and grandma, Grace, who we put into retirement homes in Miami. I purchased a gorgeous home on Roxbury Lane on Miami Beach. It was in a very high-class neighborhood.

Our lot was two hundred and ten feet wide. Actually, it was two lots. We had about a hundred and seventy palm trees on the property. The place was absolutely magnificent. Marilyn and I settled down, and I was happy being "back home." 1983 saw Marilyn and me completely settled into our new home on Roxbury in Miami Beach.

Mother was with us in a lovely retirement home. A new life had now begun. We were, as I felt, "home." I was totally content. During that time, many things happened nationally and internationally. The Nazi, nicknamed France's "Butcher of Lyon," was arrested in La Paz, Bolivia. Klaus Barbie was charged in connection with police brutality. Barbie was to be extradited to France to face charges of crimes against humanity. The French authorities had been trying for years to convince the Bolivian government to arrest Barbie, but Governor General Banzer always rejected the requests. The then-present regime of Hernán Siles Zuazo was more inclined to honor France's request to extradite him and back to France he went to face trial.

In the news also, in Arizona, Giovanni Vigliotto claimed that he had married more than one hundred and five women in thirty-three years and was found guilty of fraud and bigamy in marrying an Arizona woman in 1981. He was sentenced to thirty-four years in prison. The fifty-three year old defendant appeared surprised by the verdict. The woman testified that he vanished with thirty-six thousand, six hundred dollars of her cash and property after two weeks, abandoning her in a San Diego motel.

In Chicago, Harold Washington became the first black mayor of that city. Washington defeated Bernard Epton in one of the fiercest campaigns ever waged in the windy city. A record eighty-two percent of the city's one million six hundred thousand registered voters went to the polls. Washington received fifty-one percent of the vote. Epton gained forty-eight percent. The voting followed racial lines, as expected, but with more whites voting for Washington than blacks voting for Epton. The mayor-elect told supporters, "We have finished our course, and we have kept the faith."

Interesting also was David Anthony Kennedy, the son of the late Robert Kennedy, had died from a possible drug overdose at the age of twenty-eight. According to family members, David Kennedy had led a deeply troubled life since the assassination of his father in 1968 and had undergone treatment for alcoholism and heroin addiction. David's uncle, Senator Edward Kennedy, who had often stood in as a father for the children of Robert and President John F. Kennedy, issued a statement saying, "We all pray that David has finally found the peace that he did not find in life." These were some of the happenings of the day.

Of interest also, George Gallup of the Gallup Poll, an inquisitive Iowan who pioneered in techniques of public-opinion polling and made it a key tool of politics and business, died at his summer home in Switzerland at the age of eighty-two. Originally a teacher of journalism, Dr. Gallop's fame began with his successful prediction in 1936 that Roosevelt would beat Landon in the election. Since then, the Gallup Poll had a great record except for the prediction that Dewey would beat Truman in 1948.

Also during the early years of the 1980s, actor James Mason died at the age of seventy-five. Mason played sophisticates, bold heroes, and well-heeled heels. If he seemed unflappable on screen, he was somewhat temperamental off, criticizing hiring practices in first, the British film industry, and then in the American film industry. Mason's memorable roles include Gustave Flaubert, Brutus in *Julius Caesar*, and Hubert Humbert in *Lolita*. In the 1970s and 1980s, he made some relatively foolish pictures. *The Boys from Brazil*, about cloning Hitler, and *Frankenstein* were examples. "His stiff-lipped,

upper-crust delivery was frequently imperson-
ated."

Our lives on Roxbury Lane went quite
smoothly. We enjoyed our little two-year-old son,
who became the apple of our eye. I had purchased the Colonial Acres Mobile Home Community in Miami for a rather healthy price.
There were two hundred ninety-six mobile
homes and two houses that went with the mobile home park. I was at the community on a
daily basis, and there was a considerable
amount of tension and pressure in this job.

On July 29, 1986 I felt a very sharp pain on
the left side of my body, feared cardiac problems,
and called the cardiologist immediately to be
examined. When I went through the tests in his
office, it was determined that I had a major
blockage in my left main artery and would need
open heart surgery immediately.

The distress to my little family of Marilyn
and little Mark, who seemed to understand, was
a horrible thing. The distress I felt was no less,
and I entered surgery in great fear of not coming out.

The result of the surgery was satisfactory. I
was kept at the hospital a few days slowly healing before I was to be released. After what I

remember to be approximately five days, I was to come home. The day before coming home, Marilyn and I sat in the hospital room talking for a few hours about what might have caused this cardiac condition and there was little doubt between us that it was the heavy pressure from the business. Marilyn had suggested that if I recuperate well and become healthy once again, that we would sell our house in La Gorce Island and leave Miami.

Several months prior to this illness, we had purchased a lot, strictly for investment, in Vero Beach. The building lot was about an acre on the ocean, and Marilyn felt at the time that we purchased it that one day we would move there to retire. Retirement had never been on my mind, but I went along with her wishes, nevertheless, and the lot was ours.

In our discussions, we spoke of possibly moving to Vero Beach much sooner than I anticipated. We would put the house on the market and see how long it might take to sell it. The following day, I was taken home and put to bed. The thought of leaving Miami was very much in our minds, and I actually looked forward to it.

After about an hour and a half of resting comfortably in our bedroom, the doorbell ran. A real estate agent was at the door. The agent told Marilyn that he had been showing a home across the street and the prospect appeared interested in knowing whether our property was on the market. It was quite a coincidence, and Marilyn told the lady that, yes, the property was for sale as we were planning to move out of Miami.

That evening the broker appeared with his client. They stayed at our house for about forty-five minutes. At the end of that time, a contract was drawn and the sale of 6650 Roxbury Lane commenced. It was the oddest real estate transaction that I had ever experienced in my many years of being involved with real estate. There was no sign in front of the house, there was no advertising, there was no knowledge on anyone's part, with the exception of Marilyn's and mine, that we would even consider selling the house, and now a perfect stranger knocks on the door, brings a prospect, and that same day a contract is written for the sale of the property. One never knows what might happen in the strange real estate industry.

It took a few weeks for me to recover. The recovery was eventually complete and after a couple weeks at home, I was walking around the streets on La Gorce. Several weeks thereafter I was back on the tennis court playing tennis.

I was happy to have this behind us. The fear of not surviving and leaving a wife and a three-year-old son was at times a little bit more than I could bear. I thank God many, many times that I had survived this horrible surgery, which left a scar from my neck all the way down to my stomach. They had opened me up completely, like a chicken to be cut up for its meat.

The entire medical procedure took place at Mount Sinai Hospital in Miami, where I had been a member of the sustaining board of fellows. I had been on the board for some time. Little did I realize it was I who would be under the knife in a hospital which I visited almost weekly as a member of the group which governed it. The sustaining board of fellows is the subboard of the hospital. It was made up of younger men and a couple of ladies who would eventually become the board members. I had been on the sustaining board of fellows for some time and was scheduled to be on the board of directors of Mount Sinai Hospital had I stayed in Miami very much longer. This was not to be the case. My departure from Miami to Vero Beach, Florida, took place in October 1986, when we rented a home approximately five houses north of the building lot on the ocean that we had purchased six months prior.

We were now in Vero Beach. I still owned Colonial Acres in Miami as well as two other communities in Hallandale, which I had purchased and was operating. The communities in Hallandale, Lake Shore, and Sunnydale took very little management. They pretty well operated themselves as opposed to Colonial Acres, which took a good part of my time, caused me great pressure, and often times agony. I had made up my mind to retain Lake Shore and Sunnydale and sell Colonial Acres. I was able to sell this community and very shortly thereafter, the opportunity to purchase a similar-sized community in Lakeland appeared.

The community in Lakeland was Foxwood Village, which consisted of seventy-seven acres. It had three hundred sixty-four lots, of which about two hundred and nineteen were occupied with homes. The clubhouse was just shy of ten thousand square feet. It had six lighted shuffleboard courts and a sixty-five foot outdoor swimming pool. Inside the recreation building was an indoor pool solarium, a complete fitness center with steam rooms, a poolroom with two billiard tables, a library, laundry, and office. The main hall seated over three hundred people. The difference between Colonial Acres and Foxwood was that whereas Colonial Acres was about forty-five years old, Foxwood was brand-new and still in the developing stage. Since there were three hundred and sixty-four lots fully developed, a big job of filling these lay ahead. I looked forward to it and purchased this community with great pride in anticipation of filling a first-class, five-star park.

Shortly after our arrival in Vero Beach, we began construction on a seven-thousand-square-foot home on Ocean Way. The home was modern and absolutely magnificent in every way. It took us a little bit less than a year from start to finish, and we moved into our new home in October 1987. The job of building this home was a labor of love and it turned out to be as magnificent as I had hoped it would.

In the summer of 1987, we heard from Penny that she had been dating a psychiatrist who was about double her age. They had become serious with each other and announced an October wedding date. Penny was thirty-one and the husband-to-be, Derek Spark, had already hit his sixty-second birthday. Penny had called me on several occasions to discuss my view. Although I felt this was a mistake, I did not discourage her. Rather, I made it clear each time the subject came up that this was a decision she, and only she, alone, could make. To my disappointment, her choice was to marry him. And so it was.

Rather elaborate plans were made for the wedding day, which was set for October 10. The ceremony, beautiful as it would be, was scheduled for outdoors, and a lavish dinner after the ceremony would be held indoors.

For Laurie, Marilyn, and me, the wedding ceremony was not too far short of a disaster. I, the father of the bride, was relegated to the back of the hall and watched from the rear as another man gave the bride away. My feelings of pain cannot be described as I held back the tears. Marilyn, who sat with me, was full of sympathy regarding this terrible scenario. Laurie sat with us. She was bent out of shape since she was to be in the pictures of the bridal party, etc. Yet after two hours, no pictures had been taken and she left.

Laurie, as Penny's only sister, was not asked to be in the bridal party at all. The maid of honor was the daughter of the stepfather's brother. It was obvious that feelings were badly traumatized, as much pain was inflicted. No pictures of Laurie and Penny's father were ever taken.

I soon forgave. Not so Laurie, whose relationship with Penny has never recovered. It was also the first time in about twenty years that I saw my daughter's mother. For this part of the fractured family, it was a wedding to be forgotten.

We soon became accustomed to Vero Beach, which both Marilyn and I loved. I had many, many years before been here, when I served in the Navy in underwater demolition training in Fort Pierce, which is about twenty miles south of our address in Vero Beach.

It was now time to search for additional properties. I owned Foxwood Village, Lake Shore, and Sunnydale Mobile Home Parks, which kept us extremely comfortable financially and not overly pressured. I still had a lot of ambition left and began to search for more mobile home communities.

Over the period of the next two years, I was able to acquire a park of fifty-eight spaces in Melbourne called Hollandale. Also acquired in Melbourne was a hundred space park named Groveland. In Cocoa, I purchased Westgate Mobile Home Park and Cedar Lakes Mobile Home Communities.

This brought our holdings to seven such communities at that time. My plate was full. The business was great. Vero Beach was a joy and raising little Mark in this lovely town was also a pleasure.

19

The Bank, Travels and Holocaust

One day, I was asked to be a member of the board of directors and be a founder of a new bank that was to be built in Vero Beach. The bank was to be known as Citrus Bank. I was to put in a very hefty sum of money and become one of the owners and directors. Much work went into the creation of Citrus Bank and when it opened late in 1989, I was proud seeing what we had accomplished. I was about ten percent owner of a federally chartered bank. It afforded me great inspiration, and I looked forward to a wonderful part-time second career.

The Citrus Bank affiliation was very interesting and enjoyable. I had become a very active board member serving on various committees. The bank's progress was slow inasmuch as we had chosen a president totally lacking in drive, business acumen, and knowledge. He was a "fellow well met," popular with everyone, yet the least likely to make this bank successful in so highly a competitive business. Growth was slow, and profits were not to be had.

I became a member of the Executive Loan Committee, served it well, and after a bit over a year, was asked to be its chairman. The honor was great, and I was to do a fine job. Since our board was weak, I found the banking business difficult. If only I could inject some gas into this banking motor that stuttered constantly.

The late-1980s found much interest of variety throughout the world. In reading the newspapers, we found such things as the underage thirty divorce rate having doubled in recent years. Many saw divorce as a mid-life phenomenon, but more marriages dissolved underage thirty then at any other time. In fact, the divorce rate for young couples more then doubled the national average. It increased thirty-eight percent from 1970–1984. Unrealistic ideas of marriage, including emphasis on fantastic sex or confusing sex with intimacy and poor communication skills were cited as reasons. Also, many too young to marry did so because of premarital pregnancies.

In the news also in 1987 was an article that showed casualties in the Iran and Iraq war totaled over a million men, women, and children according to Western military sources who had followed the course of the war since it began in 1980. They estimated this totaled six hundred and fifty thousand Iranians. The Iranians had been on the offensive since 1982. Tens of thousands of half-trained schoolboys had been thrown into mass attacks against fortified Iraqi positions and suffered very heavy losses.

Meanwhile, the Iranian air force made up largely of American airplanes bought by the deposed shah had been whittled away by Iraqi attacks and poor maintenance. In Iran, there were three times as many people as its enemy. It continued to base its strategy on the "final offensive" that would defeat Iraq and topple the government of Saddam Hussein. Iraq's strategy was to defend its second city of Basra and to employ a superior air force against Iran's oil industry and petroleum exports, which supported the war effort. This was partially successful.

Also in the news was that the United States was shown to be the fifth most desirable place to live among nations in the world behind Switzerland, West Germany, Luxemburg, and the Netherlands according to a study by the Population Crisis Committee. The committee, which supported birth control and zero population growth, rated a hundred and thirty countries on job opportunities, literacy, personal freedom, and seven other criteria. The high cost of living and infant mortality weighed against the United States. The Soviet Union came in twenty-third. Extreme levels of human suffering were reported in thirty African and Asian Countries with Mozambique ranking as the worlds worst.

On the West Coast, a picture of Van Gogh's *Sunflower* on a piece of cloth with satin and gold embroidery was sold for a price of thirty-nine point nine million dollars. *Sunflower* was painted at Arles, France. In his lifetime, Vincent Van Gogh failed to find an admirer for this painting. An anonymous bidder found the painting with its original chrome yellow faded ochre and purchased it. The sale at Christy's in London surpassed the previous auction records set in 1985 of ten million point four hundred thousand dollars for sixteenth-century painter Andrea Mantegna's *Adoration of the Magi.*

Also in the news was the Soviet's heavily wired taps of the United States Embassy. Key members of Congress and the intelligence communities were demanding that the United States start from scratch and build another new embassy in Moscow. Reports were circulating that the hundred and ninety million-dollar building then under construction was riddled with listening devices. Critics said that no secret would be safe from the Soviets. "The only sensible approach was to tear down and start all over again," said Senator Bradley, New Jersey Democrat who served as vice chairman of the Intelligence Committee. There was no way possible to make the embassy secure. The new spy scandal had deeply embarrassed the Reagan administration, which was reeling from charges that marine guards in Moscow allowed KGB agents to roam at will through the present embassy.

Some officials were urging Secretary of State George Schultz to cancel his trip to Moscow. He was forced to hold all meetings and conversations in a secure trailer outside the embassy and not inside. Officials in Washington told the *New York Times* that the Soviets planted bugs in modules for the new embassy that were made in a factory closed to U.S. inspectors. The new building was already four years behind schedule and a hundred million dollars over budget. One congressman estimated that it would cost another forty million dollars to remove the bugs. Interesting times?

Another item of great interest was that Texaco had filed for bankruptcy in a desperate effort to keep the company intact until it could settle its ten point five billion dollar dispute with the Pennzoil Company. A Texas court awarded Pennzoil the money after ruling that Texaco wrongly took over Getty Oil after Pennzoil and Getty had reached a binding merger agreement. James Kinnear, Texaco's chief executive officer, said the company had no choice but to seek protection under the bankruptcy law because Pennzoil had rejected all proposals for compromise.

Texaco, the nation's third largest oil company, was the largest firm ever to enter in bankruptcy proceedings. By filing under Chapter 11, Texaco prevented Pennzoil from seizing any of its assets and ensured that most of its subsidiaries would go on operating normally but would suspend paying interest on its bonds and dividends on its common stock. It was pursuing an effort to avoid posting a twelve billion dollar bond to appeal the case in the Texas courts. Texaco reportedly had offered to pay Pennzoil two billion dollars to settle the case, but Pennzoil had said they they were demanding a minimum of five billion dollars.

Also in the news in those years was a new Soviet policy, which was encouraging small businesses. A new law went into effect in the Soviet Union, which allowed individuals to open their own businesses. There were many restrictions and not everyone was sure how the system would work. It was clear that Mikhail Gorbachev was willing to take a few chances to improve goods and services and even introduce a little competition.

In cities like Rega, small entrepreneurs were taking advantage of the Gorbachev policy. New cafés and hairdressing salons were bustling. One man was seeking a permit to open a pay-al-toilet. Another was trying to heat up the cold Russian winters by becoming a matchmaker. Soviets who wanted to open their own businesses could not quit their state jobs. For the most part, they had to moonlight. In addition to working hard, they had to overcome social attitudes, which had developed under Communism. One woman put it this way, "Russians would rather be equally poor than see somebody else get rich." And so it went as the 1980s wore on.

We found it interesting during these years to see that more than forty years after the Nazi atrocities of World War II, Klaus Barbie was convicted in a French courtroom of crimes against humanity. He was sentenced to life in prison. Barbie was found guilty of rounding up, torturing, and deporting Jews and members of French resistance during the last two years of war when he was the Gestapo chief in Lyons. Because of his acts, he was called the Butcher of Lyons. "This showed that the French people had not forgotten," Serge Klarsfeld said. The Nazi researcher led the campaign to deport Barbie to France from his hiding place in South America. "It meant that the children of Iziew would not have died in vain," Klarsfeld said. Barbie was convicted of arresting forty-four Jewish children in Iziew, a community near Lyons, and sending them to their deaths in concentration camps. He was also convicted of organizing the last convoy of Jews and resistance fighters, which left Lyons for the infamous death camps. We found also that the Nazi Rudolph Hess, who was the final survivor of Hitler's inner circle, had strangled himself with an electrical cord at the Spandau prison in West Berlin. The last prisoner at Spandau, he was ninety-three years old. It was his fourth suicide attempt. Hess, Hitler's deputy, had been in Allied custody since 1941, when he flew to Britain and bailed out in an exotic attempt to make peace with the British on the eve of Hitler's invasion of the Soviet Union. Later, at the Nuremberg trial of top Nazis, he was sentenced to life in prison for planning an aggressive war. Hess said that he had no regrets.

With my part-time involvement with Citrus Bank, my seven manufactured housing communities, tennis a few times weekly, and various and sundry other minor activities, life in our beautiful home on the ocean in Vero Beach was pretty full. Mark, my little pride and joy, was doing just fine at Beachland Elementary School, and the three of us traveled extensively.

By 1989, I felt the urge to see the world. Over the period of the next three years, Marilyn and I did just that to a point where we visited and ran around Europe three times a year. Many memories of my earlier life were relived as time was spent in Holland, particularly Scheveningen, where I grew up and attended almost four years of school.

The same with my earliest years in Magdeburg, as we visited my place of birth, all of my dad's apartment buildings, his downtown store, and the Adolph Mittagsee. Our summer getaway town of Wernigeroda was revisited and enjoyed.

During these years, I became more interested than ever in the holocaust which took place there and became a founding member of the United States Holocaust Memorial Museum in Washington, D.C. It brought back thoughts of my large family in the Ukraine where so many were murdered by the Nazis. It became my mission in those years to visit the concentration camps and the death camps.

Time was spent at Buchenwald, Dachau, Matthausen, Janovik, Auschwitz-Birkinau, Majdenik, Belzec, and the fields where slaughters took place. It was never to be forgotten, as I saw them and felt the pain that was. It brought me all the closer to the museum in Washington and to my studies of the era and the holocaust.

In one stretch of time we were in Vienna, Prague, Frankfurt, Berlin, Dresden, all through Holland's large and small cities, Paris, and most of France. Italy and Sicily were often visited along with Switzerland, Belgium, Rumania, and Yugoslavia.

One of the many trips scoured Russia, where we had gone several times, staying in Lvov, Kiev, Moscow, and St. Petersburg. A week was spent in Israel, Egypt, and Greece as we enjoyed them all. One year, we followed Hitler's life, spending some time in each of the cities in which he lived. It was hedonism indeed. We had a very good time at the Octoberfest in Munchen (Munich), my oh my, what a party as thousands of gallons of beer washed down an equal number of bratwurst, and it lasted a week.

Nuremburg was a highlight one year as we spent time on the Zeppelin Platz after being at the University in Heidelberg. Each trip and each adventure could become their own chapters.

We spent a marvelous, unforgettable New Year's Eve at Edinburg's Dal Hausie castle. Bagpiping in the New Year was surely a special experience. Mark, now eleven years old, was the hit of the party as he danced the night away with all the old ladies. Our trip to Scotland was truly a memorable experience, as was the Loche Ness monster we swear we saw.

The following year, we visited fourteen cities in China. No tours—just the two of us on adventure. We visited the cities and many small villages over a period of a month.

In Washington and nationally, a large group of dedicated people, numerous survivors of the holocaust and dignitaries from coast to coast and all walks of life, had banded together to create a museum in the capital to memorialize the deaths of 6,000,000 Jews during the war. The merciless killings over the period of not more than three to four years saw genocide practiced on a large scale with a total of over 12,000,000 people killed for no reason, excepting their religion, their way of life, and the backgrounds from whence they came. Of prime interest to the founders of what would become known as the United States Holocaust Memorial Museum was the murder of over two-thirds of European Jewry. The U.S. government, with which this very dedicated group had been working for several years, donated a plot in the heart of Washington at the mall alongside the Smithsonian Institute for the construction of the museum building.

This, with the help of the government, would become not only the hub of Holocaust education, but also the home of countless thousands of artifacts, books, and memorabilia, as well as the center of learning. It was destined to become a huge success as the nation's Jews and sympathizers opened their hearts and their pocketbooks to make it what was to eventually become, the leading museum in Washington. As a survivor of the horrible Hitler-era myself, I joined in the various efforts and became a founding member.

Countless relatives of mine, my uncles, aunts, nieces, nephews, their wives—a total of about two hundred members of my family—were slaughtered by the Nazis. My immediate family, mother, father, sister and brother, barely escaped so that we could live our lives in peace. To join those working so diligently toward remembrance was an honor. When called upon, financial help was given. In addition, with the help of my family, sister, brother-in-law, nieces, and nephews (without the help of my brother), I put together $50,000 so that that marble wall at the museum could have my father's and uncles'2 names inscribed for remembrance. With patience, when the big day we had awaited came, our wonderful museum was dedicated.

President Clinton and many more dignitaries took part in the ceremony. Marilyn and I proudly partook. All were standing in a downpour of rain almost appropriate for this great occasion. The museum had become a part of me. To this day and for the rest of my life, I am, and will be, an active member by deed and monetary support.

As I write these thoughts, I am now in my fifth year of delivering a series of lectures on the Holocaust. This past year, I taught a course and gave eight lectures for Florida Atlantic University. In a couple of months, having connected with St. Edward's School in Vero Beach, I shall teach there, and in the future, wherever I can or may be called upon, as I have in the past at various venues.

In June of 1990, my first grandson, Daniel, was born in Los Angeles. Penny became a proud mommy to an eight-pound baby boy. A big day was had in early August of 1991 as Marilyn celebrated (or suffered, take your choice) her fiftieth birthday. It was a major milestone, and I wished to celebrate it so. My wife was half a century old.

I purchased tickets on the Big Red Boat, a Disney cruise line, for Penny, Derrick, and Daniel, whom I brought in to Vero Beach from California. They stayed with us in our home on Ocean Way. Renée and Harvey came to us in Vero, and the whole crew went to Cape Canaveral outside the city of Cocoa where we boarded our cruise ship. The Disney cruise line was comfortable and great in all respects, though not as formal and fancy as some others. After the first night out, we landed in Nassau. This, after thirty-five years in South Florida, was almost a part of my neighborhood.

It was not quite so for the others. We had a great day cruising all the tourist traps, along with the old familiar sites. Nassau still had over a thousand ways to part the tourists from their money. All enjoyed the ambiance, the meals I hosted, the local goings-on, and all the sights.

The following day, "Big Red" took off and headed to an island solely owned by Disney. It was a small tropical jungle with food served continuously for our ten hours there. I can still taste the barbequed-baked beans. Hunger here surely was not possible. A highlight on the island was small boats, locally captained, which took us out to an area where the fifteen-foot deep water was so clear we could have read a newspaper were it lying on the bottom. It was the clearest water I had ever seen. Penny and I snorkeled there and played like a couple of children.

The cruise, the islands, and the few days spent together with family was a thrilling event as we all celebrated number fifty for Marilyn.

Soon thereafter, we celebrated Harvey's and Renée's forty-fifth wedding anniversary in Cleveland. Also celebrated there was our fiftieth anniversary of our confirmation class as many attended. It was like never having left Cleveland.

20

Our Boat

The early nineties saw the acquisition of what became the "Kurtell Building," my company's headquarters and home office. This was acquired in a foreclosure from Barnett Bank. At this writing, we are in our fourteenth year in our building and, God willing, will be here for years to come.

The early nineties also saw Marilyn decide to become Jewish. A marvelous conversion took place that was officiated by my dear old friend Rabbi Sam Silver, who I found in Boca Raton after not seeing him for over forty years. All this came as a surprise, as I had no idea of her wishes. Her grandmother, a devout Catholic, would have been shattered by such happenings. At age ninety-nine, she was really not sufficiently with it and never knew. It was as Marilyn had wanted. Though I was never too observant, Marilyn had already, over the years, pushed us towards religion a bit. I was elated over her decision and have always admired her for it.

We took a trip to Holland where we spent a goodly amount of time in Scheveningen. What a thrill this trip was. We went back to my old elementary school, where I had attended almost four years. Of course, time was spent in the *bosches* (a small forest) and the *strandt* (beach) where I had hung out so often as a youngster. When living in Scheveningen (Den Haag), we learned of Rotterdam and Amsterdam in school. For us, these were far-off cities of great distance somewhere in Holland. To me, as a nine-year-old there, it might have been like the distance from Baltimore to Chicago, or New York to Cleveland. To my great surprise, when we drove our car from Scheveningen to Rotterdam, the total distance between the two cities was twelve miles. I guess it's all relative.

Seeking family were ventures of the early nineties. On a trip to Israel, we spent time with my first cousin, Israel Wallach, and his wife, Judith, as well as second cousin, Steve, who was living there in Natanya. He took us throughout the country and showed us what we could never have experienced without him. He urged us to go to Cairo, which we did, and then toured down the Nile to Aswan.

Seeking family and spending time with them

took us to Messina and Castro Reale in Sicily, where we spent time with cousins Salvatore, Antonia, Marian, and Miriam. Visiting Corleone of *Godfather* fame was interesting although Mark was half-frightened to death being there.

A trip to Albany, New York, and Niagara Falls got us together with Aunt Nonnie, cousins Dan and Fran, and the crew there. We visited with cousin Carolyn, Norman, and his wife in Detroit. Mackinac Island was next and much enjoyed, although there were no relatives to be found there or at Salt St. Marie, or the Dells, Wisconsin, or Chicago, which were next.

News of the day, both domestic and international, was of much interest during the years. IBM suffered one of its darkest days in Big Blue's history as it posted its first ever annual loss. Having reported six billion in profits the previous year, it lost 364 million dollars. The company, based near Armonk, New York, said its revenues fell 6.1 percent to sixty-four billion dollars from the previous year's sixty-nine billion dollars. This was the first time that the computer giant's business had failed.

The IRA made a heinous attack in Northern Ireland as seven construction workers were killed instantly and seven others were seriously injured when a bomb destroyed a van transporting them from a British army barracks. The prime minister said the perpetrators would be punished.

Violent crimes in the United States reached epidemic proportions in the early nineties according to a report by the Senate Judiciary Committee. A total of 24,020 people were murdered that year, an increase of 580 over the previous year. California had a record 3,710 killings ahead of Texas' 2,660. New York State's numbers dropped by 2 percent.

Airlines on transatlantic flights were waging cutthroat wars to win customers. U.S. companies United and American airlines had frequent flyer programs, where regular passengers amassed points based on miles flown to qualify for free tickets. British Airways was offering free hotel bookings, while Virgin gave points to buy health club memberships and lessons in hot air ballooning.

TWA became the latest U.S. airline seeking to declare bankruptcy. The once-great carrier, owned by Carl Icahn, filed in Delaware. TWA stressed that schedules would not be affected.

The United Kingdom sank further into its longest recession since World War II. Figures released showed that the gross domestic product fell by 0.3 percent in the fourth quarter. "It all looks gloomy," a British banker said as indications showed the recession would continue.

European community environment ministers meeting in Portugal decided to back proposals to halt the production and use of chemicals harmful to the ozone layer. This followed data gathered by the highflying U2 aircraft. Michael Kuryco, manager of NASA's upper atmosphere project, said, "Everybody should be alarmed about this. We are seeing conditions primed for ozone destruction. It's in a far worse way than we thought."

A violent earthquake struck eastern Turkey. The city of Erzincan was partially destroyed by the quake, which registered 6.8 on the Richter scale. The collapse of a hospital, local police headquarters, and the loss of electricity confounded rescue efforts. An estimated 1,000 people died in the region. In 1939, Erzincan was destroyed by the worst earthquake in recorded Turkish history, which led to 40,000 deaths and a 7.3 magnitude on the Richter scale. A quake in nearby Erzurum killed 1,300 in 1983.

Late in the century after having had eleven building lots in Houston for sale actively for fifteen years, and unable to find a buyer, I made up my mind I would trade my way out of this unwanted investment. What better way then to become the owner of a huge oceangoing yacht. For several months, I scoured the papers and marinas looking for the new attraction, a new hobby, a fun adventure. Fortunately—or unfortunately, whichever the case was—I located a gorgeous fifty-two-foot Bertram yacht equipped with the latest radar, most modern equipment, beautiful galley, and furniture fit for a palace. Its decks were teak, shiny, and gorgeous. It was love at first sight.

To my good, or bad fortune, its owner was as happy to get rid of this beauty as I was to rid myself of my eleven building lots. We were both eager as I decided to become a captain and he to become a real estate investor. The deal was made quickly sans hitches or hesitation on either side.

We were both thrilled with our finds. As for my part in this fine deal, it did not take too long to find out how much my newly acquired joy would wind up costing me. I would take it out and repair it and take it out and repair it, and so it went. The teak, when finished redoing, would soon be ready for new shellac. The salt air constantly caused so much damage, it was as if a full-time maintenance man, or men, were needed. Dockage for my toy cost several hundred dollars monthly. Once I pulled in to buy gas and told the attendant to "fill her up," this he did and put nine hundred eighty dollars on my credit card. And this was when gas was still cheap. The boat was a beautiful hole in the water into which I poured money.

We had named her *Ocean Way II* after our house address. It made little sense for Marilyn and me to take it out alone. It was just too big for the two of us. Friends were eager for an afternoon outing, so when we did go out, each trip became a party. Food, plenty of it, drinks, maybe a little schnapps, and all other goodies needed to be onboard.

For this, I usually hired a captain. Oftentimes upon return, one repair or another was needed. Between the captain, the food, the booze, the gas, and all other ancillary costs, my parties averaged $700 to $1,000 dollars each. It did not take too long before the realization set in that this was not a winning horse. As my pocket book shrunk, the parties became less frequent, and after a lengthy period of time, the *Ocean Way II* mostly sat at the dock, costing dockage fees, repairs, and a very, very rare trip "out to sea."

The *Ocean Way II* had seen its day having hosted numerous friends, my daughter Laurie and family, Renée, Harvey, and others. It was an ill-fated venture. My dreamboat took over a year to sell. The financial loss was huge. I lived and learned.

As time went by, happenings of varied nature, large and small became part of our lives. Just south of Vero Beach in North Fort Pierce, an underwater demolition remembrance museum was built. The museum was laden with nostalgia and sentimental emotions for me for it featured our amphibious training base and the training I underwent here back in 1944–1945. Memories of the agony, the shipmates later to be lost overseas, and so much more were brought back. It was all about fifty years ago in a different world and a different time. Memories were to be relived here of "hitting the beaches" in mock invasions with our L.C.V.P. attack boats. It was all here although now more geared to the modern-day "Seals," to whom we gave birth, as the predecessors of this outfit. I, for one at least, attended with goose bumps. Gosh, it had been so many years and so much water over the dam. About a year or so after my first experience attending the museum, a reunion of the surviving members took place. They came here from all over the country. It was back to Ft. Pierce and its beaches, where we trained to kill the enemy. No doubt there was many a tear as we attended and remembered. Ft. Pierce Amphibious Training Base, where the war really began for so many, an experience not forgotten.

21

A Heavy Heart

At no time did our Olympians forget our high school days, our going off to war, our deep and devoted love and friendship for each other. We had had reunions, get-togethers, and small groups of two or three who remained close to each other. My very closest Olympians were Wally Page, Freddy Bram, Art Blackman, Stan Fried, Norm Landau, and Larry Klein, along with Jerry Matz. Although we had, for the most part, become geographic strangers, by no means did we not constantly stay in touch. Harvey Weiss was in St. Louis, Bram in Virginia, Page in Colorado, Matz in Sandusky, Klein, Fried, and Landau in Cleveland, etc.

Surely being physically together was difficult and not nearly as often as we would have liked. Nevertheless, we managed to do it, whether two or three at a time, or all of us. We held several such reunions, so enjoyed. To detail these is not necessary as the reader can well imagine them.

As time went on, tragedy after tragedy occurred in the nineties. My Olympian brothers were aging and the Grim Reaper came upon the scene. First, it was Alf Meyers, then Marty Surad and Bobby Pollack. All three never lived to see their sixtieth birthdays. At about sixty-one Wally Seidler committed suicide and Lenny Portman died of a heart attack. Morty Coles didn't make it as he succumbed far too early in life, too many cigarettes.

My dearest, and without question, my closest Olympian friend was Freddy Bram. Freddy, who was the nutty kid in high school, had become a psychiatrist. Unfortunately, his drinking and smoking habits were never shaken off. For, oh so many years I harped on him and fought with him to quit. I never got my way as I was told to lay off 100 times or more. The handwriting was on the wall as Freddy drank nightly and smoked three to four packs of cigarettes daily.

He practiced medicine outside of Washington and lived on twenty acres in Chantilly, Virginia. We spoke on the phone almost weekly. One day, he told me he would be checked into a hospital for a month to be "dried out." This occurred and after coming out, he found most of his patients had left him.

Financial disaster followed as the bank was going to foreclose on his homestead, leaving him broke and in bankruptcy. I had sent him a few thousand dollars. It was not enough. I could not help sufficiently to keep things going as not enough former patients came back and not enough new ones were taken on. Somehow it was just not enough. Fred never recouped financially.

One day, he told me he would have a toe removed. Gangrene had set in from poor circulation. His humor never failed as he said, "I didn't like that toe anyway." Further help was needed. I didn't fail him. It was not too much later that during one of our conversations he told me that he did not have enough money to pay for an operation needed to save his life. His left leg was gangrenous and needed to be amputated. I was greatly distressed but was there for him as my heart cried out. The drinking and smoking were doing him in. He was not able to shake these devils. There was no money to pay for the surgery. Fortunately my business was strong, and I was able to pay all the bills after his leg was amputated.

It was late in the nineties when things with Fred deteriorated even more. The circulation problems continued unabated and an almost-to-be-expected cancer appeared in his lung. Radiation, chemotherapy, and all his doctors could do were to no avail. It was too late.

One day, Joyce, his wife, called and told me Fred was in the hospital and things looked very, very bad. It was about 10:00 A.M. By 11:00, I had left the office, gone home, got dressed, bought tickets to Washington, and was on the way to the airport in Orlando. I was very late and felt I would surely miss my flight as I drove at ninety miles per hour up Route 95 in hopes of making the flight. I left my car in the entry lane, grabbed the keys, and headed in, figuring one way or another I would get my car back. I made the flight but had no idea what would happen to my car and when/if I would get it back. I didn't care. The only thing on my mind was to see Freddy one more time before it was too late.

I arrived in Washington and took a cab to the hospital. I got into Fred's room half an hour after they took his body to the morgue. The best friend I had ever had in my life was gone. I could not console myself. When meeting Joyce and their two sons, we cried more tears then I had ever seen before in all my life.

The following few hours saw me, with Joyce,

at a funeral home making arrangements. It was, of course, a new experience to both of us as we wrote the obituary for the papers, bought what was needed—coffin, urn, announcement lists, etc. I don't recall it all. The funeral was arranged and all the details handled with the help of the funeral director. I believe it was one of the saddest days of my life.

The funeral was held one day after, with an open casket. I didn't know my body held as many tears as I shed. No experience had ever rivaled this unexpected disaster. There were many people at the ceremony. I was asked to give the eulogy. No preparation was needed as I spoke for close to an hour. No one was bored as I told of Freddy's life. Tears were shed by the bucket by many as the casket was closed. I felt my life was taken from me. I stayed in town another day or so, helping Joyce before heading back to Florida. Freddy was gone and life must go on without him. It was indeed a very sad day.

In 1994, Mark, soon to be thirteen, had begun his lessons for bar mitzvah. It was obvious that he was a bright kid as he learned all at an amazing pace. Marilyn took him to his lessons, sat in, and soon became as fluent at reading Hebrew as Mark. The two of them studied together and enjoyed the learning, many times discussing the text of "Dor Vador," from generation to generation, etc. They had become a team in a much-enjoyed learning venture, at which they excelled.

One day, Rabbi Silver, who would officiate at the ceremony, seeing both Mark and Marilyn studying together, proposed that not only Mark should become bar mitzvah, but that Marilyn should partake in what would be a b'nai mitzvah. The idea took hold immediately and the two moved onto their goal. I was more than overjoyed at the happening. It was an experience to be viewed once in a lifetime, to be remembered and cherished.

The big day was to be October 15, 1994. By sheer coincidence, this day would have been my mother's 100th birthday were she still alive. It couldn't have been planned as well. How thrilled she would have been at the happening. Not only had her daughter-in-law adopted our faith, but here she was, with her now thirteen-year-old grandson, performing the ageless and solemn formality of attaining maturity in our religion. These thoughts were on my mind as I reveled in the festivities of the day. If ever one felt "family," this was that day for me. I loved them both so.

Marilyn and Mark were both on the pulpit, beautifully dressed, and both performed their role flawlessly. There was not a hitch in either one's role. Mark's speech could not have been better written, nor delivered. I was a proud peacock on that day not to be forgotten.

That evening, a 120-foot yacht I had rented was filled with over 100 dinner guests and departed the marina in Fort Lauderdale for a formal dinner cruise going north on the Indian River. Renée, Harvey, and their children, Judy, Pam, and Norman, along with a generous sprinkling of family, cousins, etc. enjoyed dinner, the six-piece orchestra, and dancing for most of the evening hours as everyone had a wonderful time celebrating the b'nai mitzvah, a marvelous event.

The year, though mostly mundane, had other events of interest. Fidel Castro's Cuba held its unhappy population in check. Communism was working, as it does, keeping the populous in semibondage, under control, and for the most part, unhappy. So many of the residents coveted and envied neighbors, friends, and relatives who had escaped an oppressive regime. Most wanted to be out of Cuba, preferably in the United States. Legally, this was not possible.

Many risked their lives, having built something of a cross between a raft and a boat, and set out to sea in hopes of landing on some friendly shores in Florida. The raft/boats were not much more than some lumber boards nailed together. By no stretch of the imagination could one call these dilapidated pieces of junk seaworthy crafts; yet many braved them out at sea, oftentimes drowning in the effort. It was amazing to me that any of them reached Florida shores safely. Empty crafts often washed ashore without their occupants, who were usually lost at sea, never to be found.

On occasion, these drifted ashore in Vero Beach. One day late that year, several washed ashore in our backyard. The occupants were never found.

1994 saw the death of Ann Stella, Marilyn's dear relative in Albany. She had long been known as "Nonnie," much beloved and much missed. It was a great loss for Marilyn. She had been like a mother to her.

Late in the year, we took a vacation trip to the Blue Ridge Mountains in western North Carolina, where neither of us had ever been. It was like a different world to us, who were used to the flatlands of Florida. Here, we found a for-

A Heavy Heart

*Kurt sits on Cuban boats (rafts) that
drifted into his back yard.*

est stretching thousands of square miles 3,000 to 4,500 feet above sea level and beautiful it was. Virgin forestland punctuated with an occasional town and scattered houses dotted in the great wooded terrain. Developers had come in and carved out some golf courses and small resort communities in this little piece of unspoiled beauty. These scattered through western North Carolina made up wonderful little areas of escape for Floridians and Georgians. Tennis, golf, restaurants, and clubhouses with pools were attractions for us Floridians who lived in so different a world.

Marilyn and I fell in love with this oasis and with little hesitation bought a small home on a lake in Sapphire Valley, outside of Cashiers, overlooking both water and mountain. The view was beautiful beyond words, the house was not. It was an A-frame with tiny rooms totaling no more than 2,000 square feet. Much renovation was in order. I hired a contractor to do the work and returned to Florida. Soon I was told that the house had so much dry rot that the floors were in danger of collapsing. The contractor was afraid to go into the house. After much delay, consternation, alarm, and dismay, a new contractor was hired, heavy equipment was brought in, and the home was all but rebuilt. It turned out to be an expensive experience, costing half again the purchase price.

Our home in North Carolina turned out well after Marilyn did a total remodeling job. Small as it was, the beautiful views, many decks, and a boat dock made up for its lack of size. Many happy days and weeks were spent here as we imported friends and relatives for R & R. As we noted originally, the house was just too small. If six to eight people were in it, walking sideways would have been a necessity. A choice needed to be made. Should we keep it or put it on the market and buy a larger home. Surely the gorgeous lake and the mountains on the other side could not easily be duplicated and would be missed. After some debate, the decision was made to sell it and purchase anew.

We had our insurance agent and his family as guests. While they were here, they wanted very much to purchase a lakefront home. None was available, though they spent much time searching. When we decided to sell, a phone call to Palm Beach was all that was necessary and a fairly priced sale was had. I now felt free to commence our search.

Waterfront property turned out not to be an

option. There simply wasn't anything available. We viewed numerous properties, many with beautiful views, none seemed to fit until we found a real beauty, almost new, on a bit under three acres of land. The home sat in back of the property, giving us a winding 545-foot driveway that curved up to the top of the land where the house sat. Three lovely ponds into which we put fountains that were lighted gave the property a marvelous "estate" look. We were thrilled and made what I felt was an exceptional purchase. The home would be called "Eagle Feather Lodge." It eventually became adorned with over 150 eagle statues and pictures. It is a home/estate of which we are both proud. Bringing guests to Eagle Feather Lodge was always a joy.

In October 1999, Mark announced that he and his girlfriend had decided to get married. My feelings can only be described as mixed emotions, something like watching your mother-in-law drive off a cliff in your brand-new sports car. His intended was a very sweet and more than lovely little girl by the name of Lianne. "Mark and Lianne Wallach" were to be almost as my parents, Mark and Lena Wallach.

To say I was deeply disturbed would likely be an accurate assessment. Mark's life was in shambles. He had, at that time, finished only the ninth grade in school. Thus, having no education at all was a great pain for me. Our family, so laden with highly educated and so many professional people, saw my son as an uneducated oaf. Furthermore, Mark had no way of making a living. He had no income and no way of supporting a family. How could he, as a married man, make the grade on any measurable level?

No education, no job, no business. Now to be married and soon to become a father. Was I expected to totally support this family that was planned? It made little or no sense.

Mark, in his nonaccomplishments, had advanced no further in his life than a fifteen-year-old boy. What sense could this marriage make? What chances did it have for success? There was much reason to say no. These were my true feelings when soon after, a wedding was planned and that took place.

I shall write little of this wedding ceremony because I felt it was tainted in so many ways and caused sadness and depression rather than elation and joy. My only son was married, lacking every entity or ingredient needed for a successful life. He took on all responsibilities of a man for a family, yet possessed no merit or standing. What chance was there for this union to find happiness? My fear was great, as I knew not what was to be expected.

A huge bright spot was however to be enjoyed, one of which we have spoken often. The evening before the wedding, I received a phone call from Penny in Los Angeles. She wanted to talk about Mark's wedding, his plans, etc. After the lengthy discussion, I felt pleased that she was taking so much interest and involvement in her half brother's future. As always, she was a kind and feeling soul.

The following morning, Marilyn left the house early to help with the coming wedding ceremony. I was at home lounging around in my robe with little to do when the doorbell rang. When opening the door, I saw facing me my daughter, Penny, who had spent the night on an airplane and had arrived in Orlando a couple of hours before in order to attend Mark and Lianne's wedding. There was much pleasure to be derived from such depth of feeling. In my mind Penny shone like a star.

The early years of the twenty-first century brought us two blessings as Mark and Lianne produced two beautiful baby boys. The first, in

2000, to be named James Vincent, a sweetheart of all sweethearts. One year later, a carbon copy to be named Vincent Anthony was born. Mark and Lianne were making us proud with this new little Wallach family.

Obviously, they were big pluses following Daniel in California and our fabulous blue-ribbon stunning Shira in Cleveland. We now had four grandchildren, of whom we were the proud grandparents.

22

The Early Twenty-first Century

There was a smidgen of joy and hope one day for Mark's success when Marilyn told me that Mark had decided to get his high school diploma and move toward college. Hope was only a glimmer, but it was there. What followed in the ensuing times was one treat after another.

Mark had begun to turn his life around. First, he got his high school diploma. Following this, he enrolled at Indian River Community College, from where he received an associates in arts degree in criminal justice. This in hand, he now added to his A.A. degree by continuing classes in hopes of adding yet a second degree. This, an associate in science, was earned in reasonably short order.

Now, having these two under his belt, great motivation had him apply to Florida Atlantic University for further study. After acceptance and two years later Marilyn, Lianne, and I stood proudly as Mark received his bachelor of arts degree. Not only this, but he received it with high honors. The diploma read magna cum laude. Proud father? I could not have been more so as Mark displayed the drive, ambition, and fortitude of a Wallach. What took place was that he had become a "Mensch." The fear of a totally uneducated son had been alleviated and allayed.

Mark had come to maturity.

At the time of graduation, likely due to frustration, Mark had gained weight month after month. Lacking exercise and feeding on junk food, Mark ballooned to a very unacceptable 309 pounds. He felt it was time to take his problem in hand and gain a normal stature. Religiously, steadfastly, and faithfully, he initiated a diet to which he totally adhered. After approximately twelve months, he lost 109 pounds, weighing in at an even 200 pounds. Again, he made us proud with his resourcefulness.

While heavily dieting, Mark began a business selling and programming two-way radios. Again, as before, he persevered and soon was the chief operating officer of a highly successful company. Now able to support his family, maintain a lovely home I had built for him and his family, Mark had turned his life around and was enjoying his marriage and life in general. His becoming a true success story was evident.

Son Mark, wife Lianne, 2002.

Now with business in hand, a happy marriage, and raising our two grandsons, James and Vincent, the whole family was slowly becoming addicted to martial arts. The two boys were doing well, as was Lianne. The four of them all excelled in one way or another. Mark had been spending countless hours, usually five days a week, working out, teaching, and practicing jiujitsu. After over four years, he became a black belt. Lianne is a bit behind him and will soon also attain that designation, no doubt to be followed by the boys in due time. Would this little family go on to emulate that of his father and grandfather? My dad was often thought and spoken of with discussions ending in adoration for him. Over the years, both Marilyn and I marveled at his foresight, fortitude, and talents.

He saw where others did not, he envisioned where others did not, and through his determined will and just plain guts, saved his family from certain death where others did not. In our eyes, he was a hero, a marvelous human being to be loved and admired. His story, his reaction to pending disaster not seen by others, was known only by few. He was the bravest of all among the brave. This, however, was known only within a small family circle, and even they never focused upon, rarely discussed and totally took for granted. What a shame, we both felt that his extraordinary deeds were to be forgotten. Greatness within his own right was never recognized, let alone appreciated. We felt something needed to be done to right the wrong of the non-recognition and lack of acknowledgment. Shout it from the rooftops—but how?

Marilyn suggested that I write a book to be titled *Mark* to tell the world, to let all know his story and his bravery. But, but, but—what an undertaking that would be. I was totally engulfed in still growing my business and working many long hours. Marilyn said something to the effect that I'm really not very busy between 11:00 P.M. and 1:00 A.M. It was a joke. But why should all these hours be wasted, I said.

And so it was. For the next eighteen months, as planned, it was those hours, worked religiously, that I researched and worked, writing about my dad and the times he lived. After completion, a number of dignitaries and publishers were made aware of this man who did so much. I received letters of endorsements. Four publishers wished to publish what became the book *Remembering Mark*.

The letters of endorsement from household

names were a great tribute. My illustrious brother soon wrote to each of them, telling them he would sue them should they not retract them. What possible reason for this could be given was and is unknown. I believe the poor bloke, phony and vicious as he is, knew no better. Antics such as this have often come from this sorry soul and repeatedly shamed our family. His letters soon made a recognized fool of him. Rather than employ any of the publishers who came forth, I decided to self-publish. My company's many connections made a market possible. Promotions and personal book reviews given in various cities followed. Barnes & Noble, Books-A-Million, and other booksellers came aboard.

I attended the annual publishers convention in Chicago and displayed there. I felt the book was a total success. It sold under a million copies and still sells some now, ten years later. The name Mark Wallach and his deeds were told to the world, at least, whoever wished to hear. Thankfully, there were many.

The same year, Heights High School had a marvelous and well-attended fiftieth reunion of our 1945 graduating class. Seeing so many of my old friends after over fifty years was a great thrill. It was, however, much negated by the absence of so many who were no longer alive. It took much of the thrill off the joy of the get-together.

The following year, on one of my infrequent opportunities to talk to my sweetheart grand-daughter, Shira, she told me that her mother was dating a psychiatrist who was somewhat of a neighbor. It appeared to me that she was try-ing to tell me that she thought they were get-ting serious with each other. The following year, I learned that they were married. My God, two daughters married to two shrinks. What does that say about the old man? It was, neverthe-less, with much anger and even greater grief that yet a second marriage for my daughter had taken place and I was neither advised of, nor invited to, either one of them. Did I not suffi-ciently provide funds? Of what was I suppos-edly guilty this time? It would have been so easy and effortless to vent my feelings and let her know how very much I resented the abuse, so ill-gotten and ill-deserved.

There was no invitation to wedding number one because of an unfaithful ex-wife who had turned my daughters against me. Now, there was wedding number two with a slap in the face equally as great. Well, that's the way it was and so by Laurie's choice. I made up my mind that I would never say anything to her about either affront, and I never have, nor will. Nevertheless, all facts speak for themselves. Only I wonder, over and over again, why has neither daughter ever asked the question "Where was my mother every Tuesday night for six months? Bowling? Dinner?" Maybe not always. This will never be known.

That same year Marilyn and I went to Atlanta to see the Olympic games. It was a once in a lifetime experience seeing various sporting events, including tennis with Mary Jo Fernandes representing the USA.

Danny Ornstein had his bar mitzvah in Washington that year. It was greatly enjoyed by all, including Marilyn and me.

I made a donation to the Jewish War Veterans of Vero Beach. They, in turn, dedicated the newly named chapter of the Jewish War Veterans as the "Mark Wallach Jewish War Veteran Post #506." To see the members wearing the newly ordered hats and to see the newly embroidered banner bearing the name "Mark Wallach, Jewish War Veterans Post #506" unfurled, was, indeed, a thrill. The *Press Journal* covered the event as I stood proud as can be, ever so satisfied that I could have played a part in remembering and memorializing Dad's name, and at the same time, help the much deserving veterans who had given so much.

My good friend Jack Bear called one evening and confided in me that he had found a lady with whom he was very compatible. He had made up his mind that he wished to marry her. Congratulations were in order and were immediately delivered. I was a bit taken aback when he said to me that he would love to be married in my backyard on the ocean and asked, since I was licensed to perform marriages as a notary public, whether I would perform the ceremony. After a bit of deep thinking about this, I told him that I would be honored to do so.

Plans were made, a lovely trellis was set up, invitations were printed, and on the appointed day, we had a bit under 100 well-dressed guests in the backyard seated on benches which had been bought. All went smoothly and I, as the priest or rabbi, was told that I had done a fine job. The party after the wedding was wonderful and beyond all expectations. It has been a number of years now and it's good to say they are living together as a happy couple. I must have tied a good knot.

Marilyn and I, 2007.

Several weeks after this happy event, Marilyn planned a big seventy-fifth birthday party for me at our home in Sapphire Valley. Vincent had just been born and bringing the whole family to North Carolina brought great pleasure. The cousins, nieces, nephews, my children, grandkids, and all were there for the big event. Seventy-five—holy mackerel, I'd become an old man! The event was fabulous. More travels were enjoyed that year as we, again, visited Cleveland and spent a couple of weeks in California, during which time we visited Penny. We ended the year on a happy note.

The following few years were mostly uneventful, excepting major illnesses that I suffered. In year 2000, Robin Atwell, my urologist, discovered a fairly well-developed cancer growing in my prostate gland. He felt attention to it was called for and an appointment for me was made in Orlando where seed radiation was administered. This procedure, tolerable as it was, saw radioactive seeds that destroy cancerous cells implanted. The seeds were permanently placed into the prostate gland. Over a period of time, the cancerous cells were destroyed. The procedure was well-administrated. A big problem arising out of such therapy is that more often than not, the radioactive seeds destroy not only the cancerous cells but also healthy ones.

This was the case with me, and the next few months produced urinary tract problems. Some were severe, others not so, on one occasion, I suffered "retention," the inability to void altogether. An immediate trip was made to the hospital emergency room, where they were unable to relieve the problem causing a filled bladder expanding. Fortunately, the urologist on call came to the hospital and was able to relieve me. Ultimately, I became incontinent, a condition which will not change the rest of my life.

On a follow-up visit, Dr. Atwell asked me when I had had a colonoscopy last. I told him not for many years. He insisted that I have one done immediately. The following week, Dr. McGovern performed the procedure. His nurse called my office two days later and said that an immediate appointment with the doctor was necessary. This appointment was kept, and he advised me that he had found a sizeable cancer in my colon. The cancer was well-developed and had gone into the wall, the other side of which was the liver. It had not gone through the wall yet. Once through the wall, survival would have become an issue. The morning I heard the news

Kurt with granddaughter, Shira, 2007.

was several hours before a lecture I was delivering to a class of about thirty-five students. About halfway through this lecture, realizing my possible mortality, I broke down almost completely. This occurring in front of so many people embarrassed me to a point that I couldn't live it down in my own mind for months. It was, however, an understandable reaction.

I had made an appointment with Dr. Heidi Gorsuch, a friend and lovely temple member. She had received a full report from Doctor McGovern and was prepared to go over all that needed to be done. She focused on the need for immediate intervention, stressing this in view of the fact that this was an aggressive cancer which must be immediately removed. She assured me that it would be painless surgery, that healing time would not be lengthy, and that I should feel comfortable and optimistic about the outcome. Within twenty-four hours, I was checked into the hospital. The surgery, as she stated, was painless and successful. She assured me that she got all of the cancer and that I was not in danger any longer. She had done a marvelous job. Recovery did not take long, and I was both lucky and grateful. Had my good friend, Robin Atwell, not pushed me into the

Son-in-law, Aaron, granddaughter, Shira, and daughter, Laurie, in 2007.

colonoscopy, I would quite likely not have survived. I had not had a colonoscopy for years and had no plans to have one. The thought of two major cancers within a couple of months still boggles my mind to this day.

In business, my ownership of too many problem mobile home parks was wearing me to a frazzle. Most particularly, Westgate, Groveland, and Hollandale communities were taking their toll. At Groveland, in Melbourne, the accounts receivable had gone completely awry. This was the only "family" park I owned and I witnessed much crime, drugs, property destruction, and the like there. Hardly a day passed that there was not one crisis or another here. Hollandale, though it had few problems of this nature, was running at twenty-five percent vacancy, and it was my conviction that this number would grow. There seemed to be no filling of empty spots. Rentals of owned homes here were too difficult to obtain. Westgate in Cocoa was almost a hybrid of the two.

With these problems causing a daily grind I couldn't stand, I decided to add Lakeshore and Sunnydale Mobile Home Parks in Broward County to the group and put the package of five on the market.

For many reasons, a very poor sale was consummated. A seven-figure second mortgage defaulted, and all in all, a loss of about three million dollars occurred. I was going through very difficult financial problems, which were taking a toll on me. Proceeds from the disastrous sale, plus the sale of Arbor Oaks Community on the west coast, were used to purchase a 256-space mobile home community in Leesburg, five medical office buildings in Port Charlotte, a 7-Eleven convenience store/gas station in Lakeland, and two Payless shoe stores in Miami. Aside from other investments, these deals changed the overall makeup of my company. Time would tell how loss from our disastrous sale could be recouped.

While involved with asset changes, I purchased a rather large piece of commercial land in Vero Beach located in a very prime and most desirable spot. My motivation was to build the most modern and beautiful medical center on the Treasure Coast. Profits from this venture were a secondary consideration. I had for a long time wished to honor and memorialize my mother and father whom I so admired. To build this edifice, the finest and the best, and have it carry the name of "The Mark–Lena Center," was my goal. Mark, my father, and Lena, my mother, would here be remembered. I am happy to write this venture was successful, so named and hopefully will remain so for many many years. The Mark–Lena Center is located in Vero Beach on Seventeenth Street, just off the corner of Indian River Blvd. A tribute to two fine people. It was in the early years of this, the twenty-first century, that my interests in the Holocaust and lecturing were aroused and expanded. Although the horrors of the Holocaust took place over sixty years ago, I was more than ever shaken by the hatred, cruelties, and repugnance of the era. How could a highly cultured and civilized nation like Germany even think of the things that happened, let alone commit to and see them through? A complete study is needed of prior history to understand it all and even after that, it would still be found incomprehensible.

In the first few years following the millennium, I undertook such a study. I read book after book, 100 or more pamphlets on the subject, and almost anything else that was written about the era. Although previously a member of the Holocaust Memorial Museum in Washington, but not too active, I revved up my motor of involvement there.

To learn, to learn, to learn was the modis

operandi. The more knowledge gathered, the less I understood the human mind. I undertook to expand my learning and awareness. This I did with many lecture series.

My first series of lectures was held at Temple Beth Shalom in Vero Beach. A major public awareness was created. All churches in the area were contacted, as were retirement communities, etc. The series of lectures was successful as I had from 100 to 175 people attend each lecture. It was an experience to see how very little the general public knew. It was viewed as one might view the Civil War, or even the Revolutionary War. The average person knew so little and thought of it as ancient history. Though much knowledge was shared, the bottom line was disappointment as so many more needed to know the truth of what happened.

My next series was held at the Vero Beach Museum of Art, with similar expectations and results. In the past year, Florida Atlantic University sponsored me for a series of eight lectures. In the coming months, I shall teach at St. Edward's Upper School. The public must know, and I practice diligently as the teacher with a message that I will continue to deliver. A new avocation had taken complete hold of me.

23

Life Goes On

In the news of the day, we read that after the breakup of the Soviet Union, there were shortages of food, medical supplies, and other much-needed goods throughout what had been the former Soviet Union. With deafening roars, giant USA Lockheed G2 Galaxy cargo aircraft rolled down the runways and took off from the Phein, a major German airport, heading east to help.

Fifty-four planned air force flights, BYC-5 and C-141 Starlifter planes from Frankfort to Incirlik Airbase flew to eastern Turkey. The cargo planes carried more than 2,500 tons of surplus military food and rations, mostly stock left over from the Gulf War, as well as pharmaceutical supplies, to be distributed in Moscow and about twenty-five cities in southern Russia. Each package of humanitarian aid carried a label in both Russian and English saying, "From the American people who hope that your fight for democracy is worth it."

U.S. Secretary of State James Baker was at the Pheinmain Base to watch the launch of "Operation Provide Hope," an airlift which lasted only three weeks and was funded by $100 million in Pentagon funds. He said that unlike the Berlin Airlift, this operation was not a long-term one. Russia and the newly independent republics were in the grips of winter and the shelves were bare. Emergency food and medical supplies were much needed, and we were happy to supply them.

In other news, Pope John Paul II came to Gorée Island off Senegal's capital at Dakar and spoke of the forgotten Holocaust. It was through here that an estimated fifteen million Africans captured along the coast of West Africa from as far south as Angola, passed on their way to slavery in America and the Caribbean for nearly 400 years, from the mid-fifteenth to the mid-nineteenth centuries. Gorée Island and its infamous prison, "The House of Slaves," was one of the continent's chief transit points for slaves. Thousands of African men, women, and children died here while waiting in overcrowded and filthy cells to be crammed aboard French or English slave ships bound for the new World.

In Washington, the American census office

stated that there were 5.5 billion people living on earth and that in twenty-five years, there would be 8 billion crammed onto a planet that is already failing to feed itself. It reported that China, alone, accounted for 1.3 billion inhabitants. They stated that despite having the worst infant death rate, African mothers produce an average of six children each. The world population is expected to double by the year 2020.

In other world news late in the century, a powerful earthquake hit Cairo, Egypt, killing about 350 people and injuring over 4,000. The center of the quake registered 5.9 on the Richter scale. This measure was taken nineteen miles outside of the city. Tremors were felt as far away as Jerusalem, 250 miles away. Panic caused many traffic accidents, and many were trampled to death in the chaos. As many as 160 buildings were demolished. The sphinx, pyramids, and other national monuments escaped damage, as did the Answan Dam in the south, which holds back Lake Nasser, the largest artificial lake in the world.

On the home front, one evening while speaking with a friend, he mentioned to me that he had read about an elderly lady who he thought grew up as a young girl in the town of

Chorostkov in the Ukraine. This, being the home of my entire paternal family, greatly aroused my interest. I asked for her name and was able to get a phone number.

Shortly thereafter, I phoned her to talk of our similar geographic background. She didn't have too much to say, but insisted on my contacting two brothers she knew well from birth, who lived in Chorostkov sometime from between 1920 to 1922 until 1941. I was happy to contact one of them, Sam Halpern, from New Jersey.

My initial discussion with Sam was very delightful and enjoyable. He told me that he was born in Chorostkov and lived there until the Nazis came in 1941, at which time he was about twenty years old. I learned that he knew my grandparents well and was also well acquainted with my uncles, my father's brothers, as well as their wives and children.

During this conversation I learned much. His early years in the farming village of 6,000 residents were happily spent until the arrival of the Nazi troops in late June of that fateful year, 1941. It took almost no time before I felt a real affinity with this person. I had never known him, nor ever seen him, yet my desire to do so became strong. I wanted to be with Sam and learn more. A few days later, I decided to phone him again. This time I asked him if he ever came to Florida and would he like to meet me. I was pleased to hear that he visited Florida frequently and was planning to come to Miami Beach to stay at the Fontainebleau Hotel for a couple of weeks. Arrangements were immediately made to get together there shortly after his arrival. He would be visiting with a number of family members, among others, his brother Ari, who I looked forward to meeting. It pleased me to no end.

The few weeks passed by, and Marilyn and I drove down to Miami Beach to meet my newfound friend. Rather than merely meeting a friend, it was more like having found and re-couped a long-lost loved relative. We couldn't get enough of each other. He told me of his growing up years, his family, their way of life, and so much more. I was learning firsthand the manner in which all my family lived there during those years. I learned of my grandfather's business, a gentleman whom I had never met. So much was learned, so much was savored. It all poured out of Sam as old memories returned. Sam's brother, Ari, had joined us and was as much a kindred spirit as Sam had become. The hours passed and before we would head back to Vero Beach, Ari, Sam, and I vowed that we would go back to our roots together.

Several weeks and a few phone calls later, we made plans for a trip together back to the old village of Chorostkov in the Ukraine. I chose to invite my daughter, Laurie, and her husband, Aaron. Sam and Ari brought some of their offspring. I had phoned Laurie that evening and told her much about her paternal family background. I detailed all I knew about my father's younger years, his growing up in the Ukraine, leaving for Holland when World War I began, and more. I attempted to tell her all I knew. It wasn't much about my relatives, uncles, aunts, nieces, and nephews in Chorostkov. It was frustrating for me to see how little I really knew. Nevertheless, after about a half hour, I realized that she had a great interest and was as excited as a little kid at the prospect of going back to the old, Old World, learning of my past and seeing in person what she had learned about Podolya and Galicia. I told her I would fund their whole trip. Her excitement moved me and when I finally hung the phone up, I realized that I had done the right thing with my offer to take her and Aaron along and pay for the journey.

All in all, there were eleven of us when we met in Warsaw, Poland, where we stayed for a day.

The following day and a short plane ride of an hour and a half or so saw us land in Lviv, once known as Lvov, (changed from prewar years from Lemberg). We had previously been in Lviv and found it no different from before, strictly third world. The people here, as we found in the rest of the Ukraine, had nothing, literally NOTHING. Owning a pen or even shoes without holes on the soles was a bonus. For the average American to fully conceive of what their national poverty level is like would be difficult.

Lviv, the big city, had wealth in comparison to Tarnopol, the next city to which we went. The city of 200,000 had two broken-down hotels, one was closed since it had no water. The other, where we stayed, was in equal sorry repair. We did, however, have electricity, from 8:00 P.M. to 10:30 in the evening—when it was available, but no more.

Our third day brought us to Chorostkov. To try to describe conditions would do no justice. Let it suffice to say that it had totally deteriorated over the years with no repairs of any kind having been made. At the entry to the town stood a huge marble statue with much lettering engraved on it in Hebrew and Ukranian. It was one of so many throughout the area. All were built and donated by Sam and Ari Halpern. At this, and at so many more memorials we visited, Ari recited a prayer for the dead in Hebrew. We stood on the ground where my grandfather's business was and then on to the family home (now a dilapidated shack).

During the occupation when 1,976 out of 2,000 Jews in Chorostkov were murdered by the Nazis (including over 200 Wallach family members here and in three surrounding towns), a gentile family gave secret haven to two Jewish girls, one of whom became Ari's wife. They were among the twenty-four survivors. For the past forty years, in gratitude for their lives, Sam and Ari sent regular payments to the surviving family. This enabled them to eat well, have plumbing, and send their son to school. The first evening in town, Ari had arranged for all eleven of us to eat a dinner in their home. It was not the type of "dining" an American is used to. It is difficult for me to describe the very substandard conditions. All were squeezed into two ten-foot square rooms. The facilities were meager, but the warmth of heart, uplifted spirits, and deep emotions would be hard to duplicate. No doubt many minds recalled the days of Nazi occupation when Jews were tortured to death and beaten to cripples for the "sin" of being of Jewish faith. Our hosts could not have been more gracious, nor could the Halpren family have been more emotionally stirred. No finer dining experience in my life has ever left a greater or deeper impression then that dinner in Chorostkov.

The following day, we strayed through the village, strangers in another world we did not know, nor could recognize, distinguish, nor with which we could identify. We stood far from anything we had ever known, further away than space. Yet, these were our roots, the homes of our forefathers.

Since my father's family, as well as that of my grandfather's, had eight siblings, the Wallach family was huge, numbering at least 220. The majority of these had remained in Chorostkov and surrounding towns and in the villages of Skalat, Tarnopol, Chortkov, Gryzmalov, and Berezeny. We visited them all. Some were similar to Chorostkov, the others not too different. In every community and in several of the "killing fields" where the Nazis murdered stood a memorial statue for the victims. Some of these memorials, though smaller, rivaled the finest to be seen anywhere. Marble structures of grace, refinement, and elegance were found in the area. Each one was built and maintained by the Halperns. We stopped at almost all of them and joined Sam and Ari as they led in a prayer for the dead at each.

Two years after our arrival back home, Ari died. It was a loss of great proportions. Few had a heart so big or a soul so great. No doubt he will be missed and remembered for the fine man that he was. I shall long remember him.

In the news in and around the world were myriad interesting events. In Miami, blacks took to the streets, rioting, looting, and burning stores in anger over the death of a black man in a police chase. Six people were shot and over 250 were arrested. The cause of it all was one Clement Lloyd, whose erratic motorcycle driving attracted attention two days earlier, and though unarmed, he was shot by police during an ensuing chase. Riots began after the mayor arrived and urged police to allow Lloyd's family to see the body.

When viewed, two dozen blacks began throwing bottles before police moved in to push the crowd back. This set off further rioting. As the clashes continued, 250 were arrested; dozens of instances of looting and arson were reported.

In Europe, the Kremlin admitted that over 43,000,000 people in Russia lived in poverty. The government claimed that poverty was an evil of capitalism. The regime acknowledged that almost twenty percent of the population were destitute and indigent, as compared to 14 percent in the United States. A newspaper reported that this was a national tragedy. They stated a person needed seventy-five rubles or $124.00 a month to maintain minimal security. Forty-three million Russians live below that line, of which one-third are retirees. A senior official asked what was to be done about the tragedy. The answer was "that there were no programs yet, but one thing we will not have is soup kitchens. We are opposed to such a system used in the United States where people get free dinners."

No country had lost more people during World War II than the Soviet Union. A new statistic was acknowledged in the Kremlin, even more horrible, that an equal number of its citizens died between 1927 and 1953 at the hand of and victims of Joseph Stalin. Over twenty million died as a result of executions, labor camps, and famine during the Soviet leader's reign. It was estimated that twenty million were arrested and driven from their homes. These calculations were in line with long standing Western estimates. Many Soviet leaders credited Stalin as the leader who prevented the Soviet state from crumbling after Lenin's death. As was pointed out, however, the methods used were pathologically harsh. Among the victims were six to seven million who starved to death during a famine he generated in the years 1932 and 1933 as an outgrowth of the drive for industrialization. Another one million were executed in 1937 and 1938, among which were his military elite. It was noted that ten to twelve million were "repressed" during World War II, most of these for little or no reason.

In 2000, facing the resurgence of neo-Nazi activity, the West German government banned the 170-member national assembly. In a series of raids on party members offices and homes, officials seized large quantities of ammunition, knives, and swastikas. The new-right Republicans who had placed well in the Berlin elections were not considered "extremists" enough to fall under the ban disallowing extreme activities.

Argentina was caught between the right and left. After warding off three army rebellions by right wing officers, the shaky government fought off a blow from the left. An armed civilian attack on an army barracks outside Buenos Aires killed twenty-one people and wounded countless more. Six soldiers and policemen were killed. More than thirty rebels were captured. Many believed that foreigners were involved. Officials said the civilians used Russian and Chinese machine guns. Meanwhile, shades of a shameful past emerged in West Berlin as election returns showed a shocking surge of support for the "Republican Citizen Party," a far right group headed by ex-Nazi Franz Schonhuber. He called for "purified patriotism," a dig against the Turks, Poles, and other foreign job seekers, who are often blamed for local housing shortages.

In Venezuela, riots erupted in numerous cities during protests over economic policies. Dozens of demonstrators were killed and hundreds injured in clashes with the National Guard. To control the unrest, the beleaguered government imposed curfews and curbed civil liberties. The riots were set off by a recent removal of price controls aimed at reducing the nation's thirty-three billion dollar debt. Prices skyrocketed, including fares for public transportation, which kindled the violence.

In other interesting news, the Japanese had added American colleges to their U.S. shopping lists, which already ranged from Manhattan skyscrapers to Honolulu mansions. At least one of the sought-after institutions said no to the mighty yen. Refusing to accept a twenty-four million dollar offer from the Kyoto Institute of Technology, officials at Phillips University declared, "Colleges are not bought like Quaker Oats." Other schools, such as financially pressed Warner Pacific College in Portland, Oregon, saw Japanese money as an opportunity too enticing to pass up, selling forty-nine percent of its physical plant to a Japanese firm. The college said it needed the six million dollars.

It was an eye-opener to see that the world's oldest profession was preparing to sell its stock. Mustang Ranch, the biggest brothel in the United States, began to sell stock to the public at twenty dollars per share. Investment bankers began to offer the stock for a total of $23,300,000. Located nine miles east of Reno, Nevada, the house of ill—but legal— repute had one hundred two rooms and thirty women available to satisfy male fantasies for eighty dollars per half hour. Profiting most from the sale was Mustang owner Joe Conforte, who owed Uncle

Sam $12,000,000 in back taxes.

Life, never mundane and dull as the twenty-first century arrived, saw vendors at major league ballparks serving tacos and sushi. Responding to the needs of bored and health-conscious fans, food services at Anaheim Stadium, Wrigley Field, and other ballparks began offering a wider variety of munchables. Hot dogs, beer, and popcorn remained popular, but last season when fans sampled sushi at San Diego Padre games, they roared for more fish.

The early years of the twenty-first century saw a huge growth in my company, Kurtell Growth Industries. I had felt manufactured housing communities, which had been our main business for almost twenty-five years, were now slowly, yet steadily, on the decline, if, in fact, they were not going into extinction. Although some of my communities had already been sold, I still owned eight, spread out throughout the state. Five of these were eventually sold, as I described previously, and I began to purchase medical office buildings. The Orlando Surgery Center was purchased. Five medical office buildings in Port Charlotte were acquired, along with the Mark–Lena Medical Center in Vero Beach.

We now owned and operated our Kurtell

Building, The Orlando Surgery Center, the triple net leased 7-Eleven, our car lot, the Payless Shoe stores in south and west Miami, along with our mobile home communities and a mortgage company. It was a plateful. At an advanced age, now in my mid- and late-seventies, selling off and slowing down would surely have been an intelligent move. The job was enough for a much younger man, and maybe too much at that.

To stop, or even slow down was not in my makeup. Opportunities glared, beckoned, and tempted me. Yes, the plate was full. My makeup and competitive drive should have succumbed and given in to common sense, reason, and the workings of a normal brain. This was not the case as only expansion was on my mind. Why? This is difficult to answer. There were enough dollars in the bank to live comfortably. My children were grown. I lacked nothing. To expand what was there now, a full-time plus large company to operate, was a big job. No answer of any intelligent nature is possible. Nevertheless, counter to the lacking of common sense, I plowed on.

In the period of the next two years, I acquired six major buildings in Nashville, Tennessee. There was not a small building in the lot as each was from three to six times the size of our Kurtell Building. Following this, I purchased the nine acre 777 Building in Vero Beach. This monster of an edifice has 125,000 square feet under roof complete with drugstore and restaurant. Its tenants include every specialty segment in the medical care business with its seventy-one resident physicians. The nine acres lie within 200 yards of Vero Beach's only hospital, a 375-bed facility. The company had grown to become likely one of the largest in Indian River County. The questions as to why, why, why were never answered as I moved forward.

During these years, we proudly watched Mark graduate with a bachelor's degree from Florida Atlantic University (magna cum laude). Mark had difficulty supporting his family. He never really found himself until his sixth anniversary. I happily write now that he is taking all financial responsibilities and is supporting his crew.

24

Hurricane Tragedies

The twenty-first century came in with a bang worldwide as George Bush was inaugurated forty-first president of the United States despite protests from those questioning the legitimacy of the election. President Clinton had handed out commutations of sentences for convicted criminals. I believe some of these were actually sold for monetary consideration as Mark Rich's ex-wife, Denise, donated $450,000 to Clinton's library to free her husband.

The first year saw veteran race driver Dale Earnhardt get killed instantly as his car, going 180 mph, slammed into the retaining wall on the last lap of the Daytona 500 NASCAR race.

On September 11, 2001, during the morning rush hour, two hijacked 757 airliners slammed into the Twin Towers of the World Trade Center in New York that created explosions and fires that led to the collapse of both towers. Moments later, a third airliner crashed into the Pentagon in Washington and a fourth crash-landed near Pittsburgh, Pennsylvania.

In what was revealed to be a coordinated terrorist attack on the United States, many thousands died. Osama Bin Laden, leader of the international terrorist network Al-Quaeda, was believed to be responsible for the attacks. The stock market reopened one week after the attack and an ailing market plummeted further as stocks fell to a three-year low with the Dow Jones average suffering its largest one-day drop in history. The NASDAQ dropped sixty-eight percent by the end of the year the market rallied beyond the 10,000 mark. The first year of the new century had come in with a bang.

The following year, the UN Food Agency issued a warning that thirty-eight million people in Africa faced the prospect of famine and starvation. They went on to say eighteen million were now starving in Ethiopia, Eritrea, and Sudan. Ironically, here in Vero Beach, it seemed everyone was on a diet.

In February of 2003, the Columbia Space Shuttle disintegrated as it reentered the earth's atmosphere, killing all seven astronauts aboard. It broke up forty miles above earth and fiery debris was showered across Texas and Louisiana. Overseas, the United States launched an invasion of Iraq. This country claimed Iraq had possessed weapons of mass destruction and was supporting international terrorism, which contributed to the September 11 attack on the United States. International cooperation was scarce except for the United Kingdom and Spain.

The year saw controversy over the revelation that the New York Stock Exchange board of directors, Chief Dick Grasso had a compensation package of over $130,000 million dollars. My personal feelings were, "How gross it was, and what an insult to the people of this country, many of whom are barely surviving, and the majority are laboring hard to lead a comfortable life."

The following year, that of our hurricanes and the destruction in Vero Beach, saw ninety-one people killed and over 1,000 injured in Madrid, Spain, as a series of bomb blasts hit four commuter trains. Evidence emerged that this was the work of the Islamic militants linked to Al-Quaeda.

Former President Ronald Reagan died at age ninety-three, having battled Alzheimer's disease for ten years. Pope John Paul II died after a bout with the flu.

The summer of 2004, began normally following spring and into the hot months starting in
June. It was much like all seasons experienced
in Florida over the past almost fifty years. Yet
something felt different. There was a question
in the air in early August. It was partially answered as Hurricane Charley battered and half-
destroyed the cities of Punta Gorda and Port
Charlotte on Florida's west coast. It roared in
with a vengeance with gusts of over 130 miles
per hour. Homes, large buildings and small ones,
cars, trucks, trees, and shrubs were blown away.
People were killed, and when it was over, the
two cities lay in ruin. Countless good citizens
and homeowners with furniture and belongings
became homeless without shelter and in many
instances, without jobs. Their little money could
not sustain them for long.

The job Hurricane Charley accomplished
likely equaled the worst bombings and destruction of life in cities in Germany in World War II.
There was little help for the unfortunate residents of the stricken cities. Disaster after disaster, catastrophe, and calamity were to be
found everywhere.

People outside the area could not imagine the
tragedy that had taken place. Two cities lying in

ruins amidst the nightmare where twenty-four hours before, happy life existed. My company, Arbor Oaks, owned five medical office buildings in this sea of distress. Of these, three had been totally destroyed. Roofs caved in and entire interiors, outside wall to outside wall, had to be rebuilt. Total damage from Charley to Arbor Oaks exceeded $3,000,000. Not all of this would be covered by insurance. Our doctors in this complex could not see their patients. At our hospital buildings, roofs were badly damaged and as a consequence, so were the interiors. Hurricane-related problems were severe, and my company's losses total six figures uninsured.

Three weeks after the disaster of Hurricane Charley, the first really major hurricane on record hit Vero Beach, just south of Oslo Road. It roared in early in the evening with winds of over 105 miles an hour, and gusts exceeding that by another twenty miles. The destruction is hard to describe as most power lines went down, cars were swept off the road, and some roofs became airborne. All were warned well in advance and told to leave areas near the river on the main land. The barrier islands had to be evacuated. No one was allowed to be there at all. Trees there and around the county were down as most roads became impassible due to this and the flooding which accompanied the storm. Marilyn and I went to the Kurtell Building, where we holed up in the hallway along with Mark and his family, Gina and her husband, the Van Sauns, and other friends.

The storm was not one that would quickly abate. Where usually hurricanes would travel at from eight to twenty miles per hour, Hurricane Frances just parked itself over the city. It moved slightly, possibly at one mile per hour, and wreaked havoc as it went. All of us spent the night in the hallway. The rains came down, and the wind blew with a velocity not often seen. Most were frightened out of their minds. It would have been a rare individual who was not. As morning came, the winds and rain left us. Going outside gave us a view similar to the disaster of Port Charlotte two weeks earlier. Trees, light poles, and such were all over impassable roads. Floods here and there restricted driving, as did the trees and downed poles.

I was eager to leave and go to the big medical center we had acquired recently, and also to go and see our home. Traveling there was difficult. After about forty-five minutes of playing "dodge'm" with our car on the roads, we got to our big building. Upon arrival, we found dozens of cars that had taken shelter in our underground parking garage sitting there under four feet of water. Soon, they would all be totaled. Our next goal was to have a successful trip to our home and the big home next door, which I had purchased. We made it in reasonable time and found both mostly undamaged except for all the missing tiles on the roofs. We had survived the big blow, although so many others had not.

Cleanup began that day all over Vero Beach and the surrounding areas. Bringing it all back to looking normal was a huge task. Many destroyed homes would soon begin repairs and as the days passed, cleaner streets were seen, debris was removed, telephone and electric poles were being worked on, and dried, unflooded streets were, once again, seen around. The area looked almost normal within two weeks when a hurricane watch was announced. Everyone scurried around. The supermarkets, Lowes, The Home Depot, etc., were, once again, full of people trying to make last-minute purchases in preparation for yet another onslaught.

The papers and TV announced another hurricane was on its way, and it was only forty-five miles out. Was it possible that *another* hurricane would hit us just two weeks after the last one? Not one major hurricane had been here in all recorded time. A second one in so short a time surely couldn't be. But that statement proved false as the following day, Hurricane Jeanne with all its fury attacked us.

Hurricane Jeanne hit our coast within exactly one mile from where Hurricane Frances had come ashore just two weeks before. This time, the winds were stronger than the last time and the velocity plus the rains wreaked havoc once more, harder and more destructive than previously. Our families, Marilyn, I, and Mark's, stayed in our houses as winds of 120 miles per hour blew down almost everything in its path. Trees not previously downed, landscaping that had survived, telephone and electric poles that had remained or had been replaced were, once again, destroyed. Was all this possible? What cruelty mother nature had inflicted upon us.

When the disaster ended, Vero Beach, once again, lay in ruins as it was two weeks ago. This time, it was worse as it compounded so much of the previous damage, a large percentage of which had not been repaired. Many felt we could never recover. The financial harm, impairments, and losses escaped no one. Hardly a soul in the county had not been hurt. Suffering the most were good people who had lost all their belongings, along with jobs, and now had nothing. Many lost all of these as businesses closed and jobs were gone, along with homes and personal property.

A disaster of major proportion had overcome us. No one was allowed on Barrier Island for five days, and those inhabitants did not know what damage they sustained. Our home received moderate damage. I considered us lucky. The Kurtell Building was to need a new roof. As for the big one, the 777 Building, things were different. Forty-three compressors that were on the roof were blown down.

This, in turn, destroyed the roof that leaked and caused the interior of the building to sustain major damage. Walls were soaked wet and had to be replaced immediately lest mold form. Getting contractors was more than just difficult. So much damage had occurred in Vero Beach that anyone who wielded a hammer was deluged with work. To get anyone to do any work was a feat and a victory. To achieve this, prices, particularly for labor, went sky high. Costs for repairs needed most particularly at the Kurtell

Medical Building had gone through the roof, as did final repair costs.

The insurance companies behaved like thieves and crooks. It seemed not to matter that they had an obligation to pay for damages. They did not come forth. They did not pay the claims though their legitimacies were without question. When payments were made, they were short and did not cover the costs to repair the damage. They dragged their feet and caused delay after delay to a point where, as I write this, a full three years have gone by and we have not recouped our insured losses. I view this insurance industry with disgust and can only think of them as low-life thieves and crooks who should have no legal rights to collect premiums.

I am told over half of homeowners with insured losses were never reimbursed. Upon the expiration of policies, new premiums were tripled and quadrupled or no insurance was possible to be obtained. As an example, our largest medical building pre-hurricane had an insurance premium of $90,000 annually. Our premium today is $385,000. These companies were destroying Florida's economies and were allowed to do so under the law. Their unconscionable rates have caused our medical office complex to operate in the red, along with numerous others.

Although our local businesses took setbacks during this period, our Nashville division was hitting home runs. The Nashville office and employees were doing well as almost 300,000 square feet of offices showed less than a five percent vacancy factor.

While vacationing in our North Carolina home that year, I found myself terribly physically distressed and was bloated. Food I had eaten did not digest, and I felt as though a shelf existed in or above my stomach, which did not allow the normal peristalsis of food traveling through the body in a normal course. Pain soon followed extreme discomfort, and Marilyn rushed me to the little local twelve room hospital between Cashiers and the Highlands. After being examined, the doctor's diagnosis was that I had a bowel obstruction. The malady is one with which I was totally unfamiliar. Simply described, it is exactly what the name implies. Although I was unaware of it, a bowel obstruction can be a very serious illness. I was much at risk.

The next five days found me in the hospital, flat on my back, with tubes in me as they were treating me back to health. I think I was extremely fortunate in that not only did we have this fine little hospital here, but that I was treated so well by a well-trained and talented physician. I recovered within seven days, and we went back home to Vero Beach.

In August of 2005, Hurricane Katrina slammed into the Gulf Coast with winds of 145 miles per hour as the levees protecting New Orleans caved in. Eighty percent of the city was flooded as 130 people died. Damage was estimated at 150 billion dollars. An earthquake measuring 7.6 on the Richter scale hit India and Pakistan, killing 80,000 people and injuring 70,000 more. It was a difficult year.

25

My Life

As I bring this book to a close, I reflect and have here reflected on an eighty-one-year life. I have lived much. I believe I was a good son in my young and teenage years. From there, a war took me into the military, where two very difficult years were lived, and then home again to study and receive a fine education at Western Reserve University. A strain within me, created in the postmilitary years, brought on an exaggerated work ethic that permeated my being and has never left me. An ingrown genie, ever present, has always egged me on saying, "You've not accomplished enough. Do more." And so it has been over the years—"Do more"—and it was never enough. "Do more. Do more." It might have been my name as I lived that role, both consciously and unconsciously. It has had rewards, and it has been a damnation as I traveled the road of life. "Do more." It was my way of living.

The years I have lived have brought much sadness and happiness both. I learned to admire and adore my father. I have always felt like this alone. But really not so. He was a great man, far beyond my state. He was a true hero, whereas though I tried, I was not. He will always be idealized.

My mother tried. She wanted to be the best and gave her all. Her total lack of understanding of Psychology 101 made her, in my mind, a difficult parent. Her temperment was opposite from my father's kindness, compassion, altruism, and unselfishness. He could not kill a fly. She took great joy in doing so. They led their lives, however, equally loving their children as they melded as one.

My sister, who I have loved all my life, was much a hybrid of the two. Many of her traits were to be found in both my parents, some good, some not quite so, but overall, she deserved a high grade. I believe she was the smartest of the three of us, i.e., she, my brother, and I.

Little can be found in this book about my brother. It is not a sin of omission, but rather an indication of my dismay, disgust, and contempt, which I felt for a mean, arrogant, and totally phony man who has charaded through life as something he wanted to be but never was. Through all my years as his brother (biologically only), I have never, even in the slightest, detected a hint or a grain of kindness or understanding of and for his fellow man. Though not overly bright, he led his life in a lie pretending at all times to be what he was not.

Life was at times cruel to me. I did not choose well in finding suitable mates, except for Marilyn. There was great marital and domestic strife and intranquility which twice ended in divorce. As I reflect and try to do so honestly and in an unbiased manner, I feel no fault for my failures. The circumstances differed, yet the common thread was uncomplicated. I was mismatched in my choices. Incompatibility was the culprit. It was not her fault. It was not mine. One does not, nor cannot, mate apples and pears. They are as incompatible as the failed marriages. I bear more grief than grudge. The human psyche is a very complex mechanism, and possibly I never fully understood it. I view the failures as tragedies, but it is events like these that make life good, bad, indifferent, kind, mean, complex, and simple. It is so that we live, each in a different yet similar way. It is so that my life was lived.

I spawned three children in my years. They, too, reflect much of what I have written here.

Laurie first, then Penny, and last Mark. Much pleasure was derived from them, as was a great deal of heartache. They are individuals, very much differing from each other with pluses and minuses galore. There seems to be very little behavior in common among them. Born of the same father, there is a common grain between father and daughters as well as father and son. Yet, I have detected little in the way of personality similarities among the three. I love them all, but must say they have all made life difficult at times.

Health-wise I have suffered. There was an operation to save my wrist, partial removal of my thyroid gland, open-heart surgery with a coronary bypass, prostate cancer, major urinary problems, surgery for an advanced cancer in my colon, and now, chronic, lymphocytic leukemia.

What will take me? We do not know.

I close the chapter of the life of Kurt L. Wallach with hopes for a better and more peaceful world. I close with the hope that my grandchildren, Daniel, Shira, James, and Vincent, will have good, happy, and productive lives, keeping the name of Wallach alive. I close my chapter knowing I have tried hard to be exemplary, good, and philanthropic.

...hday August 2007

Top, Kurt, Shira, Daniel, Marilyn and Mark.
Bottom, James, Vincent, and Lianne.

473

About the Author

Kurt Wallach brings with him a varied background not often found, ranging across a spectrum of a most manifold and wide range of callings as adult life began with a short and almost nonexistent career as a hearing and speech pathologist. He completed his master's degree studies at Western Reserve University and many weeks of practice teaching in this field, but never continued toward a career.

Not finding the future lucrative here, he incorporated an aluminum storm window company in Cleveland, Ohio, at the age of twenty-three and was inordinately successful until he sold it, and moved to Miami, Florida, where he built several subdivisions, apartment complexes, and an office building. He built Florida's first condominium in 1960, subdivided a 1,460-acre piece of land in South Dade County (Miami), and a 2,700-lot subdivision in Stuart, Florida. He patented a lady's hairstyling tool, selling over nineteen million pieces, merging his company with another, and placing it on the American Stock Exchange before retiring from it.

Wallach spent several years as a tennis professional and then built the Miami Racquet Club. It was at this time that he wrote and published his first book, a humorous tennis book called *Tennis is a Funny Racquet,* a book which became quite successful. At the same time, he wrote a weekly newspaper column, "Tennis Technique," which was syndicated in numerous magazines and newspapers throughout Florida for thirty years. He was a frequent umpire at the U.S. Tennis Open as a "chair umpire," working many major nationally televised matches. During this time, he became an avid duplicate bridge player, participating in many statewide tournaments and achieving the designation of Junior Master from the American Contract Bridge League.

In the late 1990s, Mr. Wallach authored the book *Remembering Mark,* which told the story of his father, a brave and truly marvelous man who saved the lives of many as he took his family to safety from certain death. He brought his wife's family and strangers out of Austria, taking them out of the claws of the Hitler regime. Time and time again, he gave up profitable businesses to save lives. The book *Remembering Mark* was a great success.

Kurt Wallach later reentered the real estate industry via construction and for twenty-five years was the owner of twelve manufactured housing communities, shopping plazas, a mortgage company, office buildings, and fifteen major medical plazas. His company, Kurtell Growth Industries, a real estate investment trust with assets of nine figures, became one of the largest of its kind on the Treasure Coast of Florida. He remains as president and chairman of the board.

He is a substantial contributor to the Holocaust Museum.

As a major stockholder of Citrus Bank, Mr. Wallach also served on its board of directors. He has been chairman of several major committees, including the chairmanship of the important Executive Loan Committee. He has donated fifty-five acres of land to the State of Florida for the protection of the environment. He is a sponsor of the Indian River Humane Society, a benefactor of the Treasure Coast Opera Society, and serves on its board of directors. Mr. Wallach also served on the board of directors of the Vero Heritage Center.

About the Author

He is happily married to his lovely wife, Marilyn. They will celebrate their thirtieth anniversary next year. He is the father of two daughters, Laurie Mitchell and Penny Spark, and has a twenty-six-year-old son, Mark, who was born two months after his grandfather Mark's death in 1981. Four grandchildren will carry on the Wallach legacy.

Eighty-one years old, at this writing, he remains active in business and frequently travels domestically and overseas.